# THE ACTUAL AND POTENTIAL USE
# OF LABORATORY SCHOOLS

*IN STATE NORMAL SCHOOLS AND*

*TEACHERS COLLEGES*

By E. I. F. WILLIAMS, Ph.D.

TEACHERS COLLEGE, COLUMBIA UNIVERSITY
CONTRIBUTIONS TO EDUCATION, NO. 846

*Published with the Approval of*
*Professor E. S. Evenden, Sponsor*

BUREAU OF PUBLICATIONS
TEACHERS COLLEGE, COLUMBIA UNIVERSITY
NEW YORK, 1942

COPYRIGHT, 1942, BY E. I. F. WILLIAMS

# ACKNOWLEDGMENTS

THE author is indebted to Professor E. S. Evenden, the sponsor of this study, for his encouragement and friendly counsel, his incisive, constructive suggestions during the time the study was in process, and his careful evaluation of the manuscript. He also wishes to express his appreciation to Professors F. B. O'Rear and Milo B. Hillegas, who acted as advisers and who, by their helpful suggestions, assisted in forming the pattern of the study. He is also deeply grateful to Professor William C. Bagley for his wise guidance and leadership in the study of the problems of the laboratory school.

The author also wishes to acknowledge his gratitude to Dean Thomas C. McCracken, Chairman of the Committee on Standards and Surveys of the American Association of Teachers Colleges, and to the various members of the Committee at the inception of the study who secured the cooperation of the member institutions and thus made it possible to obtain an unusually large percentage of replies to the questionnaires; and to Charles W. Hunt, Secretary of the American Association of Teachers Colleges, for his generous interest and advice.

Invaluable aid was given by Mrs. Marjorie N. Ullman, who assisted in tabulating and summarizing the data and in typing the manuscript.

Finally, the author appreciates the cooperation of executives of the state normal schools and teachers colleges, who furnished the detailed information which was needed to complete the investigation. A list of the institutions which furnished data is given in the Appendix.

E. I. F. W.

# CONTENTS

| CHAPTER | | PAGE |
|---|---|---|
| I. | INTRODUCTION AND STATEMENT OF THE PROBLEM . . . . . . . . . . . . . . | 1 |
| | A. Historical Introduction . . . . . . . . | 1 |
| | B. The Problem and the Procedure . . . . . | 13 |
| |     Importance of the Laboratory School Facilities . | 14 |
| |     Related Studies . . . . . . . . . | 16 |
| |     Need for the Study . . . . . . . . | 19 |
| |     The Problem . . . . . . . . . . | 20 |
| |     Sources of Data and Procedures . . . . | 21 |
| |     Definition of Terms Used in the Study . . . | 23 |
| II. | THE PRESENTATION AND INTERPRETATION OF THE DATA . . . . . . . . . . . | 25 |
| | A. General Information Regarding the Calendar Year, Enrollment, and Curriculums . . . . | 25 |
| |     The Calendar of the Academic Year . . . . | 25 |
| |     Enrollment According to Type and Length of Curriculum . . . . . . . . . . | 27 |
| |     Types of Curriculums Offered . . . . . . | 32 |
| |     Length of Curriculums . . . . . . . | 32 |
| |     Summary . . . . . . . . . . . | 37 |
| | B. Laboratory Courses in the Training School . . . | 38 |
| |     Time Location of Laboratory Courses in the Curriculums . . . . . . . . . . | 39 |
| |     Allocation of Special Curriculums to Certain Institutions . . . . . . . . . . | 52 |
| |     Patterns of Organization of Laboratory Courses . | 57 |
| |     Clock-Hours of Laboratory Experience Required | 63 |
| |     Flexibility in Requirement of Laboratory Experience . . . . . . . . . . . | 73 |
| |     Number of Students Completing Courses in Student-Teaching in Laboratory Schools . . . | 84 |

## CONTENTS

| | | PAGE |
|---|---|---|

Number of Grades or Subjects to Which Student-Teachers Are Assigned . . . . . . . 98
Summary . . . . . . . . . . . . 101

C. The Campus Laboratory School . . . . . 104
  The Types of Laboratory School . . . . 104
  Advantages of the Campus School . . . . . 105
  The Relation of the Off-Campus School to the Campus School . . . . . . . . . 106
  Use of Each Type of Laboratory Facility . . 109
  Purposes for Which Campus Schools Are Used . 110
  The Use of Campus Schools for Class Demonstration . . . . . . . . . . . . . 113
  How Pupils Are Secured for Campus Laboratory Schools . . . . . . . . . . . . 117
  Enrollment of the Schools . . . . . . 118
  Grade Levels in the Schools . . . . . 121
  Ratio of Student-Teacher Enrollment to Enrollment in the Laboratory School . . . . 123
  A Formula for Determining the Size of the Campus School Necessary to Accommodate Student-Teachers . . . . . . . . . . 125
  Ownership and Control of the Campus School . 128
  Summary . . . . . . . . . . . . 130

D. The Off-Campus Laboratory School . . . . . 132
  The Need for Off-Campus Schools . . . . . 133
  The Population of Communities in Which Off-Campus Laboratory Schools Are Located . . 137
  The Off-Campus School as a Supplement and Complement to the Campus School . . . . . 139
  The Types of Schools Used as Off-Campus Laboratory Schools . . . . . . . . . 141
  The Use of the "Cadet" or "Interne" Plan . . 145
  Formula for Determining the Number of Pupils Necessary in Off-Campus Schools . . . . 146
  The Pupil Enrollment and Its Distribution . . 149
  Time Required to Reach Off-Campus Schools from the Teachers College Campus . . . . . 152
  The Methods of Transportation to Off-Campus Schools . . . . . . . . . . . . 153

|  |  |
|---|---|
| The Phases of Laboratory Experience Provided in Off-Campus Schools | 155 |
| Kind and Amount of Compensation to Cooperating Schools | 162 |
| Tuition Fees Paid by Pupils in the Laboratory Schools | 168 |
| Legal and Contractual Relationships between the Teachers College and Off-Campus Schools | 171 |
| Agreements and Contracts with Off-Campus Schools | 174 |
| The Attitudes of Individuals and Groups toward the Use of Public Schools as Laboratory Schools | 183 |
| Kind and Degree of Difficulty Encountered in the Use of Off-Campus Schools | 184 |
| Summary | 189 |
| E. Off-Campus Laboratory Schools Needed and Those Potentially Available | 191 |
| Institutions Needing Additional Laboratory Facilities | 192 |
| Plans for Securing Additional Facilities Needed | 193 |
| Distance and Time of Travel to Potential Off-Campus Schools Nearest to Campus | 199 |
| The Types of School Potentially Available within a Radius of Ten Miles from the Campus | 202 |
| Rural One-Teacher and Two-Teacher Schools Potentially Available Near the Campus | 204 |
| Comparison of Pupil Enrollments of Campus and Off-Campus Laboratory Schools with Those of Schools Potentially Available within Ten Miles of College Campus | 205 |
| Private Schools as Laboratory Schools | 209 |
| Summary | 210 |
| III. SUMMARY, CONCLUSIONS, AND RECOMMENDATIONS | 212 |
| Method | 213 |
| Summary and Conclusions | 213 |
| The Calendar Year and Curriculums | 213 |
| Laboratory Courses in the Training School | 214 |

| CHAPTER | PAGE |
|---|---|
| The Campus Laboratory School | 217 |
| The Off-Campus Laboratory School | 219 |
| Off-Campus Laboratory Schools and Those Potentially Available | 220 |
| Recommendations | 221 |
| Suggested Additional Studies | 228 |

*BIBLIOGRAPHY* . . . . . . . . . . . . . 230

*APPENDIX* . . . . . . . . . . . . . . 239

A.  Institutions from Which Data Were Received Which Were Members of The American Association of Teachers Colleges, 1933-34, 1937-38 . . . . . . . . . . 241

B.  Selected Legislation Concerning Laboratory Schools . . 248

C.  Selected Contracts and Agreements between Local Boards of Education and the Authorities Governing State Teachers Colleges for the Use of Laboratory Schools in Effect in the Academic Year, 1937-38, or Later . . . . . 252

# THE ACTUAL AND POTENTIAL USE
OF LABORATORY SCHOOLS

# CHAPTER I
# INTRODUCTION AND STATEMENT OF THE PROBLEM

## SECTION A
## HISTORICAL INTRODUCTION

FOR many years student-teaching has had a recognized place in the professional preparation of teachers. The origin of this important phase of the teacher preparation program can be traced to many sources, including the schools maintained by the Jesuit order, those conducted by the Pietists, the professional preparation of teachers begun by Basedow at Dessau in 1774 (where demonstration and experimentation were emphasized), the monitorial system of instruction, and, perhaps most important of all, the Institute at Yverdon, Switzerland, where Pestalozzi set forth and applied his educational theories.[1]

Probably Duke Ernest, of Gotha, was the first to realize and explicitly express the necessity for educating teachers by giving them preparation distinctly fitting them for their profession. His proposals, which included student- or practice-teaching, were incorporated in his will executed in 1654. He wrote:

It is desirable that the teachers at their expense or with assistance remain in one central place and . . . through practice learn that . . . for which they will in the future be employed.[2]

In 1698 his grandson, Frederick II, also of Gotha, established ten teachers seminaries in which the students gave demonstrations of their teaching ability by teaching their fellow students. Two years earlier Francke had established the *Seminarium praeceptorum* in connection with his institution for the preparation of teachers at Halle and, as was true in the seminaries founded by Frederick II, prospective (student) teachers listened to lessons taught by fellow students.

---
[1] Fred McCarrel, *The Development of the Training School*, pp. 212–213. 1934.
[2] I. L. Kandel, *The Training of Elementary School Teachers in Germany*, pp. 5–7. 1910.

When the first state-supported institution for the preparation of teachers was founded (Berlin, 1788), student-teaching was a specific part of the professional curriculum for teachers. Laboratory school experience was provided, and students were given experience

through visitation and observation of the regular school work, by assisting in the class work of the regular teachers, by oversight and care of indifferent or backward pupils, and by actual teaching according to instructions and under the supervision of the director.[3]

The earliest training schools in the present territory of the United States seem to have been in operation among the Indian pueblos of New Mexico, where Franciscan friars had established schools as early as 1600 and where from the beginning the brighter students were prepared as teachers. Student-teaching was a feature of these schools. As early as 1808, Mother Seaton's teacher-training school at Emmitsburg, Maryland, required practice teaching and had many of the characteristics of present-day normal schools.[4]

However, these attempts, sporadic and temporary as they were, did not have a lasting influence upon the development of teacher preparation. It was in New England, then the seat of culture and reform, that a continuously sustained impression grew that opportunity for student-teaching must be supplied as an imperative condition underlying effective teacher preparation. Some years before the first state normal school was established, there was much sentiment in favor of teacher education and in 1823 Rev. Samuel Hall of Concord, Vermont, began to operate the first private normal school in America. From the beginning (March 11, 1823) a few children were admitted to his school for demonstration and practice purposes.[5]

In 1825 Rev. Thomas H. Gallaudet, of Connecticut, published a *Plan of a Seminary for the Education of the Instructors of Youth* in which he suggested that all students, in their turn, should instruct in the training school. During the winter of 1824–25 James

---

[3] G. W. A. Luckey, *The Professional Training of Secondary Teachers in the United States*, p. 37. 1903.

[4] McCarrel, *op. cit.*, pp. 213–214.

[5] M. S. Stone, "The First Normal School in America." *Teachers College Record*, Vol. 24, p. 263, May, 1923.

G. Carter, the father of normal schools, wrote a series of articles for the *Boston Patriot* in which he emphasized vigorously the need for practice schools in seminaries for teachers.[6] A century ago the directors of the American Institute of Instruction declared that it was essential that there be "A situation such that a school may be connected with the seminary, accessible by a sufficient number of children, to give the variety of an ordinary district school."[7] And two years later (1839) Barnard pleaded for

an institution with a suitable principal and assistants and especially a model school connected with it, in which theory could be carried into practice, and an example given of what a district school ought to be . . . (which) would by actual results, give an impulse to the cause of popular education, and the procuring of good teachers, that could be given in no other way.[8]

With this background it is not surprising that practice departments, sometimes called "experimental" or "practice" schools, were provided from the time the first state normal schools were established by legislative action in Massachusetts, April 19, 1838. Under the law which provided for the first three state normal schools, the state Board of Education made provisions for training school departments in each of them.

The first state normal school in Massachusetts (and in the United States) was formally opened at Lexington, July 3, 1839. At the beginning of the second term (October 21, 1839) the laboratory school began its work with pupils selected from the six districts comprising the town in which the school was located. The general plan of organization and procedure was described by its first principal, Cyrus Pierce, in a letter which he wrote to Henry Barnard, on January 1, 1841:

This school consists of thirty pupils, of both sexes, from the age of six to ten, inclusive, taken promiscuously from families in the various dis-

---

[6] John P. Gordy, *Rise and Growth of the Normal-School Idea in the United States*, pp. 13-14. 1891.
[7] Memorial of the American Institute of Instruction to the Legislature of Massachusetts on Normal Schools, January, 1837. Quoted in Henry Barnard, *Normal Schools, and Other Institutions, Agencies, and Means Designed for the Professional Education of Teachers*, Part I, p. 85. 1851.
[8] Henry Barnard, "First Annual Report of the Secretary of the Board of Commissioners of Common Schools of Connecticut." *Connecticut Common School Journal*, Vol. 1, p. 174, June 1, 1839.

tricts of the town. The children pay nothing for tuition; .... This school is under the general superintendence and inspection of the Principal of the Normal School. After it was arranged, the general course of instruction and discipline being settled, it was committed to the immediate care of the pupils of the Normal School, one acting as superintendent, and two as assistants, for one month in rotation, for all who are thought *prepared* to take a part in its instruction. ... Twice every day the Principal of the Normal School goes into the model school for general observation and direction, spending from one half to one hour each visit. In these visits I either sit and watch the general operations of the school, or listen attentively to particular teacher and her class, or take a class myself, and let the teacher be a listener and observer. After the exercises have closed, I comment upon what I have seen and heard before the teachers, telling them what I deem good, and what faulty, either in their doctrine or their practice, their theory or their manner. Once or twice each term, I take the whole Normal School with me into the model school room, and teach the model school myself, in the presence of the pupils of the Normal School, they being listeners and observers. In these several ways, I attempt to combine, as well as I can, theory and practice, precept and example. In regard to the materials of which it is composed, and the studies attended to, the model school is as nearly a facsimile of a *common district school* as one district school is of another.[9]

When the location of the normal school was changed from Lexington to West Newton the laboratory school was continued. By agreement with the town the public grammar school was used as its model department:

The affairs of the school are under the sole direction of a Permanent Teacher, chosen and responsible to, said district and approved by the Principal of the State Normal School. ... He is assisted in his work by the Pupils of the State Normal School—two at a time, who spend three weeks each in the service and who are subject to his general direction and supervision.[10]

Soon afterwards the facilities for laboratory teaching were enlarged by the addition of the primary school of the town. A definite, specific plan of cooperation was arranged:

By the terms of the agreement, the district furnishes schoolroom, etc., and one permanent male teacher, approved by both parties, and allows such additions to their number, by pupils from abroad, on a small tui-

---

[9] Arthur O. Norton, *The First State Normal School in America: The Journals of Cyrus Pierce and Mary Swift*, Introduction, pp. liii–liv. 1926.
[10] Eben S. Stearns and others, *Historical Sketches of the Framingham State Normal School*, p. 65. 1914.

INTRODUCTION AND STATEMENT OF PROBLEM 5

tion, as circumstances justify. The State Normal School furnishes a portion of apparatus, etc., and two assistant teachers, each to observe one week previous to teaching, and to teach two weeks under constant supervision.[11]

The institution was moved to its third and present location at Framingham, on December 15, 1853. Less than a year afterward (November 6, 1854) a formal agreement was entered into between the town of Framingham and the normal school, signed by the chairman of the School Committee of the Town of Framingham and the principal of the normal school.[12] Among other things, it provided that each student-teacher should have charge of a class or classes for discipline and instruction for not less than one hour each day, for a minimum of six consecutive weeks. Thus early the advantage of a formal written agreement over an oral understanding was seen. During the Civil War period, with its attendant necessity for economy, the practice school at Framingham was discontinued, but in 1866 it was again reopened, though parents of the town had shown some opposition and it was difficult to secure children as pupils in the school.

The second state normal school in America opened at Barre, Massachusetts, on September 4, 1839, but under difficult circumstances suspended operation in 1841. Three years later it was relocated at Westfield, where the town school was furnished for use as a model school for eleven years from 1844 to 1855; the arrangement, however, was never entirely satisfactory. Fifteen hundred dollars was raised by School District No. 1 of the town

. . . to be applied towards the erection of the edifice, on condition that a portion of it may be used as a model schoolroom for the instruction of the children of the district, to be connected with the Normal School, under the general superintendence of its Principal.[13]

The building was constructed and the first floor allotted to the model school to which pupils from the town were assigned. A written contract between the school district and the State Board of Education (reproduced in the *Tenth Annual Report of the Mass-*

[11] Massachusetts, *Fourteenth Annual Report, Board of Education*, p. 16. December 12, 1850.
[12] Massachusetts, *Eighteenth Annual Report, Board of Education*, pp. 12-16. 1855.
[13] Massachusetts, *Ninth Annual Report, Board of Education*, p. 12. 1845.

achusetts *Board of Education*, pp. 58-59) was signed. The criticism was made that the pupils of the model schools were a selected group who were not typical of actual school conditions, but this criticism was soon met by the Board of Education, which provided a typical district school as one of the model schools with the purpose of giving students teaching experience under real and usual conditions, and of testing the merits of the practice schools. In 1856 this training school arrangement was discontinued, and the students taught their own normal school classmates for practice. A "school of observation" was opened in 1867, but the plan of a special school was again abandoned in 1879 when the training school was discontinued, not to be re-established again until 1892.

At Bridgewater, Massachusetts, the Centre School District expended five hundred dollars to build a model school connected with the normal school:

A model school was connected with the school for the first eleven years of its history, in which each member of the senior class taught at least two weeks. Since 1880 the primary grades of the town school in the adjoining lot have been a school of observation for the normal students.[14]

In 1846 a new building, the first constructed by any state to house a normal school, was completed. As in other early normal schools, the model school was located on the lower floor. Soon, however, the model school was temporarily discontinued because of the sentiment expressed by the parents that they did not want their children "experimented with."

In 1844 the first state normal school in New York was opened at Albany. An "experimental" school was organized at the beginning of the second term, April 9, 1845.[15] By 1850 there were ninety-three pupils in attendance, fifty-eight of whom were free pupils. Each of the other twenty-five paid twenty dollars for instruction and books and to help defray the expenses of maintaining the school. An official document states:

Two spacious rooms in the building are appropriated to the accommodation of the two departments of this school. . . . Each member of the

[14] Bridgewater Normal School, *Semi-Centennial Exercises*. Address by Albert G. Boyden, p. 24. 1890.
[15] Henry Barnard, *Normal Schools, and Other Institutions, Agencies, and Means Designed for the Professional Education of Teachers*, pp. 203-205. 1851.

# INTRODUCTION AND STATEMENT OF PROBLEM 7

graduating class is required to spend at least two weeks in this department.[16]

At New Britain, Connecticut, a normal school authorized by the legislature in 1849 was opened on May 15, 1850. By the act founding the institution the trustees were enabled to make provision for a model primary school, and they soon exercised the power delegated to them:

> At the close of the first week there were thirty-five Normal pupils in attendance, under the immediate instruction of Rev. T. D. P. Stone, the Associate Principal of the School, and upward of three hundred pupils from the village in four Schools of Practice, under the charge of Mr. Stone, assisted by Professor Guion, three female teachers and pupils of the Normal School. The four Schools of Practice are supported by the Central District of the New Britain School Society.[17]

At Ypsilanti, Michigan, where the first normal school under state auspices west of the Allegheny mountains was established, the town engaged to pay the salary of the teacher in the model school composed of children of the village, and to furnish a temporary building until the institution could provide suitable quarters to house the institution.

> The people of Ypsilanti, in their offer of land and money to secure the location of the school in their city, proposed to defray, for a time a large part of the expense of supporting this Model Department. Such a school was opened at the commencement of the second term of the normal. . . . At the time of its organization the Board had space and conveniences for only a small number of pupils. A single room and a single teacher were all that could be provided. The attendance during the first term was twenty-seven.[18]

The plan as actually put into operation was relatively ineffective and in 1855, the Secretary of the Board of Education, Superintendent Ira Mayhew, wrote that model school pupils received instruction in elementary subjects only, "and this without any aid from Normal pupils, and without their presence and attention to school arrangements, plans of government or method of instruc-

---

[16] Annual Circular of the Executive Committee for 1850; quoted in Barnard, *op. cit.*, p. 207.
[17] *Fifth Annual Report of the Superintendent of the Common Schools of Connecticut to the General Assembly*, May Session, p. 14. 1850.
[18] Daniel Putnam, *History of the Michigan State Normal School*, p. 86. 1899.

tion." In 1870 the Michigan Board of Education arranged with the city of Ypsilanti for observation and limited practice but the plan was discontinued two years later because of the distances which students were compelled to travel, the difficulty incurred in giving adequate supervision, and the aversion which parents felt toward having their children "practiced upon" by inexperienced teachers.[19]

The state normal school at Providence, Rhode Island, an outgrowth of a private institution, was opened May 29, 1854. There was no laboratory school, but prospective teachers gave "teaching exercises" to their classmates.

The greater and more important part of the new matter introduced into the course of instruction at the Normal School consists of what are called "Teaching Exercises." These are properly experiments of the pupils in practical instruction. A scholar is assigned a particular branch for a particular time, and it is his duty to present that topic to his fellows of the school at the time. He is required, of course, to teach something new, as well as what is already known, and to do this in a manner adapted to the capacities of smaller children. After his "Exercise" he is subject to the criticisms of the class, and to the corrections and instructions of the Principal or Teacher having charge of the particular department. These "Exercises" are very popular with the scholars of the school, and are, without doubt, the most excellent part of the system of training in the school.[20]

Each student-teacher spent six months or a year in these "exercises."

A similar plan was employed in the normal school at Salem, Massachusetts, the eighth to be established in the country. But here it was augmented by using a practice school composed of children from one of the town schools.

In every study the pupils in turn occupy temporarily the place of teacher of their classmates, and are subjected to their criticism as well as those of the regular teacher. Teaching exercises of various kinds form a large and important part of the school work. During the senior term object lessons are daily given to classes of children from an adjacent primary school, so that every pupil obtains, before graduating, considerable ex-

[19] *Ibid.*, p. 96.
[20] *Annual Report of the Commissioner of Public Schools of Rhode Island*, pp. 28–29, January, 1856.

INTRODUCTION AND STATEMENT OF PROBLEM 9

perience in teaching young children to observe, think and give expression to thought.[21]

The normal school at Trenton, New Jersey, opened on October 1, 1855, and the model school was opened on March 17, 1856, about six months later. It was successful from the first.[22] The two rooms designated for the use of the model school when it opened were soon inadequate and it became necessary to provide additional rooms. In 1857 a plot of ground adjoining the normal school was purchased and a model school building was erected.

In Pennsylvania the Bill of 1857, which had been enacted by the legislature to provide for normal schools, made it mandatory, as a condition of locating a normal school in any town or city, that there be a model school with accommodations for not less than one hundred pupils. The Lancaster County Normal Institute had begun its sessions at Millersville on April 17, 1855, and had almost two hundred enrolled in its model schools. On December 2, 1859, the first state normal school in Pennsylvania became the successor of this institution.[23]

The first state normal school west of the Mississippi River was established at Winona, Minnesota. The first Board of Education of Winona was created by act of the legislature to consist of a school director elected from each of the three wards, the principal, and such members of the normal school board at Winona "as shall be residents of the city and properly qualified." "The idea was to copy somewhat after the Oswego plan of uniting the jurisdiction of the normal and public schools of Winona, using the public schools as graded and model schools."[24] In the following year, however, the law was repealed and the plan of joint jurisdiction was abandoned. In 1864 two rooms were equipped in the normal school building to accommodate the model department. Each had a capacity of about forty pupils. In 1867 there were 164 enrolled. Financial support was obtained by charging each pupil $7.50 a quarter. The model department was independent of the

[21] Henry Barnard, "State Normal School at Salem, Mass." *American Journal of Education*, Vol. 17, p. 699, 1867-68.
[22] *Ibid.*, p. 731.
[23] J. P. Wickersham, *A History of Education in Pennsylvania*, pp. 621-624. 1886.
[24] Clyde O. Ruggles, *Historical Sketch and Notes, Winona State Normal School, 1860-1910*, p. 40. 1910.

local school system and "entirely under the control of the normal school" and "an integral part of it."[25] The plan for the institution contemplated both a graded model and a graded practice school: the former a school of three grades—primary, intermediate, and grammar; the latter, one having four departments.

While in many or most of the institutions mentioned above the amount of practice teaching, judged by present standards, was small, a new epoch in the development of training schools began with the opening of the institution at Oswego, New York, for here great stress was laid on practice work. Students were expected to spend one year in observation and practice in the Model Primary School Teachers Department, half of the school day to be used in the laboratory school, the other half of the time in studying the other school subjects. In May, 1861, the training school consisted of a primary school of about two hundred children and there were nine student-teachers. "In addition to the practice school there was a model school used exclusively for observation purposes, and one school taught exclusively by members of the training class."[26]

From the foregoing it is clear that observation and student-teaching were deemed necessary by all the state normal schools which were established prior to the Civil War. Even when local or temporary conditions were such that the student-teaching program was restricted in scope, or made totally impossible, it was always a clear tenet of those charged with the duty of preparing teachers that laboratory experience is indispensable. Nowhere is this shown more clearly than in a resolution which was adopted without debate at the First Annual Convention of the American Normal School Association in Trenton, New Jersey, August 18, 1859:

Resolved, That this education of teachers should not only be theoretical, but also practical; and that, to this end, there should either be a school of observation and practice in immediate connection with the normal school, and under the same Board of Control, or that there should be in other ways equivalent opportunities for observation and practice.[27]

---

[25] Barnard, *loc. cit.*, p. 763.
[26] Ned H. Dearborn, *The Oswego Movement in American Education*, p. 15. 1925.
[27] *Proceedings of the First Annual Convention of the American Normal School Association*, p. 107. 1860.

With the outbreak of the Civil War the development of training schools was retarded.[28] Because of doubts which had arisen regarding the efficacy of the laboratory schools, and because the attention and energy of the nation were turned in other directions by the impact of the struggle, a tendency, begun earlier, to use normal school classes for practice, in which students taught their fellow students instead of training school pupils in the model school, continued. A state commissioner of public instruction, who was prominent in educational matters in America during the period, surveyed the situation immediately after the close of the war:

> Most normal schools have a model or experimental department in which students practice under the supervision and criticism of a skilled teacher. In the best training schools, these model lessons, as they are called, are made the basis of instruction in methods. In some normal schools the practice of the students is obtained by giving model lessons in their own classes.[29]

It would be incorrect to overemphasize the change in attitude toward laboratory schools. During the war only three state normal schools closed—Winona, Minn., New Orleans, La., and Charleston, S. C. Three others opened during or just following the war, each with provision for a model school—San Francisco, Calif., Emporia, Kan., and Terre Haute, Ind. In reply to a query directed to the normal schools in 1867 by the United States Commissioner of Education, twenty-five of thirty state normal schools replying indicated that they maintained practice schools. Except in some institutions in Massachusetts and Maine, where students in the normal schools were substituted for model school pupils in practice classes, student-teaching was done either in a campus school or in schools of adjacent districts.[30]

During the sixties and seventies of the last century, under the inspiration and leadership of the vigorous programs of the Oswego Movement and renewed interest resulting from the extension of

---

[28] H. H. Ryan, "A Century of Laboratory Schools in the United States," p. 4. Unpublished study. 1929.
[29] E. E. White, *Report of the Commissioner of Public Schools of Ohio to the General Assembly*. 1866.
[30] *Report of the (United States) Commissioner of Education for the Year 1867–68*, pp. 649–820. 1868.

Pestalozzian theories, the number of laboratory schools increased, and they assumed a central position in the programs of teacher education. A study of the data contained in the reports of the United States Commissioner of Education at intervals [31] indicates clearly this central position and emphasis. In the year 1873, 71.4 percent of the publicly supported normal schools had laboratory schools; in 1883–84, 71 percent; in 1893–94, 68.5 percent. In 1874 forty-seven of the sixty-seven state normal schools had laboratory schools attached to them.

In a study of sixty "representative" state normal schools—east, north, south, and west—a comparison of the same group of institutions was made over a period of a decade (1903–04 or 1904–05 and 1913–14 or 1914–15). Of these, fifty-three offered a course in practice teaching in 1905, while all did so in 1915, when 78 percent of the schools had their own campus schools, and only 22 percent used cooperating schools either of their own or adjoining school districts.[32]

With the organization of the American Association of Teachers Colleges in 1917 there came a new emphasis on standards of teacher preparation. At the meeting of the Association in Washington, D. C., February 20, 1926, the following standard was adopted:

Each teachers college shall maintain a training school under its own control as a part of its organization, as a laboratory school, for purposes of observation, demonstration, and supervised teaching on the part of students. The use of an urban or rural school system, under sufficient control and supervision of the college to permit carrying out the educational policy of the college to a sufficient degree for the conduct of effective student teaching, will satisfy this requirement. (Standard VII. A.)[33]

In reporting on compliance with these standards, a committee of the Association reported the following year that replies had been received from 113 of 150 member institutions and concluded that "Every institution with one or two exceptions affirms the main-

---

[31] *Report of the Commissioner of Education for the Year 1873*, pp. 573–580, 1874; *1883–84*, pp. 388–398, 1885; *1893–94*, pp. 2070–2079, Vol. 2, 1896; *1900–01*, pp. 1882–1893, Vol. 2, 1902.
[32] George E. Walk, "Practice Teaching and Observation in Normal Schools." *Education*, Vol. 38, pp. 69–85, October, 1917.
[33] *Yearbook of The American Association of Teachers Colleges, 1926*, p. 11.

tenance of a training school or of affiliated urban or rural schools for student teaching purposes . . . ."[34]

With further development of the Association in membership and more rigid enforcement of its standards, laboratory experience in the training schools has become a universally recognized requirement.

## SECTION B

## THE PROBLEM AND THE PROCEDURE

The development of the laboratory school, traced in the preceding section, has been conditioned and influenced by the general trend of educational thought. During the last two decades a remarkable impetus has been given to all forms of educational progress. Rapidly changing social conditions have found a correlative response in improved curriculums, more nearly scientific and adequate teaching techniques, more nearly adequate supervision, and greater skill in administration. Important as the "trappings" of the educational system may be, the briefest consideration makes it evident that the very heart and center of the educational system and of the educational process is the teacher who implements the social inheritance in instructing the pupils, other educational factors being subsidiary to the production of skilled and well-prepared teachers.

Consequently, increasingly insistent demands have been made that the institutions for the education of teachers furnish teachers of adequate scholarship, technical skill, and professional competency to educate pupils as citizens of a democracy. Social turmoil and conflict, the increased complexity of the society in which pupils are to live, and an awakened consciousness of the importance of universally diffused education have been factors in providing an impulse toward more effective schools. Teaching is now advancing rapidly toward the status of a profession in which its members increasingly assume a position in society commensurate with the importance of their work and perform their professional functions

---

[34] H. W. Rockwell, "Report of the Committee on Accrediting and Classification." *Yearbook of The American Association of Teachers Colleges, 1927*, pp. 120–121.

with greater skill and understanding. Paralleling rapid changes in other areas of educational advance, such as educational philosophy, curriculum development, techniques of teaching, supervision, and administration, there has been marked improvement in pre-service education of teachers. A more substantial and valid educational theory is being accumulated; teacher education is growing more conscious of its achievements as well as of its problems and is definitely moving toward a program of greater excellence.

## IMPORTANCE OF THE LABORATORY SCHOOL FACILITIES

Among the problems that the teachers colleges and normal schools face is that of furnishing teachers-to-be with the appropriate laboratory experience as a part of their preparation. Modern psychology affirms the value of learning through guided activity. Sound educational theory asserts that theory and practice, as two phases of the teaching process, must go hand in hand in learning. The emphasis which the normal schools and teachers colleges have traditionally placed upon the training school grows out of the "faith that the best way of learning to teach is through actual contact with real teaching, and a philosophy which declares that a usable theory will work in practice."[35]

Educational theory, the results of educational research, and the pragmatic judgments of students and teachers affirm the necessity of the laboratory experience in the preparation of teachers. An important study in 1920 declares:

> The training school constitutes the characteristic laboratory equipment of a normal school or teachers college, and the courses in observation, participation, and practice teaching should be looked upon as the central and critical elements in each of the curricula.[36]

As early as 1916 Judd and Parker asserted that the "zone of [the] normal school should be limited by [its] practice facilities."[37]

The value of student-teaching as a prediction of future teaching

---

[35] A. R. Mead, *Supervised Student-Teaching*, p. 17. 1930.
[36] William S. Learned and William C. Bagley, *The Professional Preparation of Teachers for American Public Schools*, p. 192. 1920.
[37] C. H. Judd and S. C. Parker, *Problems Involved in Standardizing State Normal Schools*, p. 47. 1916.

## INTRODUCTION AND STATEMENT OF PROBLEM 15

success has been investigated in a number of scientific studies. In a study of 1,185 students enrolled in ten normal schools, Meriam[38] found that the correlation between teaching ability and practice teaching is higher than between teaching ability and any other courses which the student takes. Whitney,[39] in a study of 1,156 graduates from twelve normal schools using the method of partial and multiple correlations and regression equations, found evidence that practice teaching is a better index of future teaching success than any other factor which he measured. Somers[40] studied the teaching success of 156 graduates of the State Normal School, Farmville, Va., as measured by ratings of supervisors, principals, and superintendents, and found a high correlation (.70) between the success of teachers and their ratings in teaching in the laboratory schools. Ullman,[41] reviewing earlier studies and investigating the same subject further concludes: "Success in practice teaching is the best single measure of teaching success."

In 1926–27 a committee of the Association of Colleges and Secondary Schools of the Southern States sent a questionnaire to the teachers in the secondary schools in the Association. Replies were received from 11,472 teachers in 838 schools. In assigning values to the professional subjects which they had taken as students in college, practice teaching was placed first by 3,909 teachers. Practice teaching ranked higher in value than any other subject, whether replies were from teachers in groups having experience of one year or less, two to six years, or over six years.[42] Though this is not conclusive evidence, it is important in showing the combined judgment of experienced teachers. Summarizing the opinions of teachers regarding the value of the course in student-teaching, Peik states:

In all recent evaluations studies based upon the judgment of teachers

---

[38] Junius L. Meriam, *Normal School Education and Efficiency in Teaching*, pp. 55, 71, 78–80. 1905.
[39] F. L. Whitney, "The Prediction of Teaching Success." *Journal of Educational Research Monographs*, No. 6, p. 19. 1924.
[40] G. T. Somers, *Pedagogical Prognosis: Predicting the Success of Prospective Teachers*, p. 48. 1923.
[41] Roy Roland Ullman, *The Prognostic Value of Certain Factors Related to Teaching Success*, p. 97. 1931.
[42] M. E. Ligon, Chairman, *Training of High School Teachers*, pp. 6, 26–41. 1931.

in which student-teaching is listed among courses evaluated, none has been found where it does not rank at or near the top.[43]

Foster, concludes:

Provision for adequate training-school facilities is an important issue in the program of teacher education.[44]

Available evidence indicates that the problem of providing laboratory facilities which are adequate in quantity and quality is still urgent. Though the college enrollments in state normal schools and teachers colleges have been decreasing in the nondegree curriculums, the number of degrees conferred steadily increases. For the year 1919-20 there were 1,296 graduates in degree courses; a decade later, in 1929-30, the number had risen to 11,073; in 1935-36, after another six years, it was 18,262.[45]

Statistics gathered by Walters[46] show that total enrollments in the teachers colleges are increasing. The enrollment of a group of sixty-nine institutions increased 4.8 percent in 1935 over 1934; of sixty institutions, 2.7 percent in 1936 over 1935; and of sixty-five colleges, 0.9 percent in 1937 over the preceding year. While the rate of growth is declining and there is a decrease in the enrollments of students in state teachers colleges preparing for teaching in the elementary schools, there is an increase in those preparing for teaching service on the secondary level.

## RELATED STUDIES

An unusually large number of studies have been made which are related to the present investigation. These fall loosely into two groups: (a) those which are concerned with an analysis of student-teaching courses and supervisory techniques; and (b) those which relate to the organization and administration of the laboratory schools.

[43] W. E. Peik, "Teacher Education Curricula in Universities, Colleges, and Junior Colleges." *National Survey of the Education of Teachers*, Vol. III, Part III, p. 269. 1935.
[44] Frank K. Foster, "The Training School in the Education of Teachers." *National Survey of the Education of Teachers*, Vol. III, Part IV, p. 387. 1935.
[45] *Biennial Survey of Education, 1934-36*, Vol. II, Chap. IV, p. 37. Office of Education Bulletin 1937, No. 2. 1939.
[46] Raymond Walters, "Statistics of Registration in American Universities and Colleges." *School and Society*, Vol. 42, p. 802, December 14, 1935; Vol. 44, p. 793, December 19, 1936; Vol. 46, p. 770, December 18, 1937.

## INTRODUCTION AND STATEMENT OF PROBLEM 17

In the first group an early study was that by Garrison,[47] who, in his dissertation, made a job analysis of the supervisor's work in fifty-five state teachers colleges. Fitch[48] used a similar procedure to study the activities and techniques employed by supervisors in the elementary schools. Flowers[49] investigated the courses in student-teaching designed to prepare teachers for service in the secondary schools of state teachers colleges. Pryor[50] proposed gradual induction of students into student-teaching by a series of graded units. Strebel[51] described the supervisory activities during induction into teaching and during responsible room teaching. He limited his investigation to a study of universities which used public schools as off-campus laboratory schools. Mooney[52] studied the supervision of student-teaching as it applied to the state teachers colleges of a single state, New York. In 1939 two similar studies appeared: the first, by Nelson,[53] investigated the content of student-teaching courses for the preparation of elementary teachers; the second, by Cole,[54] was concerned with the problem of integrating the program for teacher education by the cooperation of the members of the faculty of the laboratory school with the other members of the normal school or teachers college faculty.

Early studies, usually limited in their scope, mark the beginning of investigations into the administrative problems of laboratory schools in normal schools and teachers colleges. Greenough,[55] chairman of a committee of the Normal Department of the National Education Association, stated the conditions under which

---

[47] Noble L. Garrison, *Status and Work of the Training Supervisor.* 1927.
[48] Harry N. Fitch, *An Analysis of the Supervisory Activities and Techniques of the Elementary School Training Supervisor.* 1931.
[49] John G. Flowers, *Content of Student-Teaching Courses Designed for the Training of Secondary Teachers in State Teachers Colleges.* 1932.
[50] Hugh Clark Pryor, *Graded Units in Student-Teaching.* 1926.
[51] Ralph F. Strebel, *The Nature of the Supervision of Student-Teaching in Universities Using Cooperative Public Schools.* 1935.
[52] Edward S. Mooney, *An Analysis of the Supervision of Student Teaching.* 1937.
[53] Esther M. Nelson, *An Analysis of the Content of Student-Teaching Courses for the Education of Elementary Teachers in State Teachers Colleges.* 1939.
[54] Mary I. Cole, *Cooperation Between the Faculty of the Campus Elementary Training School and the Other Departments of Teachers Colleges and Normal Schools.* 1939.
[55] J. C. Greenough, "Training Schools in Connection with Normal Schools." *The Addresses and Journal of Proceedings of the National Education Association,* pp. 229-233. 1874.

an efficient laboratory school could be operated. Cook,[56] writing as chairman of the Committee on Normal School Education, surveyed the facilities which were available in fifty-seven state normal schools. Kelly and Scott[57] investigated the laboratory schools in sixty-eight state normal schools in the South and West. Judd and Parker[58] set forth general principles which should govern in the administration of normal schools and laboratory schools. Walk[59] made a study which was limited in scope to relatively few items, but which showed trends in the use of laboratory facilities in fifty-five representative normal schools over a ten-year period, from 1903–04 or 1905 to 1913–14 or 1915. The study is significant in indicating certain trends over a decade.

Learned and Bagley,[60] in a survey of the tax-supported normal schools of the State of Missouri, included a comprehensive statement of the problems of laboratory schools, and developed a set of principles for administering them. About the same time Wilson[61] made a rather complete study of the administration of the laboratory school, limiting his investigation to state normal schools. He urged the necessity for affiliating public schools with teachers colleges to secure laboratory facilities and the desirability of the participation of college teachers in the work of the laboratory schools. The author[62] of the present study used a questionnaire study of 295 institutions, of which eighty-five were state normal schools and teachers colleges, to survey the facilities which were available for observation and demonstration classes. Henderson[63]

---

[56] John W. Cook, "The Kind and Amount of Practice-Work and Its Place in the Normal School Course." *Journal of Proceedings and Addresses of the National Education Association*, pp. 501–509. 1895.

[57] F. J. Kelly and Ira O. Scott, "What Training School Facilities Are Provided in State Normal Schools?" *Educational Administration and Supervision*, Vol. 1, pp. 591–598, November, 1915.

[58] Judd and Parker, *op. cit.*

[59] Walk, *op. cit.*

[60] Learned and Bagley, *op. cit.*

[61] Lester M. Wilson, *Training Departments in State Normal Schools in the United States*. 1919.

[62] E. I. F. Williams, "Demonstration Teaching and Observation in the Teacher Training Institutions of the United States," pp. 103–121. Society of College Teachers of Education, *Educational Monographs*, No. XI. 1922.

[63] Joseph L. Henderson, "A Statistical Study of the Use of City School Systems by Student-Teachers in Colleges and Universities in the United States." *Educational Administration and Supervision*, Vol. 12, pp. 326–339, May, 1926.

INTRODUCTION AND STATEMENT OF PROBLEM 19

surveyed the use made of city school systems as laboratory schools by 114 state and independent colleges and universities. Armentrout[64] in a rather general study of administrative problems analyzed student-teaching activities, suggested methods of improving the supervisory techniques employed, and devoted a limited part of his study to the problems of facilities. Baugher[65] investigated practice teaching as found in the small privately endowed liberal arts college; and Jarman[66] studied the administration of laboratory schools used as university high schools by state universities. Eubank[67] studied the administration of the laboratory school in eighty-five state teachers colleges, and although this aspect of administration formed a rather minor part of his study, he discovered an inadequacy of practice facilities. Foster[68] described various aspects of teachers college administration, including curriculums, the training schools, and coordination of the work of the training school with the other departments of the institution. A recent study in the administration of student-teaching by Henderson,[69] including thirty-seven teachers colleges, dealt largely with the selection, supervision, and appointment of student-teachers and the selection, employment, and assignment to duties of faculty members to teach in the laboratory schools. In each of these studies the provision of adequate laboratory school facilities was an important, though a minor, aspect of the investigation.

### NEED FOR THE STUDY

That present facilities are inadequate for the work which state teachers colleges should ideally do is witnessed generally by those who are acquainted with the situation. Typical of the general opinion of investigators is the statement of Nelson,[70] who discov-

[64] W. D. Armentrout, *The Conduct of Student Teaching in State Teachers Colleges.* 1927.
[65] Jacob I. Baugher, *Organization and Administration of Practice-Teaching in Privately Endowed Colleges of Liberal Arts.* 1931.
[66] Arthur M. Jarman, *The Administration of Laboratory Schools.* 1932.
[67] Louis Allen Eubank, *The Organization and Administration of Laboratory Schools in State Teachers Colleges.* 1931.
[68] Foster, *op. cit.*, pp. 367–401.
[69] Elisha L. Henderson, *The Organization and Administration of Student Teaching in State Teachers Colleges.* 1937.
[70] Nelson, *op. cit.*, pp. 23–24.

ered a consensus of opinion among the administrators of fifty-seven state teachers colleges that a large proportion of the teachers colleges of the country have too limited laboratory facilities, and that the ratio of pupils to student-teachers falls far below approved standards, in some cases so low as to make the work in student-teaching relatively ineffective. Support of this view is shown in the findings of the National Survey of the Education of Teachers, which reaches this conclusion:

The improvement of student-teaching facilities, greater emphasis on student-teaching, more directed observation of it by competent persons, more nearly adequate professional treatment of the teaching field, and the correlation of student-teaching, observation and special methods constitute the urgent needs of the education of teachers.[71]

Because, then, the whole problem of the education of teachers is conditioned by the opportunity for the student-teacher to secure laboratory experience, and this, in turn, is directly related to the question of the facilities which are available for laboratory schools, it is of the utmost importance that an adequate number of classes and schools be under the control of the teachers college so as to provide student-teachers with actual experience of such quantity and quality as may be necessary in schools similar to those in which they may be expected to teach.

## THE PROBLEM

This study aims to accomplish these objectives:

1. To survey (*a*) the laboratory facilities found at present in campus and off-campus laboratory schools of state normal schools and teachers colleges; (*b*) the extent to which, and the conditions under which, they are employed; and (*c*) additional facilities which are potentially available to supplement those now being used.

2. To formulate a set of criteria, supported by reference to leading authorities, which may be used as a basis for analyzing and criticizing current practices in providing facilities for, and administering student-teaching in, the laboratory schools.

3. To make such proposals for administrative procedures as can be determined and supported by an analysis and interpreta-

[71] Peik, *op. cit.*, p. 273.

# INTRODUCTION AND STATEMENT OF PROBLEM

tion of the data, and are consistent with the principles which have been derived.

## SOURCES OF DATA AND PROCEDURES

Information regarding present situations and practices was secured as follows:

1. A survey was made by a questionnaire which was sent to 160 state normal schools and teachers colleges listed as members of the American Association of Teachers Colleges in the 1934 *Yearbook* of the Association. The questionnaire was authorized and sponsored by the Committee on Standards and Surveys of the American Association of Teachers Colleges. Data were obtained for the year 1933-34 or 1934-35, depending upon the type of information required. Out of the 160 institutions 131, or 81.9 percent, replied. The high percentage of returns was due to the cooperation of the Committee in sponsoring the study.

That the replies received are typical of the whole country is indicated by an examination of the distribution in Table I. In order that the institutions might be comparable, the study was limited to state normal schools and teachers colleges which prepare for teaching in schools for white children.

To check on former data and to establish trends, a questionnaire seeking similar information was sent again to members of the Association in the fall of 1938, asking for data for the year 1937-38. Replies were received to the second questionnaire from 137 institutions distributed throughout forty-one states. Certain tables in the study include comparative data as revealed by the replies in the two questionnaires.

2. State school laws, catalogues of teachers colleges, and bulletins of state departments of education were used to secure additional data and to verify certain answers in the questionnaires.

3. Letters were sent to state departments of education to verify statements which were made and to supplement them.

4. Copies of contracts which were furnished by the state normal schools and teachers colleges were analyzed.

5. Supplementary information was secured through interviews with directors of training and by a personal visit to eight of the institutions represented in the study.

## TABLE I

*Distribution of Members of the American Association of Teachers Colleges Included in This Study*

| Geographic Division | No. of Institutions to Which Questionnaire Was Sent | Institutions Furnishing Data No. | % | No. of States Represented in Replies* |
|---|---|---|---|---|
| New England (Conn., Maine, Mass., N. H., R. I., Vt.) | 11 | 7 | 63.6 | 4 |
| Middle Atlantic (N. J., N. Y., Pa.) | 27 | 22 | 81.5 | 3 |
| East North Central (Ill., Ind., Mich., Ohio, Wis.) | 25 | 21 | 84.0 | 5 |
| West North Central (Iowa, Kan., Minn., Mo., Neb., N. D., S. D.) | 28 | 24 | 85.7 | 7 |
| South Atlantic (Del., Fla., Ga., Md., N. C., S. C., Va., W. Va.) | 15 | 12 | 80.0 | 5 |
| East South Central (Ala., Ky., Miss., Tenn.) | 14 | 10 | 71.4 | 4 |
| West South Central (Ark., La., Okla., Tex.) | 17 | 16 | 94.1 | 4 |
| Mountain (Ariz., Colo., Idaho, Mont., Nev., N. M., Utah, Wyo.) | 11 | 8 | 72.7 | 6 |
| Pacific (Cal., Ore., Wash.) | 12 | 11 | 91.7 | 3 |
| Total | 160 | 131 | 81.9 | 41 |

*States not represented are four which have no state teachers colleges—Delaware, Florida, South Carolina, and Wyoming—and Maine, Mississippi, and Vermont.

6. Unpublished data secured by two former questionnaires, the first in 1923-24 and the second in 1929-30, were used to show certain long-term trends.

Whenever the number of replies to the questionnaire was sufficient to make it useful to do so, replies were tabulated and analyzed according to the geographic divisions of the United States as established by the Bureau of the Census. The reason for adopting this classification in this study is indicated in the report of the Census itself:

The states within each of these divisions are for the most part fairly homogeneous in physical characteristics, as well as in the characteristics of their population and in their social and economic conditions, whereas each division differs more or less sharply from most of the others in these respects.
—Fourteenth Census of the United States, Vol. I, p. 9. 1920.

Where it has seemed useful to emphasize distinctions between the different curriculums, the data are presented classified according to the length of the curriculum and the type of service for which students in the teachers college are preparing, such as teacher in the elementary schools, in the primary grades, in the rural one-teacher and two-teacher schools, and in the special subjects, for example, art and music.

As the laboratory school problems in liberal arts colleges and universities are in many respects different from those in the state teachers colleges, the former have not been included in this study. The provision of student-teaching in summer sessions is excluded in the belief that this is a temporary expedient in the preparation of teachers.

### DEFINITION OF TERMS USED IN THE STUDY

*Cadet* or *interne* plan of student-teaching is one in which the student-teacher is placed in full charge of a class in a neighboring school system, and performs the functions of a regular teacher of the system, being visited at more or less frequent intervals by a supervisor from the college campus.

*Campus laboratory school* is one which is located on the grounds of the normal school or teachers college.

*Class demonstration* is the teaching of a class of pupils in the laboratory schools by a supervisor, to illustrate techniques of teaching and management of a class to one or more student-teachers who observe the techniques used.

A *one-year curriculum*, or a *curriculum one year in length*, denotes a curriculum following in subject-matter sequence immediately after a four-year course in the secondary schools. Similarly, other curriculums, of whatever lengths, follow immediately, in their subject matter, that of the secondary school. No curriculums of graduate level are included in the study.

*General elementary curriculum* is a single undifferentiated curriculum designed to prepare teachers for teaching in all grades of the elementary school.

*Laboratory experience* means all the experience which the student-teacher receives from his contact with the laboratory school, whether in observation, in participation, or in student-teaching.

*Laboratory school* is any school, located on or off the campus of a teachers college, to which student-teachers go for their laboratory experience.

*Laboratory school facilities* is a term used to designate all schools which are available for the provision of laboratory experience to student-teachers.

*Observation* is that phase of the laboratory experience of a student-teacher in which, under direction, he goes to the laboratory school to study procedures and techniques in teaching and managing a school.

*Off-campus laboratory school* is a laboratory school, not located on the grounds of a state teachers college but affiliated with it, used to provide laboratory experience for student-teachers.

*Participation* is that phase of the student-teacher's experience in the laboratory school following his completion of observation of teaching and prior to his assumption of responsible room teaching, during which he assists the supervising teacher in such activities as grading papers, instructing individual pupils, and sharing in the instruction of a class as a whole.

*Student-teaching* is responsible room teaching in which the student-teacher assumes the complete conduct of the class under the direction of a supervising teacher.

*Supervisor* is a teacher in the laboratory schools, either on the campus or off the campus, who directs the student-teachers in laboratory experience. *Critic teacher* is an equivalent designation.

*Teachers college* is a term used to mean either a normal school or teachers college.

## CHAPTER II

## THE PRESENTATION AND INTERPRETATION OF THE DATA

IN this chapter, the data which have been secured in answer to the questionnaires, supplemented by related information which has been secured by other methods and from other sources, are presented and interpreted. The questionnaire was arranged in five sections to each of which a corresponding section of this chapter is allotted: (*a*) general information, relating to the calendar of the academic year and the student enrollment; (*b*) the laboratory courses which are offered in the laboratory or training schools; (*c*) the campus laboratory schools; (*d*) the off-campus laboratory schools; and (*e*) off-campus schools not now used for laboratory purposes, but potentially available to the institution for such use.

### SECTION A

### *GENERAL INFORMATION REGARDING THE CALENDAR YEAR, ENROLLMENT, AND CURRICULUMS*

General information concerning the normal schools and teachers colleges included in this study is presented below under four divisions: (*a*) the calendar of the academic year; (*b*) enrollment in various curriculums; (*c*) the type of curriculums offered; and (*d*) the length of curriculums.

#### THE CALENDAR OF THE ACADEMIC YEAR

Except in a few instances, whether or not the academic year of the teachers college is divided into quarters or semesters does not affect the presentation of the data. However, the calendar of the teachers college has important implications for a study of the facilities which the institution can use for laboratory purposes. An analysis of Table II indicates that more than one-half of the institutions (53.4 percent) studied organized their calendar on the semester plan in 1933–34, and that an increased number (59.1 percent) did so in 1937–38, changes having been made during the period in the direction of the semester plan in four of the nine geographic divisions of the country. The greatest shift toward the semester plan is found in New England, where fifteen institutions were reported on the semester plan in 1937–38 and no institution reporting was organized on the quarter plan; a lesser though positive trend toward the semester plan is found in the Middle Atlantic and South Atlantic divisions. The other areas, taken as a whole, show a slight movement toward the quarter plan.

TABLE II

*Number of Institutions on Quarter and Semester Plan in State Normal Schools and Teachers Colleges, 1933–34 and 1937–38*

| Geographic Division | On Semester Plan 1933–34 | On Semester Plan 1937–38 | On Quarter Plan 1933–34 | On Quarter Plan 1937–38 |
|---|---|---|---|---|
| New England | 6 | 15 | 1 | 0 |
| Middle Atlantic | 22 | 26 | 0 | 1 |
| East North Central | 10 | 19 | 11 | 11 |
| West North Central | 4 | 5 | 20 | 18 |
| South Atlantic | 5 | 8 | 7 | 7 |
| East South Central | 4 | 3 | 6 | 7 |
| West South Central | 14 | 11 | 2 | 1 |
| Mountain | 1 | 1 | 7 | 5 |
| Pacific | 4 | 3 | 7 | 6 |
| Total | 70 | 81 | 61 | 56 |
| Percent | 53.4 | 59.1 | 46.6 | 40.9 |

Total number of institutions, 1933–34............ 131
Total number of institutions, 1937–38............ 137

What division of the academic year is employed by the institution is less important than that it synchronize with that of the campus and off-campus laboratory schools. This matter is considered of such importance by some institutions that a clause is inserted in the contracts made with cooperating off-campus laboratory schools synchronizing the calendars of the public school and the teachers college. If the calendars do correspond, (*a*) schedule-making for the college student is simplified—conflicts with his college classes are prevented, and his assignment to student-teaching is facilitated; (*b*) serious loss of time and the disorganization which results from inter-quarter vacations, final examinations, and registration periods are prevented; (*c*) the planning of courses which use the laboratory schools is simplified; and (*d*) the ease with which the student-teacher can plan the units of work for his period of student-teaching or other laboratory experience in the training school is enhanced. The effective use of the laboratory school in carrying the laboratory experience load is directly influenced by proper relationships between the calendars of the college and of the laboratory schools.

Wherever, in this study, the plan of calendar organization must be considered in assembling and interpreting the data, semester hours have been expressed in quarter-hour equivalents, not because this plan is favored above the other as being more desirable, but because, by this procedure, data can be handled more effectively.

### ENROLLMENT ACCORDING TO TYPE AND LENGTH OF CURRICULUM[1]

A tabulation of the enrollment in 105 state normal schools and teachers colleges (Table III), arranged according to the type and length of the curriculums, indicates the teaching levels and areas for which students are preparing and, consequently, where facilities are needed in the training school to provide them with laboratory experience. Data were not included for twenty-six institutions which did not report the number of students enrolled.

The questionnaire included the curriculums which were most frequently offered. In some cases, the type of organization did not lend itself to answering the questionnaire completely. For example, the Central Missouri State Teachers College, Warrensburg,

---

[1] "Type of curriculum," as used in this study, refers to a curriculum designed to prepare for teaching certain grade levels or special subjects; for example, general elementary, intermediate, senior high school, rural one-teacher and two-teacher schools, or agriculture, home economics, and music. This phrase is to be distinguished from such expressions as "One-year curriculum," "Two-year curriculum," etc., which are used as a matter of convenience to indicate the length of a curriculum rather than its type.

## TABLE III

*Student Enrollment in 105 State Normal Schools and Teachers Colleges, According to Type of Curriculum, 1933–34*

| Type of Curriculum | No. of Institutions | One Year* | Two Year | Three Year | Four Year | Total |
|---|---|---|---|---|---|---|
| General elem. (gr. K or 1–8)... | 47 | 912 | 3,861 | 1,716 | 4,746 | 11,235 |
| Kindergarten-primary (gr. K-3). | 69 | 31 | 3,093 | 1,608 | 2,248 | 6,980 |
| Primary-intermediate (gr. 1–6). | 1 | | | 116 | | 116 |
| Intermediate (gr. 4–6)......... | 60 | 22 | 3,097 | 1,264 | 2,554 | 6,937 |
| Intermediate-Jr. H. S. (gr. 4–9). | 3 | | 158 | | 268 | 426 |
| Grammar (gr. 7–8)............ | 8 | | 237 | 573 | 369 | 1,179 |
| Junior high school (gr. 7–9).... | 43 | 113 | 860 | 725 | 1,931 | 3,629 |
| Jr. and sr. high school (gr. 7–12). | 27 | | | | 9,696 | 9,696 |
| Senior high school (gr. 8–11, or 9 or 10–12)................. | 43 | 41 | 81 | 167 | 10,937 | 11,226 |
| Rural one-teacher and two-teacher schools............. | 38 | 1,549 | 1,011 | 158 | 250 | 2,968 |
| Six other groupings each reported by one or two institutions.... | 12 | | 971 | 56 | 513 | 1,540 |
| Total..................... | | 2,668 | 13,369 | 6,383 | 33,512 | 55,932 |
| Percent................... | | 4.8 | 23.9 | 11.4 | 59.9 | 100.0 |
| Special subjects: | | | | | | |
| Agriculture................ | 16 | 2 | 1 | 1 | 298 | 302 |
| Art....................... | 36 | 6 | 4 | 74 | 703 | 787 |
| Business.................. | 42 | 23 | 23 | 67 | 2,710 | 2,823 |
| Home economics........... | 47 | 6 | 8 | 13 | 1,979 | 2,006 |
| Industrial arts............. | 44 | 4 | 11 | 29 | 1,461 | 1,505 |
| Music.................... | 50 | 59 | 26 | 49 | 1,416 | 1,550 |
| Physical education (men).... | 35 | 14 | 5 | 29 | 1,198 | 1,246 |
| Physical education (women).. | 36 | 5 | 8 | 23 | 774 | 810 |
| Physical education (men and women)................. | 3 | | | | 287 | 287 |
| Sixteen others each reported by one or two institutions.. | 18 | | | 34 | 432 | 466 |
| Total..................... | | 119 | 86 | 319 | 11,258 | 11,782 |
| Percent................... | | 1.0 | .7 | 2.7 | 95.6 | 100.0 |
| Grand Total................ | | 2,787 | 13,455 | 6,702 | 44,770 | 67,714 |
| Percent................... | | 4.1 | 19.9 | 9.9 | 66.1 | 100.0 |

* One year above the high school level. No fifth, or graduate year is considered in this study.

Missouri, replied: "Students do not declare a major until the beginning of the junior year; therefore, no junior college students [are included] in these figures except those completing the two year general elementary course." Western Kentucky State Teachers College, Bowling Green, Kentucky, writes: "Students are not required to select definitely a curriculum before the junior year." For different institutions the curriculum patterns ranged from those offering a single general elementary curriculum, as at the State Teachers Colleges at Florence, Jacksonville, and Troy, Alabama, at the time the data for this study were submitted, to those offering a wide variety of patterns, as at the State Teachers College, San Francisco, California. In the latter the following curriculums, a total of eighteen, are named: kindergarten-primary; kindergarten-primary and elementary; elementary; elementary and junior high school; junior high school; pre-secondary; kindergarten-primary and music; elementary and music; elementary, junior high school and music; junior high school and music; special music; elementary, junior high school and physical education for men; junior high school and physical education for men; special physical education for men; elementary and physical education for women; elementary, junior high school, and physical education for women; junior high school and physical education for women; and special physical education for women.

The table includes all data received except that from one institution in the East North Central Division which offered a curriculum two and one-half years in length in which nineteen students were enrolled to prepare themselves to teach in four special subjects—business, industrial arts, music, and physical education for men.

An analysis of the table makes certain comparisons possible. Though it is not the purpose of this study to enter into an elaborate and complete analysis of the teacher needs on different grade levels and in the various subject-matter areas, it is pertinent to call attention to certain apparent discrepancies between the numbers preparing for the different types of service and the numbers which are necessary to fill vacancies in the schools. The table shows that of the total enrolled in all the curriculums (excluding special subjects), 6.5 percent are enrolled in curriculums for junior high school teachers; 17.3 percent for junior-senior teachers; and 20.1 percent for senior high school teachers—a total of 43.9 percent in the curriculums preparing for teaching on junior and senior high school levels. The remaining 56.1 percent includes some students in curriculums for the high school level who cannot be segregated into elementary and high school levels—students pursuing the intermediate-junior high school (years 4–9) curriculum and those preparing for teaching in one-teacher and two-teacher schools. Accordingly, the number must be reduced somewhat below 56.1 percent. In contrast to these totals are those showing the number of teachers actually employed on these levels in the schools of the United States. According to data which were assembled for the corresponding academic year (1933–34), the number of teachers employed in the kindergarten and elementary schools in the United States was 520,668, or 61.5 percent of all teachers employed; in the junior high schools, 31,235, or 3.6 percent; in the junior-senior high schools, 12,417, or 1.5 percent; in the senior high schools, 13,853, or 1.6 percent; in the general and vocational subjects in the four-year high schools, 152,392, or 18.0 percent.[2] Though the latter data include all teachers, both white and colored, while the figures from the questionnaire are for white teachers only, the comparison is essentially applicable. Confirmatory evidence of the large number of teachers in the elementary schools is found in the data given by the National Survey of the Education of Teachers.[3] Of 447,917 replying, 259,694 (58.0 percent) indicated that they taught in grades below the junior high school. The contrasting figures indicate that the number enrolled in curriculums for the preparation of teachers in the elementary school divisions is too small if considered in the light of the numbers preparing in other fields and on other levels. It is true that the number of elementary pupils enrolled decreased 4.2 percent in the years 1930 to 1936, and that the high school enrollment increased 32.5 percent during the same period, but the decreased elementary enrollments occurred in the cities, the rural school enrollment ac-

---

[2] *Biennial Survey of Education, 1932–34*, Vol. II. Office of Education Bulletin, 1935, No. 2, Chap. II, pp. 66. 1937.

[3] E. S. Evenden, Guy C. Gamble, and Harold G. Blue, "Teacher Personnel in the United States." *National Survey of the Education of Teachers*, Vol. II, Part I, pp. 8–9. 1935.

## PRESENTATION AND INTERPRETATION OF DATA

tually increased.[4] The need for more teachers trained for service in the elementary schools is augmented to a considerable degree by the fact that the turnover, i.e., the ratio of the number of new teachers to the total number of teaching positions, is 1 to 4.8 for elementary teachers as contrasted with 1 to 5.3 for junior and senior high school teachers[5] (computed from Table 28 in reference cited).

It may be urged that colleges and universities or other institutions which are engaged in preparing teachers are supplying the need. However, other data show that this is not the case,[6] for 60.1 percent of the total number of graduates for the year 1933–34, who were preparing for grades below the high school, received their education in the state normal schools and teachers colleges.

Table III reveals an enrollment of 2,968 in curriculums for the preparation of teachers in one- and two-room schools. This is 4.4 percent of the total number enrolled in all curriculums in the 105 institutions reporting. An official governmental report[7] shows that there were 138,542 one-room rural schools in the United States in 1933–34, each needing a teacher; estimates made by the Office of Education in 1930 placed the number of two-teacher schools at 23,200,[8] each needing two teachers, making a total of 46,400 teachers. Accordingly, at this time there were approximately 184,950 teachers needed in one-teacher and two-teacher schools, 21.8 percent of all who were employed in the schools of the country that year, and 4.9 times the percentage enrolled in curriculums for preparation of such teachers in state normal schools and teachers colleges. The proportion of new teachers needed in rural schools each year to the whole number of rural teachers is greater than in other types of schools. The ratio of *new* teachers in elementary schools to the whole number teaching in such schools is 1 to 4.8; in rural schools it is 1 to 2.5,[9] a number

---

[4] *Biennial Survey of Education, 1934-36,* Vol. II, Chap. II, pp. 6, 9, and 50. Office of Education Bulletin, 1937, No. 2. 1939.

[5] Evenden, Gamble, and Blue, *op. cit.,* p. 92.

[6] *Biennial Survey of Education, 1932-34,* Vol. II, Chap. IV, pp. 78–82. (Computation from data in report.)

[7] *Ibid.,* Chap. II, p. 70.

[8] William McKinley Robinson, *Practices and Trends in the Preparation of Teachers for Rural Elementary Schools in the State Teachers Colleges and Normal Schools,* p. 55. 1936.

[9] Evenden, Gamble, and Blue, *loc. cit.*

1.92 times as great. It is evident that more attention should be given to preparing teachers for the rural schools.

The percentages of the total enrollment of teachers college students included in the enrollments in curriculums which are designed for teaching in the special subject fields are shown by Table III to be as follows: agriculture, 0.4 percent; art, 1.2 percent; business, 4.2 percent; home economics, 3.0 percent; music, 2.7 percent; physical education, 3.5 percent; and industrial arts, 2.2 percent. Figures adapted from a study made only two years prior to this one indicate the following percentages of white teachers actually in service in the fields named: agriculture, 0.4 percent; art and drawing, 1.2 percent; commercial, 2.4 percent; health, 1.9 percent; home economics, 2.1 percent; industrial arts, 1.4 percent; and music, 1.4 percent.[10] The number in preparation in each area corresponds well with the number of teachers needed, so far as the special subjects are concerned.

## TYPES OF CURRICULUMS OFFERED

An examination of Table IV reveals that state normal schools and teachers colleges rather generally prepare for all levels of teaching service. A greater number of institutions are included here than in Table III because in answering the questionnaire some institutions indicated the areas in which and the levels on which they offered curriculums, without stating the number enrolled. This accounts for the apparent discrepancy in numbers.

Here, again, it is seen that the percentage of institutions offering curriculums for one- and two-teacher schools is fewer than for any other curriculum (the combined junior and senior high school curriculums being combined with the previous two columns), there being only fifty-one institutions, or 38.9 percent of all which offer specialized curriculums for teachers in rural schools having one and two rooms.

## LENGTH OF CURRICULUMS

An aspect of the curriculum which has considerable bearing on the question of providing adequate facilities is its length. Table V indicates that twenty-seven of the 128 institutions which re-

[10] *Ibid.*, p. 8.

## TABLE IV

*Number of State Normal Schools and Teachers Colleges Offering Certain Types of General Curriculums, 1933-34*

| Geographic Division | No. of Institutions Reporting | General Elementary | Kindergarten-Primary | Intermediate | Junior High School | Senior High School | Junior and Senior High School | Rural One- and Two-Teacher Schools |
|---|---|---|---|---|---|---|---|---|
| New England | 7 | 6 | 3 | 2 | 4 | 3 | 1 | |
| Middle Atlantic | 22 | 6 | 19 | 16 | 6 | 2 | 11 | 8 |
| East North Central | 21 | 6 | 15 | 15 | 13 | 14 | 6 | 14 |
| West North Central | 24 | 12 | 19 | 18 | 14 | 13 | 5 | 18 |
| South Atlantic | 12 | 6 | 7 | 5 | 2 | 6 | 2 | 3 |
| East South Central | 10 | 7 | 3 | 3 | 6 | 5 | 1 | 1 |
| West South Central | 16 | 7 | 11 | 8 | 4 | 11 | 4 | 5 |
| Mountain | 8 | 4 | 5 | 5 | 4 | 5 | 1 | 2 |
| Pacific | 11 | 8 | 6 | 4 | 6 | 2 | | |
| Total | 131 | 62 | 88 | 76 | 59 | 61 | 31 | 51 |
| Percent | 100.0 | 47.3 | 67.2 | 58.0 | 45.0 | 46.6 | 23.7 | 38.9 |

ported on this item still continue to offer one or more curriculums which are only one year in length above the high school level, and that at the other end of the scale twenty-six, or 20.3 percent, offer no curriculum shorter than four years. Institutions in five of the nine geographic divisions (New England, Middle Atlantic, South Atlantic, Mountain, and Pacific), report no students enrolled in one-year curriculums. These seem to be confined, so far as the state normal schools and teachers colleges are concerned, to the four geographic divisions in the central part of the United States.

Table III indicates that almost two-thirds (66.1 percent) of all the students are enrolled in the four-year curriculums, even though (Table V) 79.7 percent of the institutions offer one or more shorter curriculums. The curriculum which is a single year in length above the high school level should be abandoned in

## TABLE V

*Minimum Length of Curriculum Offered by State Normal Schools and Teachers Colleges, 1933-34*

| Geographic Division | No. of Institutions Studied | No. of Institutions Reporting | One Year* | Two Years | Three Years | Four Years |
|---|---|---|---|---|---|---|
| New England........ | 7 | 7 | | 2 | 3 | 2 |
| Middle Atlantic....... | 22 | 22 | | 7 | 10 | 5 |
| East North Central.... | 21 | 19 | 3 | 13 | 2 | 1 |
| West North Central.... | 24 | 25 | 18 | 7 | | |
| South Atlantic........ | 12 | 12 | | 11 | 1 | |
| East South Central.... | 10 | 9 | 3 | 2 | | 4 |
| West South Central.... | 16 | 15 | 3 | 4 | 1 | 7 |
| Mountain............. | 8 | 8 | | 4 | 3 | 1 |
| Pacific............... | 11 | 11 | | 3 | 2 | 6 |
| Total................ | 131 | 128 | 27 | 53 | 22 | 26 |
| Percent............. | | 100.0 | 21.1 | 41.4 | 17.2 | 20.3 |

* Above the secondary school level. See Chap. I.

American education. For long it has been urged that a single year is insufficient for the preparation of teachers for American schools. It is now increasingly being accepted that the ultimate aim should be a four-year period of preparation for elementary teachers and a five-year curriculum for teachers preparing for service in the secondary schools. Rugg and Peik[11] declare that all curriculums of less than four years ought to be abandoned at an early date, except possibly those for rural teachers, where a curriculum two or three years in length may be approved temporarily, while moving toward a goal of a universal minimum curriculum length of four years. They also advocate an "immediate gradual extension" of the period of preparation of teachers for the secondary schools to a minimum of five years. Of the students enrolled in institutions which prepare for service in the senior high schools, 10,937, or 97.4 percent, are enrolled in four-year curriculums; for teaching in junior high schools, 53.2 percent; for the combined junior

[11] Earle U. Rugg and W. E. Peik, "The Plan and Scope of Curriculum Studies." *National Survey of the Education of Teachers*, Vol. III, Part I, pp. 19. 1935.

and senior high school, 100.0 percent. Of those preparing to teach the special subjects 11,258 out of 11,782, or 95.6 percent, are enrolled in curriculums four years in length, even though with the exception of commercial subjects, special teachers are "used extensively in the elementary schools as well as in the departmentally organized junior and senior high schools."[12] In marked contrast to this situation is that of the teachers preparing for service in the elementary schools and in the one- and two-teacher rural schools.

Of the 11,235 enrolled in the general elementary curriculum, only 4,746, or 42.2 percent, were pursuing a four-year curriculum, while 3,861, or 34.4 percent, were pursuing a curriculum to be completed in two years. A smaller number are enrolled in the three-year curriculums, and a still smaller number in the one-year curriculums.

The paucity of training is even more evident in the case of teachers preparing for service in the one- and two-teacher rural schools than in the case of those enrolled in any other curriculum. Of 2,968 students enrolled in a curriculum for the preparation of teachers in one- and two-teacher rural schools, 250 or only 8.4 percent were enrolled in a four-year curriculum. On the other hand, more than half (52.2 percent) of such students were enrolled in curriculums only one year in length and an additional third (34.0 percent) in curriculums two years long, a total of 86.2 percent who are enrolled in curriculums not to exceed two years in length.

Moreover, of all students enrolled in one-year curriculums in the 105 institutions reporting, 55.6 percent were pursuing curriculums in preparation for teaching in one- and two-teacher schools. In writing of the preparation of teachers for the rural schools, Carney[13] urges:

Standards for rural school teachers in the matter of time required for pre-service preparation should be the same as those for teachers in urban schools . . . [She recommends] the abandonment of all high-school training classes and county normal schools, and of 1-year courses in institutions preparing teachers.

[12] Evenden, Gamble, and Blue, *op. cit.*, pp. 10–11.
[13] Mabel Carney, "The Preparation of Teachers for Small Rural Schools." *National Survey of the Education of Teachers*, Vol. V, Part VII, p. 374. 1935.

It is urged by some that rural teachers should not be prepared in a separate specialized course, that all teachers in the elementary course should be required to take some preparation for rural teaching. Palmer[14] advocates the unspecialized type of course. Against the specialized curriculum it has been argued that teaching is essentially the same in any school; that rural courses do not attract students; that certification laws and the regulations of state departments of education do not require differentiation; that there is little demand for professionally trained rural teachers; and that it tends to augment and intensify rural-urban cleavages.[15] But the preponderance of opinion seems to favor specialization of courses. After surveying the opinions of hundreds of presidents and instructors in colleges, universities and teachers colleges, Peik[16] writes: "It is seldom that those in contact with problems of teaching oppose a minimum of necessary differentiation." Expressing a similar view regarding the curriculums of rural schools, Bagley, after directing attention to the fact that it is important "to consider the background experiences with which the pupil approaches the learning task," states:

Especially should the rural-school teacher be able to capitalize in the interests of education the rich natural environment of the rural child. . . . In the preparation of rural-school teachers, then, there is certainly a place for such specialized courses as are necessary to meet these needs.[17]

In an analysis of the duties of teachers in one-teacher schools and the grade teachers in cities, McGuffey[18] found "There is a real and statistically reliable difference between the activities and attitudes of the teacher in the one-teacher school and of the grade teacher of the city." Confirming the findings of McGuffey, Char-

---

[14] James B. Palmer, "The Responsibility of Teacher-Training Institutions During the Depression." *Proceedings of the National Education Association*, Vol. 70, p. 435. 1932.
[15] Robinson, *op. cit.*, pp. 59–72.
[16] W. E. Peik, "Teacher Education Curricula in Universities, Colleges, and Junior Colleges." *National Survey of the Education of Teachers*, Vol. III, Part III, p. 248. 1935. (For analysis of opinions, see pp. 246–248)
[17] William C. Bagley, "Nature and Extent of Curriculum Differentiation in the Training of Rural-School Teachers." *Professional Preparation of Teachers for Rural Schools*, p. 19. 1928.
[18] Verne McGuffey, *Differences in the Activities of Teachers in Rural One-Teacher Schools and of Grade Teachers in Cities*, p. 62. 1929.

ters and Waples[19] concluded that the activities of rural teachers vary by a significant difference from teachers in the city schools, sufficiently so as to indicate different preparation. Evenden summarizes the consensus of a jury of educational authorities:

The principle of differentiation was generally approved by teachers of representative courses who voted on it as one of the educational issues in the education of teachers. Its practical application to many courses depends very definitely upon the size of the institution and the number of prospective teachers in the different teaching fields.[20]

Robinson[21] reports that eighteen of twenty experts whose opinions were solicited believed that teachers in one-teacher schools "work under conditions sufficiently unlike those of teachers in urban schools to justify a special differentiated curriculum for their preparation."

## SUMMARY

1. About half of the institutions are organized on the semester plan. A recheck made in 1937–38 indicates a shift toward the semester plan and away from the quarter plan. The calendars of the teachers college and laboratory schools should synchronize.

2. A great variety of curriculums for the preparation of teachers are offered both as to length, ranging from one to four years, and as to type of content, ranging from a single general curriculum for teachers in the elementary school to eighteen.

3. A comparison of the numbers enrolled in the different curriculums with the needs of the schools, though of course it varies from state to state, shows that, on the whole, too few teachers are being prepared for the elementary schools, and particularly for the one- and two-teacher rural schools.

4. A gratifying number of students preparing for teaching (66.1 percent) are enrolled in four-year curriculums, but 4.1 percent are still enrolled in one-year curriculums.

5. One-year curriculums are found almost exclusively in those preparing in the general elementary field and for service in one-

---

[19] W. W. Charters and Douglas Waples, *The Commonwealth Teacher-Training Study*, pp. 493–620. 1929.
[20] E. S. Evenden, "Making the Preparation of Teachers More Professional." *National Survey of the Education of Teachers*, Vol. VI, Chap. III, p. 177. 1935.
[21] Robinson, *op. cit.*, p. 73.

and two-teacher rural schools. Curriculums in the special subjects and for the senior high school are almost universally four years in length.

6. It is the general consensus of informed educational opinion that as soon as it is feasible all curriculums offered should be upgraded to a minimum of four years.

## SECTION B
## LABORATORY COURSES IN THE TRAINING SCHOOL

In this section data are presented with respect to the following: (*a*) the time-location at which laboratory courses (observation, participation, and student-teaching) are placed in curriculums of different types and lengths; (*b*) the allocations of specialized curriculums to particular institutions; (*c*) the patterns according to which laboratory courses are organized; (*d*) the amount of laboratory experience which is required for graduation in curriculums of each type and length; (*e*) the degree of flexibility in the graduation requirements in laboratory experience, resulting either by waiving a part or all of the usual minimum requirements or by requiring them to be exceeded; (*f*) the student-teaching load carried by campus and off-campus laboratory schools for each length and type of curriculum; (*g*) the variety of student-teaching (responsible room teaching) as shown by the number of grades and subjects in which each student is furnished laboratory experience; and (*h*) the attitude of the executives of teachers colleges toward the standard of the American Association of Teachers Colleges which refers to the minimum amount of laboratory experience which that Association requires as a condition of accrediting an institution.[22] The data presented are interpreted in the light of the opinions of competent individuals and groups who have made recommendations on laboratory school policies to determine what, if any, confirmations of their recommendations or changes in policies are indicated by the facts which have been found.

[22] *Minimum Standards for Accrediting Teachers Colleges and Normal Schools*, p. 2 (Standard VI). American Association of Teachers Colleges. 1938.

## TIME LOCATION OF LABORATORY COURSES IN THE CURRICULUMS

It has been quite generally accepted by students of problems in the teachers college field that the most nearly adequate test of the effectiveness of the program for the education of teachers is the quantity and quality of the laboratory experience which prospective teachers receive. Bagley stresses its importance in stating the philosophy underlying the great emphasis which is placed upon the laboratory school:

> The training school is in many ways a microcosm of our system of universal education. . . . For the training schools set the standard for the beginning teacher and what they reflect in practice is quite likely to be what the teacher will at least have as an ideal when he enters the public-school service.[23]

There are two concepts regarding the general plan of organization of curriculums for the preparation of teachers, which reflect underlying differences in the philosophies of teacher education held by their proponents. The first, held historically and traditionally by the liberal arts colleges and universities, but less frequently by the normal schools and teachers colleges, is that during the first two years of the four-year curriculums all college education, whether for prospective teachers or others, should be general and should furnish a subject-matter and cultural structure upon which the superstructure of specialization can be erected. According to this view the consideration of professional elements in the curriculum is deferred until the beginning of the junior year of the four-year curriculums. The advocates of this conception of the curriculum believe that specialization in subject-matter and professional courses is undesirable until such time as the student has secured a thorough background and foundation of knowledge and experience upon which he can build his succeeding educational experience. Administratively, it is clear that such an educational program conforms well with the traditional program of the colleges and universities. It is well adapted to provide for the further education of students who are trans-

---

[23] William C. Bagley, "The Place of Applied Philosophy in Judging Student Teaching." *Educational Administration and Supervision*, Vol. 17, p. 335, May, 1931.

ferring to the liberal arts colleges and professional schools from the rapidly-expanding junior colleges. Educationally, the argument is advanced that since students are more mature by the opening of the junior year of college they profit more from their professional study, they are in a better position to select their courses and decide upon the particular specialized field of educational activity which they wish to enter, and the richer background resulting from longer general preparation assures more meaningful and more vital educational experience in the professional aspects of their study. Baker[24] estimates that approximately half of the state universities which maintain colleges of education do not offer courses in education prior to the beginning of the junior year. He expresses the opinion that there is little specialization in education in college curriculums before this point. Those who adopt this point of view reject the thesis of others who hold that there should be contact with educational problems and with the laboratory school throughout the entire period of college education. For example, Peik declares:

> To attempt . . . the fusion of the college level of general education with methods and content of teaching subject matter of the elementary or secondary level, handicaps the attainment of both outcomes, it invariably pulls content down to lower than college levels in college classes.[25]

Alexander, writing in similar vein, states what the European practice is in this regard:

> In recent years in America we have developed normal schools and teachers colleges in which we have attempted to fuse general academic training and professional training. This movement has not met with great success; the academic work definitely suffering as well as the professional work being inadequate. . . .
> The Europeans reject flatly the principle of organizing the teacher-training institutions which try to provide both academic and professional training at the same time. The academic instruction is thoroughly academic; this is followed by a varied period of two to four years of study devoted entirely to professional fields and allied sciences. . . .

---

[24] Frank E. Baker, "Selective Admission and Promotion." *Twenty-third Yearbook of the National Society of College Teachers of Education*, p. 63. 1935.

[25] W. E. Peik, "Integration of the Pre-Service Curriculum for Teaching in Separate and Intensive Professional Courses." *Seventeenth Yearbook of the Supervisors of Student Teaching*, p. 29. 1937.

[In this period] the German teachers college devotes 100 percent of its time to professional fields, assuming that the general academic training has been taken care of before entrance into the professional school.[26]

In European colleges and universities, as in American, the professional elements of teacher education are superimposed upon two years of prior general college education.

This view is also widely held by instructors in the subject-matter fields in this country. In a survey of opinion of more than 700 teachers in representative subject-matter fields in state normal schools and teachers colleges it was found that almost half, 47.3 percent, favor postponing the beginning of the professional study in education courses to the beginning of the junior year.[27]

The second and opposing concept regarding the organization of curriculums is held by those who support the tradition of the normal schools and teachers colleges which maintains that, from the very beginning, the educational experiences of the student in the teacher-preparing institution should be focused upon the professional aspects of his preparation. According to this point of view, there should be contact with the professional aspects of teaching and the laboratory school from the beginning of the first year of the curriculum. An orientation course, or introduction to teaching, should be given at the beginning of the freshman year, and thereafter there should be repeated and continuous contact with the problems of teaching. Many would combine the subject-matter elements and the professional aspects of teacher-preparation in single courses, called professionalized subject-matter courses. Those holding this concept would permeate the student's thinking with the professional attitude from the inception of his college career, because they believe this attitude and point of view can be secured only by means of prolonged contact with the problems of education through professional courses. Morrison[28] believes that the introduction of professional courses during the

---

[26] Thomas Alexander, "What May Teacher-Training Institutions in the United States Learn from Similar Institutions in Other Countries?" *Proceedings of the National Education Association*, Vol. 70, p. 737. 1932.

[27] Earle U. Rugg, "Curricula of Normal Schools and Teachers Colleges." *National Survey of the Education of Teachers*, Vol. III, Part II, p. 92. 1935.

[28] Robert H. Morrison, "Fundamental Issues in the Professional Education of Teachers." *Problems in Teacher-Training*, Vol. 10, pp. 259-260. 1936.

freshman year makes other courses more meaningful, motivates the student, and gives a better understanding of the extracurricular activities as they are related to the work of the teacher. Wilson[29] asserts that, if prospective teachers are to comprehend the educational process, they should have definite contact with schools similar to those in which they expect to teach throughout their entire course. Learned and Bagley[30] agree that as soon as possible after the beginning of the student's residence at the teachers college he should do systematic observation and participation in order that his interest may be aroused and his understanding of the problems of education illuminated and enhanced.

Regardless of which view is held as to the general organization of the curriculum during the first two years, there is quite general agreement that the student should have long and continuous contact with the laboratory school. Alexander,[31] Dyer[32] and Nelson[33] affirm this principle which represents a widely-accepted opinion.

A confirmation of this position is found in the experimental investigation made by Marshall to determine the type of student-teaching best designed to prepare the student for both classroom teaching and for the broader social and community activities in which teachers should participate. Her evidence on both of these aspects of teaching warrants the following conclusion: "That a given number of hours of student-teaching graded and distributed over a period of practice is more effective than concentrated practice of the same number of hours."[34]

Whether or not the ideal of long and continuous contact with the laboratory school can be effected is conditioned on the length of the curriculum as well as on the use which is made of the facilities available for laboratory experience. Recent data indicate

---

[29] Lester M. Wilson, *Training Departments in State Normal Schools in the United States*, p. 29. 1919.

[30] W. S. Learned and W. C. Bagley, *The Professional Preparation of Teachers for American Public Schools*, p. 224. 1920.

[31] Thomas Alexander, "The Training of Teachers in Europe." *National Survey of the Education of Teachers*, Vol. V, Part VIII, p. 408. 1935.

[32] W. P. Dyer, "What Changes in Our Teacher-Training Programs Need to be Made to Meet the Demands of Progressive Schools?" *Problems in Teacher-Training*, Vol. X, p. 253. 1936.

[33] Esther Marion Nelson, *An Analysis of the Content of Student-Teaching Courses for the Education of Elementary Teachers in State Teachers Colleges*, p. 278. 1939.

[34] Edna M. Marshall, *Evaluation of Types of Student-Teaching*, p. 74. 1932.

that there is a rapid movement toward a lengthened curriculum. A sub-committee of the Committee on Standards and Surveys of the American Association of Teachers Colleges[35] has found that the one- and three-year curriculums are disappearing. Of a total of 144 institutions the percentage offering each length of curriculum is: one-year, 9 percent; two-year, 49 percent; three-year, 16 percent; four-year, 95 percent. It is also indicated that the percentage of teachers college students enrolled in four-year curriculums is 66.3 percent; in one-year curriculums, 4.5 percent. As the length of the curriculums is increased, there is opportunity for longer professional study either in the junior and senior years, or throughout the four years.

In Table VI the quarter is indicated during which the first laboratory experience in the curriculums of 123 teachers colleges begins. Of nine curriculums one-year in length, five introduce students to the laboratory school in the first quarter giving a possible full year thereafter for contacts with the laboratory school. One begins during the last quarter of the year, thus restricting the contact of the student with the laboratory school to a single quarter.

In the curriculums which are two years in length the modal time of the beginning of the student's laboratory experience is the fourth quarter from the beginning of the curriculum, i.e., the beginning of the second year, both in the cases of the general curriculums and the special subjects, these being a total of 152 curriculums (55.3 percent). Laboratory experience begins with the first quarter of the first year in thirty-five curriculums (23.0 percent). Almost three-fifths (58.0 percent) defer beginning laboratory experience to the second year or later.

The modal point for the student's first laboratory contact with the laboratory school in the three-year curriculums is the beginning of the seventh quarter, i.e., the beginning of the third year, twenty-seven curriculums (38.6 percent) locating the first laboratory experience at this point. Almost a third (31.4 percent) begin the laboratory experience with the first quarter of the

---

[35] E. S. Evenden, Chairman, "Special Report on Curriculum Practices in Normal Schools and Teachers Colleges." The American Association of Teachers Colleges. Unpublished, 1940.

TABLE VI: *Location by Quarters of the First Laboratory Experience in Schools and Teachers*

| Type of Curriculum | No. of Institutions Reporting | \multicolumn{9}{c}{Number of Curriculums of All Types Beginning Laboratory Experience in Each Quarter*} |
|---|---|---|---|---|---|---|---|---|---|---|---|
| | | \multicolumn{3}{c}{One-Year† Curriculum} | \multicolumn{8}{c}{Two-Year Curriculum} |
| | | 1 | 2 | 2.5 | 3 | 1 | 2 | 2.5 | 3 | 4 | 5 | 5.5 | 6 |
| General elementary | 50 | | 1 | | | 4 | 1 | | 4 | 17 | | | 1 |
| Kindergarten-primary | 64 | | | | | 13 | 1 | 3 | 4 | 20 | 1 | | |
| Intermediate (gr. 4–6) | 53 | | | | | 11 | 1 | 3 | 1 | 19 | 1 | | |
| Jr. high school | 46 | | | | | | 1 | 1 | | 9 | | | |
| Sr. high school | 57 | | | | | | | | | 3 | | | |
| Rural one- and two-teacher schools | 31 | 5 | 2 | 1 | | 7 | | 1 | 3 | 8 | 1 | | |
| Special subjects: | | | | | | | | | | | | | |
| Agriculture | 14 | | | | | | | | | | | | |
| Art | 32 | | | | | | | | 1 | 1 | | | |
| Business | 31 | | | | | | | | | 1 | | | |
| Home economics | 40 | | | | | | | | | 1 | | | |
| Industrial arts | 37 | | | | | | | | 1 | 2 | | | |
| Music | 39 | | | | | | | 1 | 1 | 2 | | | |
| Physical education (men and women) | 33 | | | | | | | | 1 | 1 | | | |
| Physical education (men) | 4 | | | | | | | | | | | | |
| Physical education (women) | 4 | | | | | | | | | | | | |
| Total | | 5 | 3 | 1 | | 35 | 3 | 9 | 17 | 84 | 3 | | 1 |

\* Numbers indicate those of the quarters (three to the academic year) in the curriculums first quarter of the second year. Semesters are expressed in equivalents of quarters, a semester of the third year. † The one-year curriculum refers to a year which is

Note: This table should be read as follows: Among the state normal schools and teachers the first laboratory experience began in the first quarter of the curriculum and one in years in length, in which the first laboratory experience began in the middle of the fifth of the eighth quarter, one in the ninth quarter, seven in the tenth quarter, and one in the

freshman year. Most curriculums in the special subjects postpone the initial contact of the student with the laboratory school to the beginning of the seventh quarter, i.e., the beginning of the third year, this being the situation in 54.5 percent of those reported.

In the four-year curriculums the modal point falls at the beginning of the tenth quarter, the laboratory contacts, accordingly, being limited to the fourth year in 153 of 304 (37.9 percent) of the

*the Different Types and Lengths of Curriculums of 123 State Normal Colleges, 1933-34*

Number of Curriculums of All Types Beginning Laboratory Experience in Each Quarter* (*Continued*)

| Three-Year Curriculum | Four-Year Curriculum |
|---|---|
| 1 2 2.5 3 4 5 5.5 6 7 8 8.5 9 | 1 2 2.5 3 4 5 5.5 6 7 8 8.5 9 10 11 11.5 12 |
| 6      1   1 1 2 | 4  1  3      10  1   5      1 |
| 6      1 1 1 2 2 | 11 1 2  4   1 7  1  10 |
| 2      2 1 1 1 4 | 6 1 2  4 1  1 6  1 1  6 |
| 1  1 1 1     3 | 5 1   4  1 1 10  3 1  9 1 1 |
|      1      4 | 7 1   4  2 1 12  1 2 22 2 |
|             1 | 4 1          1     2 |
| 1       1 |       1  2  1 1  7 1 |
| 1    1 | 1 1  2  1 1  9  2 1 12 1 |
| 1 1 1   2 | 2  1  7  2 1 14 1 |
| 1      2 | 1  2  1 10  1 2 20 1 |
| 2      2 | 4  1  1 1 9  1 1 16 1 |
| 1      2 | 1  4  1  10  2 1 16 1 |
|       2 | 1  1 1 1 9  3 1 13 1 |
|              |                    1 |
|      1 |             1 |
| 22  1 2 6 3 4 5 27 | 44 5 7  31 1 10 7 103  19 12 153 10 1 1 |

of different lengths. For example, 4 indicates the fourth quarter of the curriculum, i.e., the semester equaling one and one-half quarters. For example, 8.5 indicates the second immediately above the high school level.

colleges studied, there was one curriculum in agriculture, three years in length, in which which it began in the seventh quarter; there was one curriculum in agriculture, four quarter, two in which it began in the seventh quarter, one in which it began in the middle eleventh quarter.

curriculums. In 306 of 404 curriculums (75.7 percent) the first laboratory courses which a student pursues is located at the beginning of the junior year or later, while only ninety-eight (24.3 percent) place it earlier.

The initial laboratory experience in curriculums for the preparation of kindergarten-primary teachers tends to be placed early. In curriculums for junior high school teachers the most common practice is to place the laboratory courses in the last two years,

TABLE VII: *Location by Quarters of the First Laboratory Experience in Teachers Colleges, According to*

| Geographic Division | NUMBER OF CURRICULUMS OF ALL TYPES BEGINNING LABORATORY EXPERIENCE IN EACH QUARTER* | | | | | | | | | | | |
|---|---|---|---|---|---|---|---|---|---|---|---|---|
| | One-Year Curriculum | | | | Two-Year Curriculum | | | | | | | |
| | 1 | 2 | 2.5 | 3 | 1 | 2 | 2.5 | 3 | 4 | 5 | 5.5 | 6 |
| New England............................ | | | | | | | | | | | | |
| Middle Atlantic......................... | | | | | 16 | | | | | | | |
| East North Central..................... | | | | | 8 | | | 4 | 3 | 11 | 3 | |
| West North Central.................... | 5 | 3 | | 1 | 5 | | | 2 | 12 | 39 | | 1 |
| South Atlantic.......................... | | | | | 5 | | | | 1 | 10 | | |
| East South Central..................... | | | | | | | | 1 | | 3 | | |
| West South Central.................... | | | | | 1 | | | 2 | | 18 | | |
| Mountain............................... | | | | | | | | | 1 | 2 | | |
| Pacific.................................. | | | | | 3 | | | | | 1 | | |
| Total................................... | 5 | 3 | | 1 | 35 | 3 | | 9 | 17 | 84 | 3 | 1 |

\* Numbers indicate those of the quarters in the curriculums of different lengths. For ex year. Semesters are expressed in equivalents of quarters, a semester equaling one and

Note: This table should be read as follows: In New England in the curriculum three primary, etc.) scheduled the first laboratory experience to begin with the first quarter of fourth quarter; one, at the middle of the fifth quarter. In the curriculum four years in begin with the first quarter of the first year.

and this is predominantly the practice in curriculums for the preparation of senior high school teachers. In the preponderant number of curriculums preparing teachers of the special subjects the initial laboratory experience occurs within the last two years (85.5 percent), and in 46.2 percent of the curriculums, within the senior year.

In Table VII the curriculums, which were classified in Table VI according to type, are arranged according to geographic divisions. Some interesting contrasts can be seen. In six of ten curriculums in New England laboratory experience is begun with the first quarter of the first year; in the Middle Atlantic Division all two-year curriculums begin with the first quarter, and thirteen of the fourteen three-year curriculums (92.8 percent) do so, none postponing the beginning as late as the third year. In the four-year curriculums of institutions in this geographic division, thirty-

## PRESENTATION AND INTERPRETATION OF DATA 47

*All Types and Lengths of Curriculums in 123 State Normal Schools and Geographic Division, 1933–34*

Number of Curriculums of All Types Beginning Laboratory Experience in Each Quarter* (*Continued*)

| Three-Year Curriculum | | | | | | | | | | Four-Year Curriculum | | | | | | | | | | | | | |
|---|---|---|---|---|---|---|---|---|---|---|---|---|---|---|---|---|---|---|---|---|---|---|---|
| 1 | 2 | 2.5 | 3 | 4 | 5 | 5.5 | 6 | 7 | 8 | 8.5 | 9 | 1 | 2 | 2.5 | 3 | 4 | 5 | 5.5 | 6 | 7 | 8 | 8.5 | 9 | 10 | 11 | 11.5 | 12 |
| 3 | | | 1 | | 2 | | 1 | | | | | 3 | | | | | | | | | | | | | | | |
| 13 | | | | | 1 | | | | | | | 31 | 1 | | 5 | | | | 4 | | | | 1 | | | | |
| 6 | | | | 3 | 2 | | 6 | | | | | 4 | 1 | | 1 | 1 | | | 21 | | 11 | | 33 | | | | |
| | 2 | | | | | | 6 | | | | | 3 | | | 5 | | | | 7 | 33 | | 10 | 15 | 9 | | | 1 |
| | | | | 1 | 2 | | | | | | | | | | | | | | 2 | | 1 | | 15 | | | | |
| | | | | | | | | | | | | | 1 | | 7 | | | | | | 1 | | 11 | 1 | 1 | | |
| | | | | | | 12 | | | | | | | 5 | 4 | 13 | 10 | | | 4 | | | | 53 | | | | |
| | | | | 5 | | | | | | | | | | | 3 | | | | 9 | | 1 | | 25 | | | | |
| | | | 3 | | 1 | | | | | | | | | | | | | | 30 | | 7 | | | | | | |
| 22 | 1 | 2 | 6 | 3 | 4 | 5 | 27 | | | | | 44 | 5 | 7 | 31 | 1 | 10 | 7 | 103 | | 19 | 12 | 153 | 10 | | 1 | 1 |

ample, 4 indicates the fourth quarter of the curriculum, i.e., the first quarter of the second one-half quarters. For example, 8.5 indicates the second semester of the third year. years in length, three curriculums of different types (i.e., general elementary, kindergarten-the curriculum; one, at the middle of the second quarter; two, at the beginning of the length, three curriculums of different types scheduled the first laboratory experience to

one of the forty-two curriculums (73.8 percent) begin laboratory experience in the first quarter of the first year, and only one defers beginning to the senior year. In the East North Central Division almost an equal number begin in the final year, whatever the length of the curriculum, and in earlier years. In this division laboratory experience begins after the first two college years in 90.2 percent of the four-year curriculums. For all other divisions of the country, except in New England, it is the prevailing practice to postpone the beginning of laboratory experience to the last year. Judging from this table, either practical or theoretical considerations result in marked contrasts in the time when laboratory experience is begun in various sections of the country.

Comparative data for 1937–38 were secured for the two-year and four-year curriculums on items covered in Tables VI and VII. In the two-year curriculum a tendency is noticeable, still greater than in 1933–34, to begin laboratory experience in the fourth quarter, i.e., the beginning of the second year, and less tendency to begin at the first quarter of the first year. In the four-year curriculums, the mode still remains at the first quarter of the fourth year, but the proportion beginning laboratory experience at this point has risen from 37.9 to 42.0 percent. The proportion of all curriculums in which laboratory work is begun with the first quarter of the junior year or later has risen from 75.7 to 84.6 percent.

Tables VIII and IX show the place in the curriculums where first student-teaching rather than first laboratory experience begins. In the tables all one-year curriculums and the first years of all other curriculum lengths are omitted. There are only nineteen of the former, of which sixteen are curriculums for the preparation of teachers in one-teacher and two-teacher rural schools. Of these, six schedule student-teaching in the first quarter, six in the second quarter, six in the second semester, and three in the last quarter of the year. In a negligible number, two in the two-year and two in the three-year curriculums, student-teaching begins before the second year. Student-teaching does not occur before the first quarter of the second year in any four-year curriculum.

In 74.1 percent of the two-year curriculums, student-teaching begins with the fourth term, i.e., the beginning of the second year; in 61.8 percent of the three-year curriculums, in the seventh quarter; in 63.1 percent of the four-year curriculums, in the tenth quarter. Including the curriculums omitted from the table (see paragraph above), student-teaching occurs in the final year of all two-year, three-year, and four-year curriculums combined in 81.0 percent of all the curriculums. Table IX reveals no significant differences to be found in the various geographic divisions.

Accepting the principle that it is desirable for the student to have long and continuous contact with the laboratory school, a study was made of the time span from the beginning of the first contact to the completion of student-teaching, to discover how far this principle is applied in practice. It should be explained that the time span does not necessarily indicate *continuous* contact in every quarter in all cases, as Table X indicates only the time span from the beginning of the laboratory experience to its completion. There may have been quarters during which no lab-

## TABLE VIII

*Location by Quarters of the Beginning of Student-Teaching in the Different Types and Lengths of Curriculums in 123 State Normal Schools and Teachers Colleges, 1933–34*

| Type of Curriculum | No. of Institutions Reporting | Two-Year Curriculum |||||| Three-Year Curriculum |||||||| Four-Year Curriculum |||||||||||||
|---|---|---|---|---|---|---|---|---|---|---|---|---|---|---|---|---|---|---|---|---|---|---|---|---|---|
| | | 4 | 5 | 5.5 | 6 | | | 4 | 5 | 5.5 | 6 | 7 | 8 | 8.5 | 9 | | 4 | 5 | 5.5 | 6 | 7 | 8 | 8.5 | 9 | 10 | 11 | 11.5 | 12 |
| General elementary | 43 | 10 | 3 | 1 | | | | | 2 | | | 8 | | 1 | | | 1 | | | | 2 | 2 | 2 | | 13 | | 2 | |
| Kindergarten-primary | 63 | 31 | 4 | 5 | 2 | | | | 1 | 1 | | 8 | 1 | | | | 4 | | | | 5 | 1 | 2 | | 24 | 1 | 2 | 1 |
| Intermediate (gr. 4–6) | 53 | 29 | 4 | 5 | 1 | | | | 1 | 1 | | 9 | | 1 | | | 2 | 1 | | 1 | 2 | 1 | | | 21 | 1 | 2 | 1 |
| Junior high school | 48 | 10 | 1 | 3 | | | | | | | | 4 | | 1 | 1 | | 1 | | | 1 | 5 | 1 | 3 | | 30 | 1 | 1 | 1 |
| Senior high school | 63 | 2 | | 1 | | | | | | | | 2 | | 1 | 1 | | | | | 1 | 9 | 1 | 3 | 2 | 36 | 8 | 4 | 2 |
| Rural one-teacher and two-teacher schools | 39 | 16 | 3 | 2 | 1 | | | | | | | 2 | | 1 | | | 1 | | | | | 1 | | | 12 | 1 | 1 | |
| Special subjects: | | | | | | | | | | | | | | | | | | | | | | | | | | | | |
| Agriculture | 16 | | | | | | | | | | | | | 1 | | | | | | | | 1 | | | 11 | 1 | 1 | 1 |
| Art | 37 | 1 | | | | | | 1 | | | | 2 | | 1 | 1 | | | | | | 3 | 2 | 1 | | 23 | 2 | 1 | 1 |
| Business | 36 | 1 | | | | | | | | | | 1 | 1 | 1 | 1 | | | | | | 2 | 1 | 3 | 1 | 21 | 1 | 5 | 1 |
| Home economics | 39 | 1 | | | | | | 1 | | | | 2 | | 1 | 1 | | | | | | 4 | 1 | 3 | 1 | 22 | 3 | 5 | 1 |
| Industrial arts | 40 | 2 | | | | | | | | | | 4 | | 1 | 1 | | | | | | 3 | 1 | 3 | | 24 | 4 | 3 | 1 |
| Music | 42 | 2 | | 1 | | | | | | | | 3 | | 1 | 1 | | | | | | 6 | 1 | 3 | | 24 | 3 | 2 | 1 |
| Physical education (men and women) | 35 | 1 | | | | | | | | | | 2 | | 1 | 1 | | | | | | 3 | 1 | 2 | | 23 | 3 | 2 | 1 |
| Physical education (men) | 4 | | | | | | | | | | | | | | | | | | | | 1 | | | | 1 | | 1 | |
| Physical education (women) | 4 | | | | | | | | | | | 1 | | | | | | | | | 1 | | 1 | | | | 1 | |
| Total | | 106 | 12 | 20 | 5 | | | 6 | 2 | 3 | | 47 | 1 | 5 | 12 | | 9 | 1 | 4 | | 49 | 12 | 28 | 4 | 285 | 29 | 33 | 12 |

*Numbers indicate those of the quarters (three to the academic year) in the curriculums of different lengths. For example, 4 indicates the fourth quarter of the curriculum, i.e., the first quarter of the second year. Semesters are expressed in equivalents of quarters, a semester equaling one and one-half quarters. For example, 8.5 indicates the second semester of the third year. The one-year curriculum and the first year of each of the others are omitted.

Note: This table should be read in a manner similar to Table VI.

## TABLE IX

*Location by Quarters of the Beginning of Student-Teaching in Different Types and Lengths of Curriculums in 123 State Normal Schools and Teachers Colleges, According to Geographic Division, 1933–34*

| Geographic Division | Two-Year Curriculum |||||| Three-Year Curriculum |||||||| Four-Year Curriculum ||||||||||
|---|---|---|---|---|---|---|---|---|---|---|---|---|---|---|---|---|---|---|---|---|---|---|---|
| | 4 | 5 | 5.5 | 6 | | | 4 | 5 | 5.5 | 6 | 7 | 8 | 8.5 | 9 | 4 | 5 | 5.5 | 6 | 7 | 8 | 8.5 | 9 | 10 | 11 | 11.5 | 12 |
| New England......... |  |  |  |  |  |  |  |  |  |  | 2 |  | 5 |  |  |  |  | 3 |  |  |  |  | 1 |  | 2 |  |
| Middle Atlantic....... | 16 |  | 3 |  |  |  | 2 |  |  |  | 16 |  |  |  | 3 |  |  | 4 |  | 4 |  |  | 47 | 7 | 9 |  |
| East North Central.... | 25 | 6 |  | 1 |  |  |  | 2 |  |  | 16 |  |  | 11 | 3 |  | 1 |  |  | 1 | 1 | 2 | 72 | 10 | 2 | 12 |
| West North Central... | 40 | 4 | 4 | 1 |  |  | 3 |  |  | 2 | 4 |  |  |  |  | 1 |  | 22 |  | 4 |  | 2 | 65 | 3 | 2 |  |
| South Atlantic........ | 11 | 2 | 1 |  |  |  | 1 |  |  |  | 3 |  |  |  | 1 |  |  | 5 |  |  |  |  | 15 | 1 |  |  |
| East South Central.... | 1 |  | 3 |  |  |  |  |  |  |  |  |  |  |  |  |  |  | 6 |  | 2 |  |  | 10 |  | 4 |  |
| West South Central... | 5 |  | 9 |  |  |  |  |  |  |  | 1 |  |  |  | 2 |  | 4 |  |  | 5 |  |  | 34 | 8 | 14 |  |
| Mountain............ | 5 |  |  |  |  |  |  |  |  |  | 5 | 1 |  |  |  |  |  | 2 |  | 7 |  |  | 14 |  |  |  |
| Pacific.............. | 3 |  | 3 |  |  |  |  |  |  | 1 |  |  |  | 1 |  |  |  | 3 |  | 10 |  |  | 27 |  |  |  |
| Total............... | 106 | 12 | 20 | 5 |  |  | 6 | 2 | 3 | 47 | 1 | 5 | 12 | 9 | 1 | 4 | 49 | 12 | 28 | 4 | 285 | 29 | 33 | 12 |

*Numbers indicate those of the quarters (three to the academic year) in the curriculums of different lengths. For example, 4 indicates the fourth quarter of the curriculum, i.e., the first quarter of the second year. Semesters are expressed in equivalents of quarters, a semester equaling one and one-half quarters. For example, 8.5 indicates the second semester of the third year. The one-year curriculum and the first year of each of the others are omitted.

Note: This table should be read in a manner similar to Table VII.

## TABLE X

**Time Span by Quarters from the Beginning to the Close of Laboratory Courses in Various Types and Lengths of Curriculums in 119 State Normal Schools and Teachers Colleges, 1933-34**

| Type of Curriculum | Two-Year Curriculum No. of Institutions | Two-Year Curriculum Quarter Range | Two-Year Curriculum Median | Three-Year Curriculum No. of Institutions | Three-Year Curriculum Quarter Range | Three-Year Curriculum Median | Four-Year Curriculum No. of Institutions | Four-Year Curriculum Quarter Range | Four-Year Curriculum Median |
|---|---|---|---|---|---|---|---|---|---|
| General elementary | 31 | 1.0-6.0 | 2.1 | 14 | 1.5-9.0 | 3.7 | 30 | 1.0-12.0 | 2.9 |
| Kindergarten-primary | 53 | 1.0-6.0 | 2.5 | 15 | 1.0-7.5 | 2.9 | 63 | 1.0-10.5 | 2.8 |
| Intermediate (gr. 4-6) | 48 | 1.0-6.0 | 2.7 | 11 | 1.0-7.5 | 2.9 | 46 | 1.0-12.0 | 2.8 |
| Junior high school | 17 | 1.0-4.5 | 2.6 | 9 | 1.0-7.5 | 2.4 | 51 | 1.0-12.0 | 2.8 |
| Senior high school | 4 | (1) | (1) | 7 | 1.0-6.0 | 2.2 | 73 | 1.0-12.0 | 2.6 |
| Rural one-teacher and two-teacher* | 27 | 1.0-6.0 | 2.1 | 4 | (1) | (1) | 17 | 1.0-12.0 | 2.4 |
| Special subjects: | | | | | | | | | |
| Agriculture | 1 | (1) | (1) | 3 | (1) | (1) | 17 | 1.0-7.5 | 2.4 |
| Art | 3 | (1) | (1) | 4 | (1) | (1) | 42 | 1.0-10.5 | 2.7 |
| Business | 1 | (1) | (1) | 6 | 1.0-7.5 | 2.3 | 38 | 1.0-9.0 | 2.3 |
| Home economics | | | | 3 | (1) | (1) | 50 | 1.0-6.0 | 2.5 |
| Industrial arts | 3 | (1) | (1) | 7 | 1.0-7.5 | 2.5 | 48 | 1.0-12.0 | 2.6 |
| Music | 5 | 1.0-4.0 | 2.4 | 6 | 1.0-7.5 | 1.8 | 48 | 1.0-7.5 | 2.7 |
| Physical education (men and women) | 3 | (1) | (1) | 4 | (1) | (1) | 44 | 1.0-10.5 | 2.5 |
| Physical education (men) | | | | | | | 3 | (1) | (1) |
| Physical education (women) | | | | | | | | | |
| All curriculums in all schools | | 1.0-6.0 | 2.2 | | 1.0-9.0 | 2.3 | | 1.0-12.0 | 2.7 |

(1) Fewer than five cases. Range and median not computed for this type, but included in computing the total.
* In 16 one-year curriculums not shown in the table the range is 1.0-3.0 quarters; the median, 1.3 quarters.

oratory experience was scheduled, although in most instances this is unlikely. This table reveals great individual differences among the various institutions. For nearly every type of curriculum there were certain institutions in which the total laboratory experience extended over only a single quarter, and others in which it extended throughout the entire length of the curriculum, the time span including the twelve quarters of the four-year curriculum of the student's contact with the laboratory school. The time span of the laboratory experience increases with the length of the curriculums, but in no curriculums does the median equal a full year of contact. A comparison was made with corresponding data for 1937-38. At that time sixty-one institutions reported a median of 3.5 quarters as the time span for the two-year curriculum, and 118 institutions a median of 4.3 quarters for the four-year curriculum, a considerable increase in the amount of contact provided at the later period compared with the former. No change occurred in the range.

Along with a rather definite trend toward postponing the education courses to a later time in the curriculum and with an increase in the time span of laboratory experience, there has been a tendency toward lengthening the curriculum. It is the opinion of the writer that all curriculums for the preparation of teachers in the elementary and high schools should be lengthened to a minimum of four years, and that eventually a five-year curriculum should be constructed for teachers on all levels. Without such a lengthening of the period of preparation, it is impossible to provide the long and continuous contact with the laboratory school which experience and the opinion of many teachers college administrators believe is necessary to prepare teachers to serve efficiently in teaching in modern democratic schools designed to meet the needs of a complex progressive society.

## ALLOCATION OF SPECIAL CURRICULUMS TO CERTAIN INSTITUTIONS

A quarter of a century ago it was urged by Judd and Parker[36] that the best policy for a state to pursue in preparing teachers

[36] C. H. Judd and S. C. Parker, *Problems Involved in Standardizing State Normal Schools*, pp. 105-121. 1916.

of the special subjects is to develop adequate facilities for the preparation of teachers of a given subject in *one* of the regular normal schools of the state. It is now generally accepted as a principle that an institution should not prepare teachers in areas in which it does not have the necessary facilities. In replies from 1,666 administrators and instructors in universities, teachers colleges and normal schools, colleges and junior colleges, more than 80 percent expressed their approval of the following statement:

It is desirable where several State-supported educational institutions exist that each should limit its curricular offerings to types of teacher education most feasible for each of the respective institutions.[37]

The principle was approved by 84 percent of the presidents of state normal schools and teachers colleges, of whom 40 percent approved the statement unqualifiedly, and 44 percent with certain reservations. Supplementing this statement with particular reference to the laboratory school, Evenden declares:

Approved institutions should be designated for specialization in the education of those types of teachers for which there is a very limited demand or which require a highly specialized and expensive type of laboratory or other equipment.[38]

The general principle of allocation of specialized functions to particular institutions seems sound. To determine the practice which prevails, each institution was asked to state in answer to the questionnaire which subjects, if any, were allocated to it, and what policy the state department of education followed in the matter of the allocation of special subjects. Later a letter was sent to the state officials concerned, as revealed by the questionnaire, to secure definite information about the allocations which were made. Table XI indicates the status of allocations so far as these apply to state normal schools and teachers colleges. No information was sought regarding allocations of special functions to state universities, land-grant colleges, and other types of institution, nor was a study made of allocations of grade divisions, such as

[37] Rugg and Peik, *op. cit.*, p. 16.
[38] E. S. Evenden, "The Education of Teachers in the United States: Principles and Problems." *Problems in Teacher-Training*, Vol. X, p. 7. 1936.

## TABLE XI
*Allocation of Special Subjects to Designated State Normal Schools and Teachers Colleges, 1934–35*

| State | Location of Normal School or Teachers College | Subject |
|---|---|---|
| Connecticut | Danbury | Business |
|  | New Britain | Industrial Arts |
|  | New Haven | Atypical |
| Maine | Farmington | Home Economics |
|  | Gorham | Industrial Arts |
| Massachusetts | Boston | Art |
|  | Bridgewater | Library |
|  | Fitchburg | Practical Arts |
|  | Framingham | Household Arts |
|  |  | Vocational Household Arts |
|  | *Hyannis | *Physical Education |
|  | Lowell | Music |
|  | Salem | Atypical |
|  |  | Commercial |
| New Hampshire | Keene | Home Economics |
|  |  | Trades and Industry |
|  | Plymouth | Commerce |
| New Jersey | *Jersey City | *Health Education |
|  |  | *Nursing |
|  | Newark | Fine Arts |
|  |  | Industrial Arts |
|  | Trenton | Business |
|  |  | Health and Physical Education |
|  |  | Industrial Arts |
|  |  | Music |
| New York | Albany | Commercial |
|  |  | Library |
|  | Buffalo | Art |
|  |  | Home Economics |
|  |  | Industrial Arts |
|  | Cortland | Physical Education |
|  | Fredonia | Music |
|  | Geneseo | Atypical |
|  |  | Library |
|  | Oswego | Industrial Arts |
|  | *Plattsburg | *Home Economics |
|  | Potsdam | Music |

* The addition of an institution or a special subject, 1935–40.

TABLE XI (*Continued*)

| State | Location of Normal School or Teachers College | Subject |
|---|---|---|
| Pennsylvania | Bloomsburg | *Atypical |
| | | Business |
| | California | *Atypical |
| | | Industrial Arts |
| | *Clarion | *Library |
| | East Stroudsburg | Health Education |
| | Edinboro | Art |
| | Indiana | Art |
| | | Business |
| | | Home Economics |
| | | Music |
| | Kutztown | Art |
| | | Library |
| | *Lock Haven | *Health and Physical Education |
| | Mansfield | Home Economics |
| | | Music |
| | Millersville | Industrial Arts |
| | | Library |
| | Shippensburg | *Adult Education |
| | | *Business |
| | | Cooperative Education |
| | Slippery Rock | Health Education |
| | West Chester | Health Education |
| | | Music |
| Wisconsin | La Crosse | Physical Education |
| | *Menonomie | *Home Economics |
| | | *Industrial Arts |
| | Milwaukee | Art |
| | | Atypical |
| | | Music |
| | Platteville | Agriculture |
| | | *Industrial Education |
| | River Falls | Agriculture |
| | Stevens Point | Home Economics |
| | Whitewater | Commercial |

elementary schools and senior high schools. It was found that eight states allocate one or more special subjects to each of forty-five institutions. Four of the states which allocate functions to particular institutions are in the New England, three in the Middle Atlantic, and one in the East North Central Divisions. No institutions which had allocations made to them in 1934–35 had had them withdrawn in 1937–38, but there were a number of new ones made as the table indicates. The number of allocations made for each subject are as follows: art, 7; agriculture, 2; business, 9; home economics, 9; industrial arts, 11; music, 8; physical education (health), 9; atypical, 6; library, 6; trades and industry, 1; nursing, 1; adult education, 1; and cooperative education, 1.

Although the information was not sought in the questionnaire, statements were volunteered in a number of instances that allocations are made on grade levels. The states of Massachusetts, New Jersey, and New York are typical of those which restrict the preparation of secondary school teachers to certain designated institutions. On the other hand, Wisconsin, with nine teachers colleges, allows all of them to engage in the preparation of teachers for the secondary schools. Certain difficulties emerge when allocations are made. For example, the president of one institution to which the preparation of commercial teachers is assigned states that to secure student-teaching facilities it is necessary to go as far away as 100 miles from the campus, often to the home town of the student. The same institution reports that to secure laboratory facilities in the education of the mentally retarded, it is necessary to go as far as thirty miles. Whether or not, in a given case, an allocation should be made depends upon many factors, including the number of institutions in the state, the density of population, the accessibility of the institution to students, the adequacy of the student-teaching facilities which are available, the degree of specialization of the courses which are allocated, the number of special teachers who are needed in the field by the schools, and various local school conditions. With the addition of a greater number of specialized teaching fields in the schools, easier means of transportation for students attending the institutions, and greater central control of the output of teachers by the state, the needs of the teaching service indicate an extension of some plan of allocation to other institutions not now involved, especially in thickly populated homogeneous areas, thus eliminating much needless institutional competition in the interest of preparing teachers more efficiently for their profession.

# PRESENTATION AND INTERPRETATION OF DATA

## PATTERNS OF ORGANIZATION OF LABORATORY COURSES

To develop teachers who have a unified experience and an integrated point of view toward the educational problems and processes, it is important that the whole educational experience of the student be correlated and integrated. While in the final analysis the student must integrate his experiences for himself by means of his own thinking, he is assisted in making his integration if the courses which he pursues are so organized that he is brought to see the relationships between them, and to appreciate the relationships between theory and practice, subject-matter and professional theory, and principles and applications. For this purpose the curriculum must be planned to produce educational and professional competence rather than to secure logical organization.

It is believed that the student's most efficient teaching results when the phases of laboratory experience—observation, participation, and student-teaching—are integrated with one another and with other professional and subject-matter courses, i.e., when the *functional* view of professional education is employed in arranging and organizing the curriculums. Schorling, writing on this point, concludes:

If the primary objective of directed teaching is the control of pedagogical principles, then the extent to which those in charge of the program can integrate and correlate their efforts in subject matter, observation, participation, directed teaching, and regular teaching, with theory will determine the efficiency of the program.[39]

Jarman asserts that 93.3 percent of the thirty jurors to whom he submitted the following principle indicated their assent to it:

Observation, participation and directed teaching should be accompanied by a systematic effort to integrate theory and practice.[40]

Rutledge found unanimous agreement among thirty-five jurors who were state superintendents of public instruction, professors of normal school education, state directors of teacher preparation, and presidents of state normal schools and teachers colleges with the following principle:

[39] Raleigh Schorling, "Directed Teaching." *Twenty-Third Yearbook of the National Society of College Teachers of Education*, pp. 154–155. 1935.
[40] A. M. Jarman, *The Administration of Laboratory Schools*, p. 114. 1932.

The president of the teachers college or the normal school should secure an intimate relationship between the theory and practice departments, through a close coordination of all the activities in these departments.[41]

To determine the extent to which the principle and ideal of integration is realized in practice, the institutions represented in this study were asked to indicate which of eleven patterns submitted to them best described the organization of the laboratory courses in their respective institutions. In case none of the eleven patterns listed gave a satisfactory description, the official replying was asked to add his own pattern and description. In reply 128 institutions listed twenty-seven different patterns, employed in a total of 177 instances, certain institutions in some cases using more than a single pattern. Table XII summarizes those which were being used. To check the situation for changes four years later, a column is added in the table showing the number of institutions using the patterns in 1937–38. Eight patterns, each used only in a single institution, are combined in a single classification in the table which is placed immediately following the other listings in each of the four groups.

An outstanding characteristic of the situation is the variety of patterns to be found. In some instances the differences between patterns are small, but in others they are marked. Variations are found even within the institutions themselves, each of forty-one of them using either two or three different patterns in connection with either its different laboratory schools or the different divisions of the same school. However, despite differences in details, all the patterns can be assembled in four groups: those laboratory courses which are self-contained; those which are combined with other professional courses; those which are combined with subject-matter courses; and those which are combined with both subject-matter courses and other professional courses. In view of the criterion of integration of theory and practice adopted in this study, it is clear that much is yet to be accomplished in unifying the work of the laboratory courses and of subject-matter and other professional courses. Almost half the patterns (45.2 percent) are reported as being in the group of self-contained laboratory

---

[41] Samuel A. Rutledge, *The Development of Guiding Principles for the Administration of Teachers Colleges and Normal Schools*, p. 50. 1930.

PRESENTATION AND INTERPRETATION OF DATA 59

TABLE XII

*Patterns According to Which Laboratory Courses Were Organized in State Normal Schools and Teachers Colleges, 1933–34 and 1937–38*

| Pattern | Group | Number of Patterns 1933–34 | 1937–38 |
|---|---|---|---|
| | **I. Laboratory Courses Are Self-Contained, i.e., Not Combined with Subject-Matter Courses or Other Professional Courses** | | |
| A | Observation, participation, and student-teaching (responsible room teaching) are combined in a single course. | 40 | 45 |
| B | Observation is given as a separate course. Participation and student-teaching are combined in one course. | 15 | 10 |
| C | Observation and participation are combined in a single course. Student-teaching is a separate course | 13 | 14 |
| D | Observation is a separate course. Student-teaching is a separate course. (No work in participation).... | 5 | 7 |
| E | Observation is a separate course. Participation is a separate course. Student-teaching is a separate course. | 3 | 5 |
| F | Observation is a separate course. Observation, participation, and student-teaching form a separate course. | 2 | 0 |
| Misc. | Other combinations, each in use in a single institution | 2 | 2 |
| | Total | 80 | 83 |
| | Percent of grand total | 45.2 | 45.9 |
| | **II. Laboratory Courses Are Combined with Other Professional Courses** | | |
| G | Observation is combined with professional courses in theory, such as principles of teaching or educational psychology, without separate credit. Student-teaching is a separate course. | 23 | 24 |
| H | Observation is combined with professional courses in theory, without separate credit. Participation and student-teaching are combined in a single course.. | 22 | 24 |
| I | Observation is combined with professional courses in theory without separate credit. Student-teaching is a separate course. (No work in participation).... | 12 | 4 |
| J | Observation is combined with professional courses. Observation, participation, and student-teaching are combined in a single course. | 6 | 6 |

## TABLE XII (*Continued*)

| Pattern | Group | Number of Patterns 1933–34 | 1937–38 |
|---|---|---|---|
| K | Observation and participation are combined with other professional courses. Student-teaching is a separate course.................................. | 2 | 4 |
| L | Observation is combined with professional courses without separate credit. Participation is a separate course. Student-teaching is a separate course..... | 1 | 2 |
| M | Observation, participation, and student-teaching are combined with professional courses in a single course.......................................... | 2 | 6 |
| N | Observation is combined with other professional courses. Observation and student-teaching are a separate course.................................. | 0 | 2 |
| O | Observation and participation are combined with other professional courses. Observation, participation, and student-teaching form a separate course | 2 | 0 |
| Misc. | Other combinations, each in use in a single institution | 2 | 4 |
|  | Total....................................... | 72 | 76 |
|  | Percent of grand total..................... | 40.7 | 42.0 |

### III. *Laboratory Courses Are Combined with Subject-Matter Courses*

| Pattern | Group | 1933–34 | 1937–38 |
|---|---|---|---|
| P | Observation is combined with subject-matter courses without separate credit. Student-teaching is a separate course. (No work in participation)......... | 7 | 5 |
| Q | Observation is combined with subject-matter courses without separate credit. Participation and student-teaching are combined in a single course......... | 4 | 6 |
| R | Observation is combined with subject-matter courses without separate credit. Participation is a separate course. Student-teaching is a separate course..... | 3 | 2 |
| Misc. | Other combinations, each in use in a single institution | 1 | 1 |
|  | Total....................................... | 15 | 14 |
|  | Percent of grand total..................... | 8.5 | 7.7 |

### IV. *Laboratory Courses Are Combined with Both Subject-Matter Courses and Other Professional Courses*

| Pattern | Group | | |
|---|---|---|---|
| S | Observation is combined with professional courses and subject-matter courses without separate credit. | | |

## TABLE XII (*Continued*)

| Pattern | Group | Number of Patterns 1933-34 | 1937-38 |
|---|---|---|---|
| T | Participation and student-teaching are combined in a separate course. | 4 | 0 |
|  | Observation is combined with professional courses in theory and subject-matter. Observation, participation and student-teaching are combined in a single course. | 3 | 2 |
| *Misc.* | Other combinations, each in use in a single institution | 3 | 6 |
|  | Total. | 10 | 8 |
|  | Percent of grand total. | 5.6 | 4.4 |
|  | GRAND TOTAL. | 177 | 181 |
|  | Number of institutions studied. | 131 | 137 |
|  | Number replying on this item. | 128 | 134 |
|  | Number each using two or three different patterns. | 41 | 37 |

courses. Pattern A, a course which consists of a combination of observation, participation, and student-teaching is the most common, being found in 22.6 percent of all cases. Observation is listed as a separate course in 14.1 percent of the patterns, being combined with other laboratory courses in 85.9 percent of them. Observation and participation are combined in a single course in 7.3 percent of the patterns. Observation is combined with professional courses other than participation and student-teaching in 37.3 percent and with subject-matter courses in 7.3 percent of all the patterns.

Participation is organized as a separate course in 4.5 percent of the patterns, is combined with student-teaching in 27.7 percent of them, is not reported as a phase of laboratory experience in 40.2 percent. Student-teaching is organized as a course separate from observation and participation in 32.2 percent of all patterns included in this study.

A comparison of the data received in 1937-38 and those secured in the original study indicates that there is no significant trend in the direction of greater integration. Some study of the permanence of the patterns was made by investigating the length of time the different patterns have been in operation in the institutions. Of those now employed forty-three were organized prior to 1924; fifty-seven between 1924 and 1934; and thirty-one between 1934 and 1938. So far as can be judged by the length of time the various patterns have been in operation there seems no discernible trend toward more integration of these courses with others in the curriculum in the courses established at the later periods as compared with the earlier ones.

In the light of the data, the group of institutions studied on the whole still fall far short of their possibilities in integrating the laboratory courses with subject-matter courses and other professional courses, particularly in integrating with the former. In view of the prevailing sentiment as expressed by the beliefs of individuals and juries, they should make plans which will effectively integrate the laboratory courses with other aspects of the student's educational experience.

How one institution has achieved such integration is described in a letter from a president:

In the kindergarten and elementary divisions we use what we call the experience method of educating teachers. Under this method the student gets all of his professional training, philosophy and principles of education, techniques of teaching, and all those skills, professional and social knowledge that a teacher is supposed to have as a direct outgrowth of professional experiences. The students spend a full year in our training school, campus and off-campus, each under the direction of a guide. The students are put into groups of about ten or twelve each, with a professional guide in charge of each group. The students have no schedule except their schedule of conferences with their training teachers and their professional guides. They spend an hour or two hours or a half day in the training school and the remainder of the time reading in the library, visiting other schools, in conferences with their training teachers and their professional guides.

Of course the methods of integration will differ on different levels, the procedure being different in preparing teachers for the senior high school from what it is in preparing for service in the elementary school. There is obviously a necessity of adapting patterns to the varying situations which are found in the different institutions.

## CLOCK-HOURS OF LABORATORY EXPERIENCE REQUIRED

The term "student-teaching," as it applies both in theory and practice, is ambiguous. One of the standards[42] of the American Association of Teachers Colleges places the minimum amount of student-teaching which may be required of students in institutions which are members of the Association at 90 clock-hours. This is interpreted and administered by the Association to mean 90 clock-hours of actual responsible room teaching, exclusive of observation and participation. However, in determining the effectiveness of the program of teacher education and the service load which the laboratory school must carry, it is important to know what proportions of observation, participation, and student-teaching are included in the total laboratory experience of the student.

Certainly no student should graduate who has not proved his ability to handle a class independently. On this point Henderson's conclusion may be quoted:

No number of observations and conferences should be permitted to take the place of actual classroom teaching by the student teacher.[43]

In an inquiry which secured the opinions of between seven and eight hundred subject-matter instructors, the majority opinion was that supervised observation is not a substitute for supervised courses in actual student-teaching.[44] Marshall, as a result of her experimental study reaches the conclusion:

That a given number of hours of student-teaching graded and distributed over a period of practice is more effective than the same number of hours divided between directed observation and actual teaching.[45]

Yet observation and participation are seen to play an important role in furnishing a suitable background for the understanding of educational problems.[46] To allow a teachers college student to en-

---

[42] American Association of Teachers Colleges, *loc. cit.*

[43] Elisha L. Henderson, *The Organization and Administration of Student Teaching in State Teachers Colleges*, p. 120. 1937.

[44] Rugg, *op. cit.*, p. 94.

[45] Marshall, *op. cit.*, p. 74.

[46] Alonzo F. Myers, "The Course in Observation and Participation in Its Relationship to Courses in Principles of Teaching, Methods, School Management, etc." *Educational Administration and Supervision*, Vol. 14, p. 410, September, 1928.

gage in responsible student-teaching prior to the time when he has observed and studied superior teaching is "like forcing the surgeon's instruments into the hands of the medical student who has never witnessed an operation."[47] Observation, too, may well be continued while the student is carrying on his student-teaching.[48]

The principle of gradual induction into responsible control of a room in student-teaching has been widely advocated. Pryor[49] strongly urges gradual induction into teaching by a gradation in difficulty from the simpler to the more complex activities of the teacher's work beginning with observation, and continuing through graded participation to complete charge of the class as a student-teacher. Learned and Bagley,[50] Mooney,[51] and Mead[52] believe that properly administered and supervised participation is a useful technique. Rutledge[53] found that thirty-four out of the thirty-five jurors whom he selected as being outstanding in the field of educational administration supported the thesis that "the students of the teachers college or the normal school should be introduced gradually to the activities of the teaching job."

The amount of student-teaching which should be required in the pre-service education of the teacher has never been determined by exact experimentation. Rutledge's study[54] showed that in his poll of thirty-five jurors all but one voted assent to the proposition that the student should spend at least enough time in the demonstration and practice school to master the skills that are necessary in the work of a thoroughly prepared teacher. However, he does not attempt to determine what the amount should be. Mead[55] recommends a minimum of ninety class periods of actual teaching for secondary school teachers and 90 clock-hours for elementary teachers and teachers of special subjects in the elementary grades. In addition he recommends ninety periods of

---

[47] Learned and Bagley, *op. cit.*, p. 211.
[48] Thomas Alexander, "Application of Some Principles Which Underlie Practice Teaching." Address Delivered before the New York Association of Teachers Colleges and Normal School Faculties. Syracuse, New York, October 13, 1930.
[49] Hugh C. Pryor, *Graded Units in Student-Teaching.* 1926.
[50] Learned and Bagley, *op. cit.*, p. 394.
[51] Edward S. Mooney, *An Analysis of the Supervision of Student Teaching*, p. 29. 1937.
[52] A. R. Mead, *Supervised Student-Teaching*, p. 241. 1930.
[53] Rutledge, *op. cit.*, p. 51.
[54] *Idem.*
[55] Mead, *op. cit.*, pp. 461–463.

PRESENTATION AND INTERPRETATION OF DATA  65

observation and participation for secondary teachers, but makes no definite recommendation on this point for elementary teachers. Bagley, Alexander, and Foote[56] recommend a half day of practice each day for a period of twelve weeks for teachers in both the elementary school and the high school.

In the present study the institutions were asked to state the amount of each type of laboratory experience—observation, participation, and student-teaching—which they required under the patterns which they listed themselves as using. (See Table XII.) In the great diversity of patterns which was found, different combinations of the three phases of laboratory experience were made in reporting. For example, in some the clock-hours of observation and participation were expressed as a single sum; in others, observation was isolated as a course with separate credit; in still others, observation and participation were combined, while student-teaching was isolated. After an examination of the data provided on the questionnaires, it was concluded (*a*) to present the data for the two-year and four-year curriculums, analyzed according to geographic divisions; (*b*) to present another set of tables, showing the distribution of clock-hours of observation and participation in one division and student-teaching in the other for the two-year and four-year curriculums of different types; and (*c*) to show the trends, if any, which were found in the four-year curriculum between the years 1933–34 and 1937–38. It was thought best to make a more detailed study of the two-year and four-year curriculums because the trend seems to be toward curriculums of these lengths. Rugg and Peik[57] found that the rural curriculum is the only one which is offered on the one-year level by 5 percent or more of the normal schools and teachers colleges which they studied. They believe that the three-year curriculum may be an intermediate step in the upgrading tendency from the two-year to the four-year curriculum. In fact, an examination of the status of institutions replying in 1933–34 and again in 1937–38 indicates that this is the case. For the most part the

---

[56] W. C. Bagley, Thomas Alexander, and J. M. Foote, *Report of the Survey Commission on the Louisiana State Normal College, The Louisiana Polytechnic Institute, and The Southwestern Louisiana Institute*, pp. 199 and 213. 1924.

[57] Rugg and Peik, *op. cit.*, p. 55.

three-year curriculum was found in 1933-34 in the New England, Middle Atlantic, and Pacific divisions where a number of the institutions have already abandoned the three-year curriculum and others are planning to do so soon.

There was another reason for omitting the one-year and three-year curriculums from this aspect of the study. The number of cases was rather small, so that any conclusions which might be drawn from the data would be inconclusive. For example, data were available for only five three-year elementary curriculums and for only three one-year curriculums. Data were not available for the special subjects in the three-year curriculums in sufficient quantity to warrant any adequate conclusions. A similar condition prevailed with respect to one-year curriculums. As it is one of the purposes of this study to determine general practices and trends, this section is limited to the general curriculums two years in length and to four-year curriculums in both the general fields and in special subjects.

In Table XIII there is presented an analysis of total laboratory experience required by seventy-nine institutions in the two-year curriculums. The median requirement varies greatly, ranging from 36 clock-hours to 594 clock-hours for different institutions, and the range is surprisingly large. There is noticeable variation among the geographic divisions, the requirement in the East South Central Division being considerably lower than in other areas. No two-year curriculums were offered in the New England Division.

A similar tabulation, shown in Table XIV, was made for four-year curriculums. Here 107 institutions gave reports on 678 curriculums and again considerable differences in requirements are to be noted. As in the case of the two-year curriculums the differences in median amounts in the different geographic divisions are striking, these ranging from the large total of 390.0 clock-hours in the New England Division and 365.1 in the Middle Atlantic Division to the meagre 99.6 clock-hours in the East South Central Division and 115.0 clock-hours in the South Atlantic Division. The amount of laboratory experience required in the four-year curriculums is greater than in the two-year curriculums, the excess being 28.3 clock-hours.

## TABLE XIII

*Total Laboratory Experience Required in the Two-Year Curriculums of All Types in State Normal Schools and Teachers Colleges, Analyzed According to Geographic Divisions, 1933–34*

| Geographic Division | No. of Institutions Reporting | No. of Curriculums | Clock-Hours of Laboratory Experience Required Range | Median |
|---|---|---|---|---|
| New England............ | | | | |
| Middle Atlantic.......... | 9 | 25 | 77–330 | 146 |
| East North Central....... | 15 | 50 | 90–594 | 144 |
| West North Central....... | 24 | 68 | 45–228 | 120 |
| South Atlantic........... | 9 | 17 | 45–190 | 120 |
| East South Central....... | 6 | 9 | 36–135 | 72 |
| West South Central....... | 11 | 22 | 45–312 | 130.5 |
| Mountain................ | 3 | 9 | 96–234 | 180 |
| Pacific.................. | 2 | 3 | 130–270 | 130 |
| Total................... | 79 | 203 | 36–594 | 131.6 |

$Q_1 = 97.2$  $Q_3 = 178.7$

Table XV (page 69) exhibits the experience required in two-year curriculums. For thirty-one institutions it was possible to separate the number of clock-hours required in observation and participation from those in student-teaching. These data, covering a smaller group of institutions than were included in Table XIII, again indicate a wide range in the total amount of laboratory experience, and also a diversity equally great in the proportionate time allotted to observation and participation and to student-teaching. In observation and participation there is a range from 12 to 120 clock-hours; in student-teaching from 30 to 315 clock-hours. In one institution as little as 12 clock-hours (4.5 percent) of a total of 330 clock-hours of laboratory experience is devoted to observation and participation. At the other extreme is another institution in which 90 (66.7 percent) of 135 clock-hours of laboratory experience are devoted to observation and participation. For the thirty-one institutions studied, the median amount of observation and participation was 60 clock-hours

## TABLE XIV

*Total Laboratory Experience Required in the Four-Year Curriculums of All Types in State Normal Schools and Teachers Colleges, According to Geographic Divisions, 1933-34*

| Geographic Division | No. of Institutions Reporting | No. of Curriculums | Clock-Hours of Laboratory Experience Required Range | Median |
|---|---|---|---|---|
| New England............ | 7 | 24 | 180–540 | 390.0 |
| Middle Atlantic.......... | 15 | 75 | 100–748 | 365.1 |
| East North Central....... | 18 | 149 | 54–700 | 161.1 |
| West North Central....... | 20 | 148 | 30–264 | 129.3 |
| South Atlantic........... | 10 | 33 | 90–240 | 115.0 |
| East South Central....... | 7 | 49 | 90–144 | 99.6 |
| West South Central....... | 15 | 97 | 60–300 | 132.5 |
| Mountain................ | 7 | 51 | 90–405 | 173.2 |
| Pacific.................. | 8 | 52 | 60–712 | 206.2 |
| Total................... | 107 | 678 | 30–748 | 159.9 |

$Q_1 = 105.7$  $Q_3 = 230.9$

(40.1 percent) while that of student-teaching was 89.5 clock-hours (59.9 percent). By a striking coincidence it happens that the median amount of student-teaching is 90 clock-hours for each type of curriculum listed in the table. Of the total of 78 curriculums, 90 clock-hours are required in twenty-three; 120 clock-hours in eleven; 108 clock-hours in seven; and 60 clock-hours in seven. The others show considerable scatter in the amounts required.

Comparable data collected in 1937–38 on the basis of fifty-three curriculums in twenty-five institutions indicate that there is a trend toward requiring a greater proportion of the laboratory experience in actual teaching, 45.3 clock-hours (32.5 percent) being indicated for observation and participation, 94 clock-hours (67.5 percent) for student-teaching, a total of 139.3 clock-hours. This indicates a median decrease of 10.2 clock-hours in the requirement during the four years.

In a similar way it was possible to segregate data for forty-seven

## TABLE XV

*Clock-Hours of Total Laboratory Experience Required in Two-Year Curriculums in State Normal Schools and Teachers Colleges, According to Type of Curriculum, 1933–34*

| Type of Curriculum | No. of Curriculums | Observation and Participation Range | Median | % | Student-Teaching Range | Median | % |
|---|---|---|---|---|---|---|---|
| General elementary.. | 8 | 12– 90 | 51 | 36.2 | 45–300 | 90 | 63.8 |
| Kindergarten-primary | 25 | 15–116 | 50 | 35.7 | 45–315 | 90 | 64.3 |
| Intermediate......... | 24 | 15–116 | 53 | 37.1 | 30–315 | 90 | 62.9 |
| Junior high school... | 9 | 18–108 | 60 | 40.0 | 30–120 | 90 | 60.0 |
| Senior high school.... | | | | | | | |
| Rural one-teacher and two-teacher schools | 12 | 30–120 | 87 | 49.1 | 47–175 | 90 | 50.9 |
| Total............... | | 12–120 | 60 | 40.1 | 30–315 | 89.5 | 59.9 |
| Total number of institutions replying.... | 31 | | | | | | |

institutions which offered a four-year curriculum. Table XVI summarizes the situation in these institutions. Here the special subjects are included. The range is even greater than in the case of the two-year curriculums, it being from 10 to 423 clock-hours of observation and participation, and from 32 to 632 clock-hours of student-teaching. Again the institutional differences are striking. One institution which requires a total of 400 clock-hours of laboratory experience allots 250 clock-hours (62.5 percent) to observation and participation, and 150 clock-hours (37.5 percent) to student-teaching; another devotes two-thirds of the total 270 clock-hours required to observation and participation; still another, 144 (80.0 percent) of 180 clock-hours to observation and 36 (20.0 percent) to student-teaching. A similar variation prevails whether elementary or high school curriculums are considered. At the other extreme is one institution which requires only 10 clock-hours (6.9 percent) of observation and participation and 135 clock-hours (93.1 percent) of student-teaching; and still another which requires no observation or participation but assigns each student 90 clock-hours of student-teaching.

TABLE XVI

Clock-Hours of Total Laboratory Experience Required in Four-Year Curriculums in State Normal Schools and Teachers Colleges, According to Type of Curriculum, 1933–34

| Type of Curriculum | No. of Curriculums | Observation and Participation |||  Student-Teaching |||
|---|---|---|---|---|---|---|---|
| | | Range | Median | % | Range | Median | % |
| General elementary.. | 11 | 30–144 | 72.0 | 36.0 | 45–360 | 128.0 | 64.0 |
| Kindergarten-primary | 27 | 16–360 | 90.0 | 33.3 | 32–630 | 180.0 | 66.7 |
| Intermediate........ | 22 | 16–270 | 71.0 | 27.9 | 32–630 | 180.0 | 72.1 |
| Junior high school... | 27 | 10–275 | 60.0 | 31.4 | 32–632 | 126.0 | 68.6 |
| Senior high school.... | 33 | 10–275 | 60.0 | 37.5 | 32–400 | 100.0 | 62.5 |
| Rural one-teacher and two-teacher schools | 6 | 30–144 | 87.5 | 28.0 | 60–336 | 225.0 | 72.0 |
| Special subjects: | | | | | | | |
| Agriculture....... | 4 | 30– 90 | 72.0 | 44.9 | 45–120 | 90.0 | 55.1 |
| Art.............. | 10 | 30–144 | 72.0 | 40.7 | 45–360 | 105.0 | 59.3 |
| Business.......... | 14 | 18–144 | 65.0 | 41.9 | 45–360 | 90.0 | 58.1 |
| Home economics... | 19 | 15–180 | 54.0 | 37.5 | 45–360 | 90.0 | 62.5 |
| Industrial Arts.... | 12 | 18–145 | 75.0 | 45.5 | 45–630 | 90.0 | 54.5 |
| Music............ | 18 | 15–423 | 60.0 | 33.3 | 45–360 | 120.0 | 66.7 |
| Physical education (men).......... | 16 | 30–180 | 60.0 | 37.7 | 45–360 | 99.0 | 62.3 |
| Physical education (women)........ | 17 | 10–180 | 60.0 | 33.3 | 45–360 | 120.0 | 66.7 |
| Total.............. | | 10–423 | 67.3 | 35.9 | 32–632 | 120.2 | 64.1 |
| Total number of institutions replying.... | 47 | | | | | | |

The median amounts of laboratory experience required in the institutions for all four-year curriculums is 187.5 clock-hours. Comparing this table with Table XV, which refers to two-year curriculums, it can be seen that the requirement of laboratory experience in the four-year curriculum exceeds that of the two-year curriculum by 42 clock-hours. While the median amount of ob-

## PRESENTATION AND INTERPRETATION OF DATA 71

servation and participation in the four-year curriculum is 7.3 clock-hours per institution more than in the curriculum two years in length, the median amount of responsible student-teaching is 30.7 clock-hours more, the percentage of observation and participation being 35.9 and of student-teaching, 64.1. It is to be noted that the greatest median amount of total laboratory experience (observation, participation, and student-teaching) as well as the greatest median amount of student-teaching of all curriculums is required in the case of one-teacher and two-teacher rural schools, the former being 312.5 (87.5 + 225), the latter, 225 clock-hours.

To determine whether there is any discernible trend in the amounts, comparable data were secured for the year 1937–38. They are presented in Table XVII. A comparison of this table with Table XVI indicates that the range, both of the combined observation and participation and of student-teaching in the four-year curriculums has been somewhat reduced during the four years. In Table XVI data for forty-seven institutions, in twenty-five states, are reported; in Table XVII there are data for forty-nine institutions in twenty-six states. A comparison of the two tables indicates that the range, both in observation and participation and in student-teaching, has been somewhat reduced. It is also noteworthy that the required median amount of observation and participation has been reduced from 67.3 clock-hours to 59.4 clock-hours; the amount of student-teaching from 120.2 to 108.1 clock-hours; the total required laboratory experience from 187.5 to 167.5 clock-hours, a reduction of 20.0 clock-hours.

To check the validity of these comparisons, thirty institutions which had furnished data for both 1933–34 and 1937–38 were studied. Confirmation of the trend toward a reduction of the clock-hour requirement in laboratory experience was evident. The reduction in the amount of observation was from 66.0 to 58.3 clock-hours, a difference of 7.7 clock-hours; in student-teaching, from 141.9 to 113.9 clock-hours, a difference of 28 clock-hours; in the total laboratory experience, from 207.9 to 172.2 clock-hours, a reduction of 35.7 clock-hours of 17.2 percent during the four-year period. The percentage of observation and participation remained approximately the same for the two academic

## TABLE XVII

*Clock-Hours of Total Laboratory Experience Required in Four-Year Curriculums in State Normal Schools and Teachers Colleges, According to Type of Curriculum, 1937–38*

|  |  | CLOCK-HOURS OF LABORATORY EXPERIENCE ||||||
|---|---|---|---|---|---|---|---|
| Type of Curriculum | No. of Curriculums | Observation and Participation ||| Student-Teaching |||
|  |  | Range | Median | % | Range | Median | % |
| General elementary.. | 20 | 10–250 | 85.5 | 36.3 | 60–450 | 150.0 | 63.7 |
| Kindergarten-primary | 35 | 0–360 | 72.0 | 37.5 | 40–360 | 120.0 | 62.5 |
| Intermediate........ | 28 | 0–360 | 65.0 | 35.2 | 40–300 | 120.0 | 64.8 |
| Junior high school... | 29 | 0–360 | 64.0 | 34.7 | 36–450 | 120.0 | 65.3 |
| Senior high school.... | 28 | 0–180 | 52.5 | 33.5 | 30–270 | 104.0 | 66.5 |
| Rural one-teacher and two-teacher schools | 8 | 0–180 | 37.5 | 29.4 | 45–270 | 90.0 | 70.6 |
| Special subjects: |  |  |  |  |  |  |  |
| Agriculture....... | 6 | 30– 60 | 42.5 | 30.7 | 60–150 | 96.0 | 69.3 |
| Art.............. | 11 | 30–108 | 46.0 | 38.9 | 44–120 | 72.0 | 61.1 |
| Business.......... | 13 | 30–150 | 60.0 | 40.0 | 30–300 | 90.0 | 60.0 |
| Home economics... | 16 | 28– 75 | 57.5 | 41.1 | 30–160 | 82.5 | 58.9 |
| Industrial arts..... | 15 | 30–360 | 60.0 | 40.0 | 44–300 | 90.0 | 60.0 |
| Music............ | 18 | 30–180 | 60.0 | 40.0 | 30–300 | 90.0 | 60.0 |
| Physical education (men).......... | 19 | 12–180 | 55.0 | 37.9 | 44–190 | 90.0 | 62.1 |
| Physical education (women)........ | 19 | 12–180 | 55.0 | 37.9 | 44–190 | 90.0 | 62.1 |
| Total.............. |  | 0–360 | 59.4 | 35.5 | 30–450 | 108.1 | 64.5 |
| Total number of institutions replying.... | 49 |  |  |  |  |  |  |

years, 35.9 percent for 1933–34, and 35.5 percent for 1937–38. It was proportionately less in the curriculums for one-teacher and two-teacher rural schools. In both years the amount of student-teaching required for prospective senior high school teachers is less than for the other general curriculums with the exception of the curriculum for rural one- and two-teacher schools.

It was possible to isolate the respective amounts of each of the three phases of laboratory experience—observation, participation and student-teaching—in the case of twenty institutions offering sixty-four curriculums in 1933–34, and thirty institutions offering 129 curriculums in 1937–38. In 1933–34 the relative amounts of each of the three phases were as follows: observation, 32.4 clock-hours (17.8 percent); participation, 34.6 clock-hours (19.0 percent); student-teaching, 114.9 clock-hours (63.2 percent). In 1937–38 the corresponding amounts were: observation, 33.3 clock-hours (20.8 percent); participation, 30.4 clock-hours (19.0 percent); student-teaching, 96.1 clock-hours (60.2 percent). Little or no trend is indicated by these amounts because the small differences may be due to the relatively small number of cases which could be isolated.

From the data in the tables the conclusion may be drawn that there is a general tendency to decrease the amount of laboratory experience required for graduation in the four years intervening between the collection of the two sets of data. The wide range and the variation between individual institutions in the absolute and relative amounts of the different phases of laboratory experience which are required indicate that there is need for a separate study which will determine the optimum amounts which will best equip the student effectively for entering upon his career as a teacher. Pending the information to be secured from such a study an explanation of the varying amounts may be found in the difficulties which certain institutions experience in supplying laboratory facilities as well as in differing judgments of those responsible regarding the optimum amount. If the median of the requirements of the different institutions represents their judgment as to what the standard amount ought to be, the conclusion must be drawn that the present minimum standard of the American Association of Teachers Colleges is too low and that the requirement should be increased.

FLEXIBILITY IN REQUIREMENT OF LABORATORY EXPERIENCE

There has been a general movement in education in America to recognize individual differences and to make requirements more flexible. This is indicated by the present practices and proposals for college admission, variations in the difficulty of courses, standards for graduation, "honors courses," sectioning classes according to ability, and by the greater freedom allowed in the student's election of courses. Standardizing agencies such as the North Central Association of Colleges and Secondary Schools have allowed greater flexibility in meeting their standards for accrediting. Practices similar to those in the liberal arts colleges and universities have been employed by the normal schools and teachers colleges as well.

In accordance with their acceptance of the desirability of flexibility, many educators who have responsibility for the preparation of teachers believe that this principle should be applied in determining the nature and amount of laboratory experience which students should be required to have. Thus Peik writes:

> Student teaching should be a flexible assignment so that all students may be given the opportunity to reach a satisfactory quality of performance to pass or to be excused from more of it, but superior people should be allowed to continue long enough to have had a chance to develop and demonstrate their superiority to capitalize upon it.[58]

Rugg, writing on the subject, concludes:

> But periodic tests of competency should be given which should result in variations in amounts and lengths of practice teaching for individual students in a given teacher-preparing institution. . . . Student teaching requirements should be flexible in amount so that all students may be expected to reach satisfactory standards of performance before being approved for certification as teachers.[59]

Schorling is in agreement with the general view held by Peik and Rugg:

> The course in directed teaching as regards kind, amount, and rate of induction should be adjusted to the ability, experience, and need of the individual student teacher. . . . A training school should not only employ a graduated program in directed teaching but it should be adjusted to the individual student teacher.[60]

Also in conformity with these views is that of Alexander, who declares:

> Student teaching should be differentiated in every respect, time, content, variety, and sequence, according to the needs of the student and other factors concerned.[61]

[58] Peik, in *National Survey of the Education of Teachers*, Vol. III, *op. cit.*, p. 362.
[59] Rugg, in *National Survey of the Education of Teachers*, Vol. III, *op. cit.*, p. 96.
[60] Schorling, *op. cit.*, p. 155.
[61] Alexander, in *National Survey of the Education of Teachers*, Vol. V, *loc. cit.*

These views are representative of a number of others which are expressed elsewhere in the report of the *National Survey of the Education of Teachers*, and by other writers.

To determine the attitude of the normal schools and teachers colleges toward a policy of flexibility in the requirement of laboratory experience, the question was asked, after stating the present standard regarding the amount of student-teaching, "If this standard were changed so as to allow it, would you, in your institution, favor a policy of flexibility in the student-teaching requirement to adapt the amount required to the individual needs of the student-teachers?" A similar query asked for the institution's opinion on the matter of flexibility in the requirement of observation and participation. The question, which was asked in the original questionnaire, was repeated four years later to determine whether there was any modification of the earlier opinion. An exhibit of the answers is presented in Table XVIII. More than 50 percent of those replying favored flexibility in two phases of laboratory experience, observation and student-teaching, in 1933–34, and in all phases of laboratory experience, observation, participation, and student-teaching, in 1937–38. The replies received in both academic years indicate less disposition to favor flexibility in observation than in student-teaching, for the country as a whole. The figures for 1937–38 indicate an increased number in favor of flexibility, whether each phase of laboratory experience is considered separately or all in their entirety. At the later date there are 100 institutions which favor flexibility in student-teaching compared with seventy-eight found to do so four years earlier. In general, the institutions in the New England States oppose modifying definite fixed requirements. One president, fearing that standards will be lowered, writes, "Absolutely *no*. Standard is absurdly low, should be increased." On the other hand, the institutions of the Mountain and Pacific Divisions generally favor flexibility. In the East Central and West Central Divisions there were twenty-six of thirty-nine institutions (66.7 percent) favoring flexibility in student-teaching in 1933–34 as against thirty-six of forty-one (87.8 percent) who did so in 1937–38. The data in the table, taken as a whole, indicate that the opinion of administrators is moving in the direction of the position held by those whose opinions are quoted earlier in the chapter, although it is a position still held far from unanimously.

To check the actual practices regarding flexibility against the opinions which were expressed regarding its advisability, the institutions were asked to indicate whether, under certain conditions, any students were excused from any or all of the three

TABLE XVIII

*State Normal Schools and Teachers Colleges Favoring Flexibility in Laboratory School Requirements in the Standards of the American Association of Teachers Colleges, 1933–34 and 1937–38*

| Geographic Division | No. of Institutions Studied | Reporting | Institutions Favoring Flexibility in: Observation | Participation | Student-Teaching |
|---|---|---|---|---|---|
| *1933–34* | | | | | |
| New England............. | 7 | 6 | 4 | 2 | 1 |
| Middle Atlantic........... | 22 | 19 | 14 | 12 | 15 |
| East North Central........ | 21 | 17 | 8 | 8 | 12 |
| West North Central........ | 24 | 22 | 12 | 13 | 14 |
| South Atlantic............ | 12 | 11 | 8 | 8 | 10 |
| East South Central........ | 10 | 9 | 2 | 2 | 6 |
| West South Central........ | 16 | 15 | 8 | 8 | 8 |
| Mountain................. | 8 | 8 | 4 | 5 | 7 |
| Pacific................... | 11 | 10 | 2 | 3 | 5 |
| Total................. | 131 | 117 | 62 | 41 | 78 |
| Percent............... |  | 100.0 | 53.0 | 35.0 | 66.7 |
| *1937–38* | | | | | |
| New England............. | 15 | 14 | 4 | 4 | 5 |
| Middle Atlantic........... | 27 | 23 | 10 | 11 | 16 |
| East North Central........ | 20 | 19 | 10 | 12 | 15 |
| West North Central........ | 23 | 22 | 15 | 14 | 21 |
| South Atlantic............ | 15 | 15 | 10 | 9 | 13 |
| East South Central........ | 10 | 10 | 4 | 8 | 8 |
| West South Central........ | 12 | 12 | 6 | 6 | 9 |
| Mountain................. | 6 | 5 | 3 | 3 | 5 |
| Pacific................... | 9 | 9 | 3 | 3 | 8 |
| Total................. | 137 | 129 | 65 | 70 | 100 |
| Percent............... |  | 100.0 | 50.4 | 54.3 | 77.5 |

phases of laboratory experience. A summary of the replies is given in Table XIX. It is likely that the standards of the American Association of Teachers Colleges act as a deterrent to flexibility in cases where only the minimum amount of student-teaching is required for graduation. In any event the greater number of institutions do not practice excusing students from any part of the

TABLE XIX

*Number and Percent of State Normal Schools and Teachers Colleges Waiving Part or All of the Usual Requirements in Laboratory Experience Under Certain Conditions, 1933–34 and 1937–38*

| Type of Experience | No. of Institutions Reporting | Waiving None No. | Waiving None % | Waiving Part No. | Waiving Part % | Waiving All No. | Waiving All % |
|---|---|---|---|---|---|---|---|
| *1933–34* | | | | | | | |
| Observation | 106 | 62 | 58.5 | 30 | 28.3 | 14 | 13.2 |
| Participation | 104 | 62 | 59.5 | 29 | 27.9 | 13 | 12.5 |
| Student-teaching | 125 | 62 | 49.6 | 51 | 40.8 | 12 | 9.6 |
| *1937–38* | | | | | | | |
| Observation | 117 | 85 | 72.6 | 16 | 13.6 | 16 | 13.6 |
| Participation | 100 | 67 | 67.0 | 19 | 19.0 | 14 | 14.0 |
| Student-teaching | 129 | 64 | 49.6 | 45 | 34.9 | 20 | 15.5 |

requirement. There is a greater disposition to waive requirements in student-teaching than in observation and participation, indicating that the practice of the institutions in this respect agrees with the opinions which they hold as expressed in Table XVIII. However, a smaller percentage of the institutions waived the requirements in observation and participation in 1937–38 than did four years earlier in 1933–34, while an equal percentage waived part or all of the student-teaching requirements in each of the academic years. A greater percentage of the institutions waived the whole requirement in the year 1937–38. There is a greater tendency to excuse either from no part or from all the laboratory experience, and less to excuse from a part only. This practice con-

## TABLE XX

*Maximum Amount of Laboratory Experience from Which Students May Be Excused in State Normal Schools and Teachers Colleges, 1933–34 and 1937–38*

| Type of Experience | No. of Institutions 1933–34 | No. of Institutions 1937–38 | Range 1933–34 | Range 1937–38 | Median 1933–34 | Median 1937–38 |
|---|---|---|---|---|---|---|
| Observation | 17 | 9 | 8– 54 | 10– 90 | 20.0 | 45.0 |
| Participation | 10 | 10 | 8–108 | 10–225 | 33.0 | 17.5 |
| Student-teaching | 39 | 38 | 8–420 | 10–400 | 60.0 | 82.5 |

flicts with the statements regarding the need of flexibility to provide for individual differences which the institutions have expressed. It would no doubt be desirable to adjust the amount of laboratory experience required from which the student is excused to his need as shown by his previous accomplishment. Difficulties in making the laboratory school schedule, in adjustments of the amount of college credit, in providing standards for determining accurately the competence of student-teachers, in varying standards imposed by supervisors, and the general difficulties in making distinctions between students in setting up requirements are factors which enter into determining actual practices, whatever theories are held. However, in spite of the difficulties to be overcome, it seems clear that the application of a more flexible requirement will make for more effectiveness in the use of the student's time and consequently for an improvement in his educational preparation.

A relatively small number of institutions indicated the number of clock-hours from which they permitted students to be excused. As indicated in Table XIX, a large number of institutions refuse to excuse their students from any part of the laboratory experience whatsoever. In Table XX the range and median number of clock-hours from which excuse is given by a limited number of institutions are presented. The trend is toward excusing from a greater number of clock-hours in observation and student-teaching, and from fewer in participation. Here, as elsewhere in the tables, one is impressed by the great range showing wide differences between institutions. There is need to determine what amount of laboratory experience the teacher should have in his pre-service education.

Whenever the requirement of laboratory experience is waived, it is the general practice to refuse the student credit toward graduation for it. Of seventy-five institutions which gave information on this subject in 1933–34, only fifteen (20 percent) assigned credit for it, while sixty (80 percent) did not. Of sixty-one institutions replying in 1937–38, eight (13.1 percent) gave credit for the work from which the student was excused, and fifty-three (86.9 percent) did not. The trend is clearly in the direction of refusing credit for the laboratory experience from which the student is excused.

A study was made of the conditions under which the usual requirements in observation, participation, and student-teaching were waived. To determine if any changes had occurred in the four-year period, figures are presented in Table XXI for each of the academic years 1933–34 and 1937–38. The reasons for excusing are listed in order of their frequencies. For all three phases of laboratory experience three factors determine almost exclusively whether or not a student shall be excused. In order of rank the reasons are: prior teaching experience, general excellence of scholarship, and superior intelligence. Prior teaching experience occurs more often than all other reasons combined, being assigned in 86.2 percent of the excuses from observation, 89.7 percent of those from participation, and 82.4 percent of those from student-teaching. No particular trend during the four-year period is discernible in the reasons for waiving the requirements.

Typical conditions under which excuses from student-teaching requirements may be granted are stated by institutions as follows:

*Institution A.* A teacher with five years of successful teaching experience may substitute some other professional subject for the third term of student-teaching if he has made two term grades not less than "A" in student-teaching. In rare cases a teacher who has taught five years is required to do only one term of teaching if his grade in that term is "A."

## TABLE XXI

*Reasons for Waiving a Part or All of the Graduation Requirement in Observation, Participation, and Student-Teaching, 1933–34 and 1937–38*

| Reason | 1933–34 | 1937–38 |
|---|---|---|
| *Observation* | | |
| Total number of institutions stating reasons for waiving requirement | 35 | 26 |
| Reasons for waiving requirement: | | |
| Prior teaching experience | 35 | 25 |
| General excellence of scholarship | 8 | 1 |
| Superior intelligence | 4 | 1 |
| Excellence in early part of course in student teaching | 2 | |
| Illness | 1 | |
| Conflict in program | | 1 |
| Substitution of other courses | | 1 |
| *Participation* | | |
| Total number of institutions stating reasons for waiving requirement | 31 | 27 |
| Reasons for waiving requirement: | | |
| Prior teaching experience | 31 | 26 |
| General excellence of scholarship | 5 | |
| Superior intelligence | 2 | 1 |
| Excellence in early part of course in student teaching | 1 | 1 |
| Illness | 1 | |
| Substitution of other courses | | 1 |
| *Student-teaching* | | |
| Total number of institutions stating reasons for waiving requirement | 60 | 61 |
| Reasons for waiving requirement: | | |
| Prior teaching experience | 51 | 56 |
| General excellence of scholarship | 11 | 3 |
| Superior intelligence | 4 | 1 |
| Excellence in the early part of the course in student teaching | 3 | 1 |
| Illness | 1 | |
| Prior teaching experience and general excellence of scholarship | | 3 |
| Prior teaching experience and excellence in student teaching | | 1 |
| Limited facilities | | 1 |
| Conflict in program | | 1 |
| Substitution of other courses | | 1 |

*Institution B.* The student, at his request, may be excused from all the usual requirements of the student-teaching courses, provided he has had forty months of successful teaching experience in the public school.

*Institution C.* State regulations allow a candidate with five years of teaching experience to substitute other education courses for practice teaching.

*Institution D.* No student is excused who has not had at least three years of successful public school experience certified to by professionally trained people.

These typical comments indicate different policies. In the first instance the teacher is excused only after proving his competence by prior teaching in the laboratory school of the college; in the last two, by evidence of experience deemed "successful." It is suggested that the student who applies for an excuse from any of the requirements should not be released until such time as he has demonstrated his ability to do successful teaching by actually giving a demonstration of his teaching in the laboratory schools.

The total number of students excused for the reasons stated in the preceding paragraph is small compared with the total number of student-teachers. Table XXII indicates, too, that the relative number excused has decreased during the four-year interval be-

TABLE XXII

*Number of Students Excused from a Part or All of Certain Phases of Laboratory Experience in State Normal Schools and Teachers Colleges, 1933–34 and 1937–38*

| Type of Experience | No. of Institutions Reporting 1933–34 | No. of Institutions Reporting 1937–38 | Students Excused 1933–34 No. | Range | Median | 1937–38 No. | Range | Median |
|---|---|---|---|---|---|---|---|---|
| Observation.. | 31 | 23 | 254 | 1–89 | 9.5 | 260 | 1–150 | 4.0 |
| Participation. | 30 | 22 | 229 | 1–89 | 10.5 | 136 | 1– 35 | 4.5 |
| Student teaching... | 48 | 47 | 375 | 1–89 | 6.0 | 289* | 1– 50 | 4.0 |

*One institution estimates 50 to 75 excused; the lower figure is included here.

tween 1933-34 and 1937-38. In 1937-38 the institutions which reported indicated that they excused a median of four students from observation, four and a half from participation and four from student-teaching, a small percentage of the total, when it is considered that the mean number of student-teachers per institution is 186.9 (Table XXIX, page 89).

Whenever a minimum requirement is stated, there is a tendency for the minimum to become the maximum or approved standard. In the preceding paragraphs of the study the concern has been with *waived* requirements. But the institutions were asked also to indicate whether students, except to repeat a course after receiving failing grades, were ever required to *exceed* the usual requirements in the three phases of laboratory experience. Table XXIII shows that in only nineteen (18.3 percent) of the 104 institutions reporting was there a requirement to exceed the usual requirement in observation; in twenty-one (23.3 percent)

TABLE XXIII

*Number of Normal Schools and Teachers Colleges Which Required Some Students to Exceed the Normal Institutional Course Requirements in Laboratory Experience, 1933-34 and 1937-38*

| Reason | 1933-34 | 1937-38 |
|---|---|---|
| *Observation* | | |
| Number of institutions reporting.................... | 104 | 103 |
| Number requiring some students to exceed the normal requirements.................................. | 19 | 14 |
| *Participation\** | | |
| Number of institutions reporting.................... | 90 | 91 |
| Number requiring some students to exceed the normal requirements.................................. | 21 | 15 |
| *Student-Teaching* | | |
| Number of institutions reporting.................... | 125 | 130 |
| Number requiring some students to exceed the normal requirements.................................. | 41 | 41 |

\* Of 131 institutions studied in 1933-34 in this investigation, 114 required participation; of 137 studied in 1937-38, 127 required participation.

## TABLE XXIV

*Number and Percent of Students Completing a Course in Student-Teaching in State Normal Schools and Teachers Colleges, Distributed According to Geographic Divisions and Type of Laboratory School in Which Student-Teaching Was Done, 1923-24*

| Geographic Division | No. of Institutions Reporting | In Campus Schools No. | In Campus Schools % | In Off-Campus Schools No. | In Off-Campus Schools % | Part in Campus, Part in Off-Campus Schools No. | Part in Campus, Part in Off-Campus Schools % | Total |
|---|---|---|---|---|---|---|---|---|
| New England | 11 | 465 | 55.2 | 226 | 26.8 | 152 | 18.0 | 843 |
| Middle Atlantic | 18 | 1,974 | 64.8 | 1,050 | 34.5 | 22 | 0.7 | 3,046 |
| East North Central | 19 | 5,305 | 72.8 | 1,857 | 25.5 | 121 | 1.7 | 7,283 |
| West North Central | 24 | 4,005 | 75.8 | 1,270 | 24.1 | 6 | 0.1 | 5,281 |
| South Atlantic | 10 | 639 | 51.5 | 601 | 48.5 | | | 1,240 |
| East South Central | 11 | 492 | 89.1 | 60 | 10.9 | | | 552 |
| West South Central | 11 | 1,871 | 90.1 | 145 | 7.0 | 60 | 2.9 | 2,076 |
| Mountain | 8 | 1,073 | 75.9 | 332 | 23.5 | 9 | 0.6 | 1,414 |
| Pacific | 7 | 1,191 | 73.5 | 414 | 25.5 | 16 | 1.0 | 1,621 |
| Total | 119 | 17,015 | | 5,955 | | 386 | | 23,356 |
| Percent | | | 72.9 | | 25.5 | | 1.6 | 100.0 |

of the ninety institutions reporting, in participation; in forty-one (32.8 percent) of the 125 institutions reporting, in student-teaching. Little change was noticeable four years later, and there was no observable important trend. There was some decrease in the percentage of students who exceeded the requirements in observation and participation, and a slightly smaller decrease in percentage of those who exceeded the requirement in student-teaching. The greater number of the institutions did not require any students to exceed the minimum requirements in any phase of laboratory experience. A comparison of Tables XIX and XXIII indicates that it is a more usual practice for institutions to waive a part of the usual requirements set up by the institution than it is to require them to be exceeded.

## TABLE XXV

*Number and Percent of Students Completing a Course in Student-Teaching in State Normal Schools and Teachers Colleges, Distributed According to Geographic Divisions and Type of Laboratory School in Which Student-Teaching Was Done, 1929-30*

|  | No. of Institutions Reporting | \multicolumn{6}{c|}{Students Completing Student-Teaching} | Total |
|---|---|---|---|---|---|---|---|---|
| Geographic Division | | In Campus Schools | | In Off-Campus Schools | | Part in Campus, Part in Off-Campus Schools | | |
| | | No. | % | No. | % | No. | % | |
| New England | 11 | 578 | 71.9 | 226 | 28.1 | | | 804 |
| Middle Atlantic | 17 | 2,249 | 50.3 | 1,807 | 40.4 | 415 | 9.3 | 4,471 |
| East North Central | 18 | 3,774 | 58.1 | 2,656 | 40.9 | 64 | 1.0 | 6,494 |
| West North Central | 23 | 5,085 | 73.5 | 1,513 | 22.8 | 44 | 0.7 | 6,642 |
| South Atlantic | 11 | 706 | 44.0 | 825 | 51.5 | 72 | 4.5 | 1,603 |
| East South Central | 7 | 777 | 100.0 | | | | | 777 |
| West South Central | 10 | 3,928 | 84.2 | 736 | 15.8 | | | 4,664 |
| Mountain | 8 | 836 | 60.9 | 442 | 32.2 | 95 | 6.9 | 1,373 |
| Pacific | 7 | 843 | 40.3 | 1,248 | 59.7 | | | 2,091 |
| Total | 112 | 23,776 | | 9,453 | | 690 | | 33,919 |
| Percent | | | 70.1 | | 27.9 | | 2.0 | 100.0 |

### NUMBER OF STUDENTS COMPLETING COURSES IN STUDENT-TEACHING IN LABORATORY SCHOOLS

In studying the use of the campus and off-campus laboratory schools it is desirable to determine the total laboratory experience load which must be carried by the campus and off-campus schools. Some institutions use campus schools only, some off-campus only, while others use both campus and off-campus schools as laboratory schools. It is believed that a truer picture is obtained of the situation which prevails by investigating how many students do their student-teaching in each type of curriculum than by noting merely the number of institutions which use both campus and off-campus schools.

Four tables (Tables XXIV to XXVII inclusive) show the number of students who did their student-teaching in campus and off-

## TABLE XXVI

*Number and Percent of Students Completing a Course in Student-Teaching in State Normal Schools and Teachers Colleges, Distributed According to Geographic Divisions and Type of Laboratory School in Which Student-Teaching Was Done, 1933-34*

| Geographic Division | No. of Institutions Reporting | In Campus Schools No. | % | In Off-Campus Schools No. | % | Part in Campus, Part in Off-Campus Schools No. | % | Total |
|---|---|---|---|---|---|---|---|---|
| New England | 5 | 204 | 29.1 | 199 | 28.4 | 298 | 42.5 | 701 |
| Middle Atlantic | 21 | 1,680 | 33.6 | 2,129 | 42.5 | 1,194 | 23.8 | 5,003 |
| East North Central | 21 | 2,242 | 35.2 | 2,417 | 38.0 | 1,710 | 26.8 | 6,369 |
| West North Central | 24 | 3,467 | 63.9 | 1,676 | 30.9 | 281 | 5.2 | 5,424 |
| South Atlantic | 11 | 956 | 51.3 | 897 | 48.2 | 9 | 0.5 | 1,862 |
| East South Central | 10 | 1,733 | 100.0 | | | | | 1,733 |
| West South Central | 15 | 1,823 | 66.9 | 829 | 30.4 | 73 | 2.7 | 2,725 |
| Mountain | 7 | 420 | 37.5 | 550 | 49.1 | 150 | 13.4 | 1,120 |
| Pacific | 11 | 662 | 34.0 | 910 | 46.7 | 377 | 19.3 | 1,949 |
| Total | 125 | 13,187 | | 9,607 | | 4,092 | | 26,886 |
| Percent | | | 49.1 | | 35.7 | | 15.2 | 100.0 |

campus schools in four different academic years at distributed intervals. Two were made from data collected prior to the time the present study was begun, and a fourth was made in 1937-38 to determine any tendency which might have developed in the four years following the collection of data for the original study in 1933-34. Taken together the tables show enrollments in student-teaching courses at four intervals during a period of fourteen years, from 1923-24 to 1937-38. In each year data were secured from a relatively large number of institutions, there being more than one hundred represented in each of the four academic years studied. The reports include all types and lengths of curriculums.

From the four tables the mean number of students for whom student-teaching was provided per institution in each of the academic years can be computed as follows: 1923-24, 196.3;

## TABLE XXVII

*Number and Percent of Students Completing a Course in Student-Teaching in State Normal Schools and Teachers Colleges, Distributed According to Geographic Divisions and Type of Laboratory School in Which Student-Teaching Was Done, 1937-38*

| Geographic Division | No. of Institutions Reporting | In Campus Schools No. | In Campus Schools % | In Off-Campus Schools No. | In Off-Campus Schools % | Part in Campus, Part in Off-Campus Schools No. | Part in Campus, Part in Off-Campus Schools % | Total |
|---|---|---|---|---|---|---|---|---|
| New England | 14 | 595 | 38.8 | 886 | 57.7 | 54 | 3.5 | 1,535 |
| Middle Atlantic | 24 | 1,550 | 36.7 | 1,794 | 42.4 | 881 | 20.9 | 4,225 |
| East North Central | 18 | 1,719 | 42.5 | 1,396 | 30.3 | 1,164 | 27.2 | 4,279 |
| West North Central | 22 | 2,777 | 61.6 | 1,508 | 33.4 | 225 | 5.0 | 4,510 |
| South Atlantic | 15 | 965 | 42.3 | 1,197 | 52.5 | 118 | 5.2 | 2,280 |
| East South Central | 10 | 1,809 | 93.4 | 81 | 4.2 | 47 | 2.4 | 1,937 |
| West South Central | 10 | 2,274 | 78.0 | 596 | 20.5 | 45 | 1.5 | 2,915 |
| Mountain | 5 | 236 | 41.9 | 251 | 44.5 | 77 | 13.6 | 564 |
| Pacific | 9 | 603 | 40.6 | 604 | 40.6 | 280 | 18.8 | 1,487 |
| Total | 127 | 12,528 | | 8,313 | | 2,891 | | 23,732 |
| Percent | | | 52.8 | | 35.0 | | 12.2 | 100.0 |

1929-30, 302.8; 1933-34, 215.1; 1937-38, 187.0. During the eight years from 1930 to 1938 there has been a decrease in the total student-teaching load which the laboratory school carries. A relatively large proportion of student-teaching was done in campus schools during the years 1923-24 and 1929-30, the proportion for those years being 72.9 and 70.1 percent respectively. The mean number of students per institution teaching on the campus each year was as follows for the respective academic years: 1923-24, 143; 1929-30, 212.3; 1933-34, 105.5; and 1937-38, 98.6. During the first three of the academic years mentioned the relative number of students doing student-teaching in off-campus schools gradually increased, the proportion being 25.5 percent, 27.9 percent, and 35.7 percent respectively. It remained at 35.0 percent for the academic year 1937-38. The mean number per institution

PRESENTATION AND INTERPRETATION OF DATA 87

was 50.0, 84.4, 76.9, and 65.5 students for the respective academic years. The number of students doing a part of their student-teaching on the campus and part off-campus was proportionately small for the first year studied, being a mean of 3.2 (1.6 percent) in 1923–24, and a mean of 6.2 (2.0 percent) in 1929–30. In 1933–34 there was a large increase to a mean of 32.7 per institution (15.2 percent), and in 1937–38 the mean decreased again to 22.8 students per institution (12.2 percent).

Of the students in the whole country whose student-teaching was divided between campus and off-campus schools, the greater number are found to be in the Middle Atlantic and East North Central Divisions. In 1933–34 71.0 percent were found in these two divisions, in 1937–38, 70.7 percent. Other sectional differences are found. In the East South Central Division all the students doing student-teaching were reported as doing it in the campus laboratory schools in 1933–34, 93.4 percent of them in 1937–38. The West South Central Division ranks next highest in the proportion of students doing their teaching in campus schools. A striking reduction in the proportionate number of students whose student-teaching was distributed between campus and off-campus schools is shown in New England, the percentage falling from 42.5 percent of all students in 1933–34 to 3.5 percent in 1937–38.

By comparing Tables XXVI and XXVII it can be seen that there has been a decrease of 3,154 in the number of student-teachers for the institutions reporting in the period between 1933–34 and 1937–38, an average decrease of 28.2 students, or 13.1 percent, per institution. Other things being equal this decrease in the laboratory service load which the training school must carry should make it possible for the institutions to strengthen the quality of the student-teaching for the fewer students who are now enrolled.

In Tables XXVIII and XXIX the data which were arranged in Tables XXVI and XXVII by geographic divisions are arranged by types of curriculums. The data secured from the original questionnaire in 1933–34 (Table XXVIII) can be checked by that of 1937–38 (Table XXIX) to determine whether any significant trends are indicated. Comparison of the two tables shows some definite changes in addition to those already mentioned. In 1933–34

## TABLE XXVIII

*Number and Percent of Students Completing a Course in Student-Teaching in 125 State Normal Schools and Teachers Colleges, Distributed According to Curriculum and Type of Laboratory School in Which Student-Teaching Was Done, 1933–34*

| Type of Curriculum | No. of Institutions Reporting | In Campus Schools No. | % | In Off-Campus Schools No. | % | Part in Campus, Part in Off-Campus Schools No. | % | Total |
|---|---|---|---|---|---|---|---|---|
| General elementary | 57 | 2,580 | 43.9 | 2,266 | 38.6 | 1,029 | 17.5 | 5,875 |
| Kindergarten-primary | 87 | 2,374 | 59.2 | 1,016 | 25.4 | 617 | 15.4 | 4,007 |
| Intermediate | 76 | 2,235 | 57.6 | 1,092 | 28.2 | 554 | 14.2 | 3,881 |
| Grammar (gr. 4–8) | 1 | 36 | 73.5 | 11 | 22.4 | 2 | 4.1 | 49 |
| Junior high school | 60 | 1,068 | 46.9 | 873 | 38.4 | 335 | 14.7 | 2,276 |
| Senior high school | 52 | 1,926 | 56.1 | 1,227 | 35.8 | 278 | 8.1 | 3,431 |
| Junior and senior high school | 27 | 981 | 49.2 | 541 | 27.2 | 470 | 23.6 | 1,992 |
| Rural | 43 | 416 | 21.1 | 1,395 | 70.7 | 163 | 8.2 | 1,974 |
| Total | | 11,616 | | 8,421 | | 3,448 | | 23,485 |
| Percent | | | 49.4 | | 35.9 | | 14.7 | |
| Special subjects: | | | | | | | | |
| Agriculture | 16 | 86 | 80.4 | 18 | 16.8 | 3 | 2.8 | 107 |
| Art | 37 | 168 | 31.6 | 302 | 56.9 | 61 | 11.5 | 531 |
| Atypical | 5 | 17 | 11.6 | 111 | 75.5 | 19 | 12.9 | 147 |
| Business | 33 | 192 | 40.2 | 270 | 56.5 | 16 | 3.3 | 478 |
| Home economics | 40 | 255 | 53.3 | 179 | 37.5 | 44 | 9.2 | 478 |
| Industrial arts | 40 | 248 | 58.4 | 108 | 25.4 | 69 | 16.2 | 425 |
| Music | 42 | 227 | 46.4 | 104 | 21.3 | 158 | 32.3 | 489 |
| Physical education (men) | 40 | 181 | 45.7 | 44 | 11.1 | 171 | 43.2 | 396 |
| Physical education (women) | 38 | 184 | 56.8 | 40 | 12.3 | 100 | 30.9 | 324 |
| Four other groupings each reported by one or two institutions | 6 | 13 | 50.0 | 10 | 38.5 | 3 | 11.5 | 26 |
| Total | | 1,571 | | 1,186 | | 644 | | 3,401 |
| Percent | | | 46.2 | | 34.9 | | 18.9 | |
| Grand total | | 13,187 | | 9,607 | | 4,092 | | 26,886 |
| Percent | | | 49.1 | | 35.7 | | 15.2 | |

## TABLE XXIX

*Number and Percent of Students Completing a Course in Student-Teaching in 127 State Normal Schools and Teachers Colleges, Distributed According to Curriculum and Type of Laboratory School in Which Student-Teaching Was Done, 1937-38*

| Type of Curriculum | No. of Institutions Reporting | In Campus Schools No. | In Campus Schools % | In Off-Campus Schools No. | In Off-Campus Schools % | Part in Campus, Part in Off-Campus Schools No. | Part in Campus, Part in Off-Campus Schools % | Total |
|---|---|---|---|---|---|---|---|---|
| General elementary | 76 | 2,920 | 46.0 | 2,354 | 37.1 | 1,070 | 16.9 | 6,344 |
| Kindergarten-primary | 69 | 1,689 | 61.2 | 758 | 27.4 | 315 | 11.4 | 2,762 |
| Intermediate | 58 | 1,259 | 57.1 | 707 | 32.1 | 238 | 10.8 | 2,204 |
| Grammar (gr. 4-8) | 11 | 229 | 64.1 | 116 | 32.5 | 12 | 3.4 | 357 |
| Junior high school | 43 | 845 | 58.6 | 448 | 31.0 | 148 | 10.4 | 1,441 |
| Senior high school | 52 | 1,857 | 54.5 | 1,250 | 36.7 | 299 | 8.8 | 3,406 |
| Junior and senior high school | 30 | 1,591 | 63.6 | 873 | 34.9 | 38 | 1.5 | 2,502 |
| Rural | 27 | 271 | 26.6 | 549 | 53.8 | 200 | 19.6 | 1,020 |
| Total | | 10,661 | | 7,055 | | 2,320 | | 20,036 |
| Percent | | | 53.2 | | 35.2 | | 11.6 | |
| Special subjects: | | | | | | | | |
| Agriculture | 9 | 19 | 20.0 | 76 | 80.0 | | | 95 |
| Art | 32 | 121 | 52.2 | 58 | 25.0 | 53 | 22.8 | 232 |
| Atypical | 4 | 14 | 25.0 | 35 | 62.5 | 7 | 12.5 | 56 |
| Business | 36 | 358 | 51.1 | 303 | 43.2 | 40 | 5.7 | 701 |
| Home economics | 43 | 226 | 40.6 | 239 | 43.0 | 91 | 16.4 | 556 |
| Industrial arts | 38 | 173 | 50.1 | 141 | 40.9 | 31 | 9.0 | 345 |
| Music | 46 | 339 | 55.6 | 183 | 30.0 | 88 | 14.4 | 610 |
| Physical education (men) | 44 | 199 | 44.9 | 103 | 23.3 | 141 | 31.8 | 443 |
| Physical education (women) | 42 | 151 | 46.3 | 93 | 28.5 | 82 | 25.2 | 326 |
| Eleven other groupings each reported by one institution | 11 | 267 | 80.4 | 27 | 8.1 | 38 | 11.5 | 332 |
| Total | | 1,867 | | 1,258 | | 571 | | 3,696 |
| Percent | | | 50.5 | | 34.0 | | 15.5 | |
| Grand total | | 12,528 | | 8,313 | | 2,891 | | 23,732 |
| Percent | | | 52.8 | | 35.0 | | 12.2 | |

TABLE XXX

*Number and Percent of Students Who Completed a Course in Student-Teaching in 125 State Normal Schools and Teachers Colleges, Distributed According to Type of Curriculum, 1933–34*

| Type of Curriculum | No. of Institutions Reporting | STUDENTS COMPLETING STUDENT-TEACHING ||||||||| Total |
|---|---|---|---|---|---|---|---|---|---|---|
| | | In One-Year Curriculum || In Two-Year Curriculum || In Three-Year Curriculum || In Four-Year Curriculum || |
| | | No. | % | No. | % | No. | % | No. | % | |
| General elementary............ | 57 | 527 | 9.0 | 2,429 | 41.3 | 1,288 | 21.9 | 1,631 | 27.8 | 5,875 |
| Kindergarten-primary.......... | 87 | 382 | 9.5 | 2,134 | 53.3 | 637 | 15.9 | 854 | 21.3 | 4,007 |
| Intermediate.................. | 76 | 318 | 8.2 | 2,466 | 63.5 | 530 | 13.7 | 567 | 14.6 | 3,881 |
| Grammar (gr. 4–8)............. | 1 | | | 46 | 93.9 | | | 3 | 6.1 | 49 |
| Junior high school............. | 60 | 80 | 3.5 | 596 | 26.2 | 522 | 22.9 | 1,078 | 47.4 | 2,276 |
| Senior high school............. | 52 | 2 | 0.1 | 2 | 0.1 | 45 | 1.3 | 3,382 | 98.5 | 3,431 |
| Junior and senior high school... | 27 | 21 | 1.1 | | | 39 | 2.0 | 1,932 | 96.9 | 1,992 |
| Rural one-teacher and two-teacher schools............... | 43 | 1,080 | 54.7 | 556 | 28.2 | 14 | 0.7 | 324 | 16.4 | 1,974 |
| Total....................... | | 2,410 | | 8,229 | | 3,075 | | 9,771 | | 23,485 |
| Percent..................... | | | 10.2 | | 35.0 | | 13.1 | | 41.7 | |
| Special subjects: | | | | | | | | | | |
| Agriculture................. | 16 | | | 1 | 0.9 | | | 106 | 99.1 | 107 |
| Art......................... | 37 | | | 36 | 6.8 | 32 | 6.0 | 463 | 87.2 | 531 |
| Atypical.................... | 5 | | | 4 | 2.7 | 124 | 84.4 | 19 | 12.9 | 147 |
| Business.................... | 33 | | | 6 | 1.3 | 29 | 6.1 | 443 | 93.7 | 478 |
| Home economics............. | 40 | | | 3 | 0.6 | 12 | 2.5 | 463 | 96.9 | 478 |

TABLE XXX (*Continued*)

STUDENTS COMPLETING STUDENT-TEACHING

| Type of Curriculum | No. of Institutions Reporting | In One-Year Curriculum |  | In Two-Year Curriculum |  | In Three-Year Curriculum |  | In Four-Year Curriculum |  | Total |
|---|---|---|---|---|---|---|---|---|---|---|
|  |  | No. | % | No. | % | No. | % | No. | % |  |
| Industrial arts.............. | 40 |  |  | 12 | 2.8 | 25 | 5.9 | 388 | 91.3 | 425 |
| Music...................... | 42 |  |  | 17 | 3.5 | 66 | 13.5 | 406 | 83.0 | 489 |
| Physical education (men)..... | 40 |  |  | 14 | 3.5 | 1 |  | 381 | 96.5 | 396 |
| Physical education (women)... | 38 |  |  | 32 | 9.9 | 5 | 1.5 | 287 | 88.6 | 324 |
| Four other groupings each reported by one or two institutions................. | 6 |  |  |  |  | 3 | 11.5 | 23 | 88.5 | 26 |
| Total...................... |  |  |  | 125 | 3.7 | 297 | 8.7 | 2,979 | 87.6 | 3,401 |
| Percent.................... |  |  |  |  |  |  |  |  |  |  |
| Grand total................. |  | 2,410 | 9.0 | 8,354 | 31.1 | 3,372 | 12.5 | 12,750 | 47.4 | 26,886 |
| Percent.................... |  |  |  |  |  |  |  |  |  |  |

70.7 percent of the student-teaching for rural one- and two-teacher schools was done in off-campus schools while 21.1 percent was completed in campus schools. In 1937–38 the amount in off-campus schools had dropped to 53.8 percent. Meanwhile the relative number of students in rural curriculums completing their student-teaching on the campus had increased, as did the proportion doing a part of it on the campus and a part off-campus. It is also to be noted that although there were two more institutions reporting in 1937–38 than in 1933–34, there were only twenty-seven reporting enrollment in student-teaching in the curriculum for one- and two-teacher rural schools, compared with 43 four years earlier, and that the total enrollments in these curriculums decreased from 1,974 to 1,020, or 48.3 percent, during the four-year period. There is somewhat less tendency than formerly to distribute the student-teaching in special subjects between the campus and off-campus schools, the percentage being reduced from 18.9 to 15.5. There is also a tendency, on the whole, to have a relatively larger part of the student-teaching done on the campus. In the case of student-teaching in the curriculum in agriculture the opposite tendency is quite marked. In 1933–34, 80.4 percent of the students enrolled in a curriculum in agriculture did their student-teaching on the campus, in 1937–38 this was reduced to 20 percent, while 80 percent did their laboratory teaching in off-campus schools.

Table XXX indicates the number of students who completed a course in student-teaching of each type and length of curriculum in 125 normal schools and teachers colleges in 1933–34. The greater part of the laboratory school service load in student-teaching in the general curriculums is found to be in the two-year and four-year curriculums, 35.0 percent and 41.7 percent, respectively, a total of 76.7 percent. Of student-teaching in the special subjects 87.6 percent is by students in the four-year curriculums. Of the total number of students enrolled in general curriculums, 13,812 (58.8 percent) are in grades below the junior high school; 1,974 (8.4 percent) in one-teacher and two-teacher rural schools; and 7,699 (32.8 percent) in junior and senior high schools.

A comparison of Table XXX with a similar table for 1937–38,

Table XXXI, reveals a rapid shift toward longer curriculums at the later date, when almost three-fifths (59.8 percent) of the students doing student-teaching are enrolled in the four-year curriculums, and only 26.3 percent in curriculums less than three years in length. Especially significant is the increased percentage of teachers preparing for junior high school who complete their student-teaching in the four-year curriculum. With this decided shift toward the four-year curriculum, the ratio of students doing student-teaching to the total enrollment of the institution becomes smaller, a situation which will make it possible to inaugurate a more nearly adequate program of laboratory experience for those who are completing the four-year course. It is likely that the chief factor in explaining the decrease in the number of student-teachers between 1933–34 and 1937–38, even though total enrollments in the teachers colleges are increasing, results from the decrease in the proportionate number enrolled in the laboratory courses as compared with the total enrollment of the institution.

In Table XXXII student-teaching enrollments are distributed according to geographic divisions. In five of the geographic divisions no student-teaching is found in any curriculums which were only one year in length. By far the greater number of student-teachers in one-year curriculums are located in the West North Central Division. On the whole, student-teaching in the three-year curriculums is found in New England, Middle Atlantic, Mountain, and Pacific Divisions. In only two divisions, the West North Central and South Atlantic, are more than one-half of the student-teachers securing their laboratory experience in curriculums which are less than three years in length.

A comparison of data collected in 1937–38 with that given in the table for 1933–34 shows a situation similar in most respects. Only eight of the institutions studied enroll student-teachers in one-year curriculums; and two of the twenty-two institutions of the West North Central Division include 78.7 percent of the enrollment. Exactly 50 percent of the student-teachers of this division are enrolled in curriculums not more than two years in length, the minimum for any geographic division in the country. In the Pacific Division, no student-teachers in the nine institu-

## TABLE XXXI

*Number and Percent of Students Who Completed a Course in Student-Teaching in 127 State Normal Schools and Teachers Colleges, Distributed According to Type of Curriculum, 1937-38*

| Type of Curriculum | No. of Institutions Reporting | In One-Year Curriculum No. | % | In Two-Year Curriculum No. | % | In Three-Year Curriculum No. | % | In Four-Year Curriculum No. | % | Total |
|---|---|---|---|---|---|---|---|---|---|---|
| General elementary | 76 | 104 | 1.6 | 2,378 | 37.5 | 1,754 | 27.7 | 2,108 | 33.2 | 6,344 |
| Kindergarten-primary | 69 | 67 | 2.4 | 1,254 | 45.4 | 322 | 11.7 | 1,119 | 40.5 | 2,762 |
| Intermediate | 58 | 58 | 2.6 | 1,103 | 50.1 | 265 | 12.0 | 778 | 35.3 | 2,204 |
| Grammar (gr. 4-8) | 11 | | | 204 | 57.2 | 18 | 5.0 | 135 | 37.8 | 357 |
| Junior high school | 43 | | | 162 | 11.2 | 232 | 16.1 | 1,047 | 72.7 | 1,441 |
| Senior high school | 52 | | | 34 | 1.0 | 94 | 2.8 | 3,278 | 96.2 | 3,406 |
| Junior and senior high school | 30 | | | | | 206 | 8.2 | 2,296 | 91.8 | 2,502 |
| Rural one-teacher and two-teacher schools | 27 | 472 | 46.3 | 389 | 38.1 | 42 | 4.1 | 117 | 11.5 | 1,020 |
| Total | | 701 | | 5,524 | | 2,933 | | 10,878 | | 20,036 |
| Percent | | | 3.5 | | 27.6 | | 14.6 | | 54.3 | |
| Special subjects: | | | | | | | | | | |
| Agriculture | 9 | | | | | | | 95 | 100.0 | 95 |
| Art | 32 | | | 2 | 0.9 | 40 | 17.2 | 190 | 81.9 | 232 |
| Atypical | 4 | | | | | | | 56 | 100.0 | 56 |
| Business | 36 | | | | | 46 | 6.6 | 655 | 93.4 | 701 |
| Home economics | 43 | | | | | 25 | 4.5 | 531 | 95.5 | 556 |

## TABLE XXXI (Continued)

| Type of Curriculum | No. of Institutions Reporting | In One-Year Curriculum No. | % | In Two-Year Curriculum No. | % | In Three-Year Curriculum No. | % | In Four-Year Curriculum No. | % | Total |
|---|---|---|---|---|---|---|---|---|---|---|
| Industrial arts | 38 | | | | | 40 | 11.6 | 305 | 88.4 | 345 |
| Music | 46 | | | | | 36 | 5.9 | 574 | 94.1 | 610 |
| Physical education (men) | 44 | | | 2 | 0.5 | 17 | 3.8 | 424 | 95.7 | 443 |
| Physical education (women) | 42 | | | 4 | 1.2 | 26 | 8.0 | 296 | 90.8 | 326 |
| Eleven other groupings, each reported by one institution | 11 | 7 | 2.1 | | | 135 | 40.7 | 190 | 57.2 | 332 |
| Total | | 7 | 0.2 | 8 | 0.2 | 365 | 9.9 | 3,316 | 89.7 | 3,696 |
| Percent | | | | | | | | | | |
| Grand total | | 708 | 3.0 | 5,532 | 23.3 | 3,298 | 13.9 | 14,194 | 59.8 | 23,732 |
| Percent | | | | | | | | | | |

TABLE XXXII

*Number and Percent of Students Who Completed a Course in Student-Teaching in Curriculums of Different Lengths in 125 Normal Schools and Teachers Colleges, Distributed According to Geographic Division, 1933–34*

| Geographic Division | No. of Institutions Reporting | Students Completing Student-Teaching ||||||||| Total |
|---|---|---|---|---|---|---|---|---|---|---|
| | | In One-Year Curriculum || In Two-Year Curriculum || In Three-Year Curriculum || In Four-Year Curriculum || |
| | | No. | % | No. | % | No. | % | No. | % | |
| New England | 5 | | | 35 | 5.0 | 338 | 48.2 | 328 | 46.8 | 701 |
| Middle Atlantic | 21 | | | 1,272 | 25.4 | 1,863 | 37.3 | 1,868 | 37.3 | 5,003 |
| East North Central | 21 | 232 | 3.7 | 2,294 | 36.0 | 614 | 9.6 | 3,229 | 50.7 | 6,369 |
| West North Central | 24 | 1,438 | 26.5 | 2,026 | 37.3 | 3 | 0.1 | 1,957 | 36.1 | 5,424 |
| South Atlantic | 11 | 381 | 20.5 | 761 | 40.9 | 38 | 2.0 | 682 | 36.6 | 1,862 |
| East South Central | 10 | | | 812 | 46.9 | | | 921 | 53.1 | 1,733 |
| West South Central | 15 | 359 | 13.2 | 542 | 19.9 | 114 | 4.2 | 1,710 | 62.7 | 2,725 |
| Mountain | 7 | | | 235 | 21.0 | 157 | 14.0 | 728 | 65.0 | 1,120 |
| Pacific | 11 | | | 377 | 19.3 | 245 | 12.6 | 1,327 | 68.1 | 1,949 |
| Total | 125 | 2,410 | | 8,354 | | 3,372 | | 12,750 | | 26,886 |
| Percent | | | 9.0 | | 31.1 | | 12.5 | | 47.4 | |

tions were enrolled in one-year or two-year curriculums in 1937–38. This division is the only one in which the number of student-teachers in the three-year curriculums exceeds those in the four-year, the percentages of each being 65.3 and 34.7 respectively.

An examination of the curriculums by types shows that decided changes have occurred between 1933–34 and 1937–38. Although the total number of student-teachers reported has decreased (see Tables XXVIII and XXXI) during the four-year period, there is a relatively small increase (10.8 percent) of those who are student-teachers in the general elementary curriculum. Of the total number of student-teachers 12.6 percent did their laboratory teaching in the special subjects in 1933–34, while 15.6 percent did so in 1937–38. A slightly larger percentage of all were enrolled as student-teachers in senior high schools. There was an increase of 25.6 percent in those doing student-teaching in the junior-senior high school curriculums. By contrast, there were decided decreases in the numbers of student-teachers in the kindergarten-primary, intermediate, grammar, and junior high school levels, these being 68.9 percent, 56.8 percent, 13.7 percent, and 63.3 percent, respectively, of the numbers reported in 1933–34. Even a more decided difference is shown in the decreased number of student-teachers in curriculums for the preparation of teachers in the one- and two-teacher rural schools, the number of student-teachers in 1937–38 being only 51.7 percent of the total for 1933–34.

From the data it can be concluded that there is a definite movement for a larger proportion of students to do their student-teaching in the longer curriculums. The student-teaching in the one-year curriculum has almost entirely disappeared.

Considerable differences are found between certain phases of student-teaching in the different geographic divisions. In both academic years it was a much more nearly general practice to divide the student-teaching for each student between the campus and off-campus schools in the Middle Atlantic, East North Central, Mountain, and Pacific Divisions than in the other five divisions, in which it was the policy to assign the student *either* to the campus laboratory school *or* to the off-campus school, but not to both.

There is a decided decrease in the number of student-teachers in the curriculums which prepare for the lower grade levels of instruction and also a decrease in such more highly specialized curriculums as kindergarten-primary and intermediate grades, while there is an increase in the numbers doing student-teaching in the general elementary curriculums. There is also some increase of those who do their student-teaching in the special subjects.

## NUMBER OF GRADES OR SUBJECTS TO WHICH STUDENT-TEACHERS ARE ASSIGNED

The teacher in the elementary grades or in the rural one- and two-teacher schools must teach a wide array of subjects. The teacher in the secondary schools usually has an assignment of more than one subject, particularly in the small high school in which the beginning teacher usually starts her teaching career. For this reason it is desirable that the prospective teacher in the teachers college be given wider experience in handling classes and instructing pupils than can be obtained by doing student-teaching in a single grade or subject. Likewise the teacher of a special subject who usually must cover several different fields or grade levels in his teaching should have experience on several levels or in several areas. For example, a teacher of commercial subjects may have such diverse courses as typing, stenography, bookkeeping, and commercial law, and it may be that courses are offered at different years in the junior and senior high school. It would be impossible within the time available to assign the student to laboratory teaching in all the levels or areas in which he may teach if he enters service in a small school, even were it desirable. However, there should be a reasonable variety in his teaching experience to assure flexibility of procedure even though he cannot have direct experience in all subjects.

Foster, in his study of the training school, states:

Student teachers should be afforded the opportunity to do practice teaching in more than one subject and in more than one grade if they are preparing for work in the elementary or rural schools and in at least their major and first minor subjects if they are preparing to be secondary teachers.[62]

[62] Frank K. Foster, "The Training School in the Education of Teachers." *National Survey of the Education of Teachers*, Vol. III, Part IV, p. 400. 1935.

More than two decades ago a Committee of the Society of College Teachers of Education[63] recommended that student-teaching on the high school level should include two high school subjects or different years in one subject. At a later time Mead[64] concluded that student-teachers preparing for service in the high schools ought to be required to do student-teaching in a minimum of three subjects, stating that four might be even better, because it is only in the cities that the number of subjects each teacher is assigned is two or less, and the larger number of beginning teachers must enter the profession in small schools.

In the questionnaire used in the present study data were sought to determine the number of grades to which each student preparing to teach in the elementary schools was assigned for student-teaching, and in how many subjects, if he was preparing to teach on the secondary level, he was given pre-service teaching experience. In connection with the special subjects, such as art and music, typically taught in both the elementary and the high school, information was sought as to whether or not the student-teacher taught classes both in the elementary grades and on the high school level, and regarding the typical number of grades or subjects in which student-teaching was required. On the latter point the question as put in the questionnaire was somewhat ambiguous, permitting two different interpretations. Some institutions understood it to mean art, music, or similar subjects which are taught as one subject of a general curriculum such as the kindergarten-primary or intermediate. Others answered in terms of the subject considered as a special subject in which a differentiated curriculum was offered. In Table XXXIII, which summarizes the data received in answer to the questionnaire, only those institutions were considered which had special curriculums for the preparation of teachers in the subject.

Inspection of the table shows that the modal number of grades or subjects in all of the three divisions is two. In 1933–34, half of the institutions (49.5 percent) required prospective elementary teachers to secure laboratory experience in student-teaching in two grades, while an additional 20.9 percent required it in three

[63] A. R. Mead, *Practice Teaching for Teachers in Secondary Schools*, p. 73. 1917.
[64] A. R. Mead, *Supervised Student-Teaching*, p. 457. 1930.

## TABLE XXXIII

*Typical Number of Grades or Subjects to Which Each Student Was Assigned for Student-Teaching in State Normal Schools and Teachers Colleges, 1933–34 and 1937–38*

| Number of Grades or Subjects | Elementary Grade Level 1933–34 | Elementary Grade Level 1937–38 | High School Level 1933–34 | High School Level 1937–38 | Special Subjects 1933–34 | Special Subjects 1937–38 |
|---|---|---|---|---|---|---|
| One............. | 31 | 25 | 19 | 17 | 4 | 5 |
| Two............. | 52 | 55 | 56 | 55 | 19 | 22 |
| Three........... | 9 | 22 | 5 | 8 | 9 | 11 |
| Four............ | 8 | 7 |   | 1 | 4 | 6 |
| Five............ |   | 1 |   |   | 1 |   |
| Six............. | 3 | 1 |   |   |   | 2 |
| Seven........... |   | 1 |   |   |   |   |
| Eight........... | 1 | 6 |   |   |   |   |
| Nine or more.... | 1 |   |   |   | 1 | 1 |
| Total........... | 105 | 118 | 80 | 81 | 38 | 47 |

or more grades, the range being from one to nine grades. Thirty-one institutions (29.5 percent) required student-teaching in a single grade.

On the secondary level fifty-six of the eighty institutions (70.0 percent) assigned student-teachers to two subjects; five (6.3 percent) to three subjects; and nineteen (23.7 percent) to one only. In the special subject fields nineteen (50.0 percent) required student-teaching on two grade levels, four on one grade level only.

Approximately a fourth (24.2 percent) of all student-teachers, whether on the elementary or high school levels or in the special subjects, secured their laboratory experience in student-teaching in a single grade or subject.

There is, in a number of cases, flexibility in the number of subjects to which students are assigned within a given institution. For example, several institutions replied "one or two," "two or three," "two to four," "three to six," or "three or four." These answers are omitted from the tabulations as the typical situation was the one on which information was desired.

A comparison of the situation in 1937–38 with that of 1933–34 shows some change in the four-year period. The percentage of students doing student-teaching in a single grade on the elementary level dropped from 29.5 to 21.2; the percentage of those in three grades rose from 8.6 percent to 18.6 percent. There was relatively little change in the situation on the high school level and in the preparation of teachers for the special subjects.

In reply to the question: "Do student-teachers in such subjects as art and music, typically taught in both elementary schools and high schools, do student-teaching in both elementary grades and high school?" an affirmative answer was given for 1933–34 by sixty-one (62.9 percent) of the institutions which replied; for 1937–38 an affirmative answer was given by fifty-seven (70.4 percent) of all.

From the data the conclusion can be drawn that the typical number of grades or subjects to which students are assigned is two, for elementary grades, high schools, or special subjects. The group judgment as revealed in the answers to the questionnaire is in agreement with the position of Foster in his recommendation quoted above (see page 98). In conformity with the criterion which he establishes, a considerable number of institutions should provide a greater degree of variety in grades and subjects to each student in their assignment in the laboratory schools.

## SUMMARY

1. The modal point at which the student-teacher secures his first laboratory experience is the beginning of the first quarter of the final year of the curriculum whether in the two-year, the three-year, or the four-year curriculums. In three-fourths of the four-year curriculums the first laboratory experience occurs at the beginning of the third year or later. In curriculums which prepare teachers for junior and senior high schools, it is the most common practice to begin the laboratory experience at the beginning of the third year or later, and in those which prepare for teaching the special subjects, at the beginning of the fourth year. In the New England and Middle Atlantic geographic divisions, laboratory experience is most commonly begun at the beginning of the first year. In all other divisions, except the East North Central, where about half begin in the final year and half earlier

in the course, it is the prevailing practice to postpone the laboratory experience to the first quarter or semester of the last year of the curriculum. During the four years between 1933-34 and 1937-38 there has been some tendency to defer the beginning to a later period in both the two-year and the four-year curriculums.

2. Though institutions differ in their practices, student-teaching begins in the final year of the curriculum in approximately four-fifths of all two-year, three-year, and four-year curriculums.

3. The time span of laboratory experience, i.e., the period from its beginning to its close, ranges from a single quarter in some institutions to the entire length of the curriculum in others. The median is 3.5 quarters for sixty-one institutions in the two-year curriculum and 4.3 quarters for 118 institutions in the four-year curriculum.

4. In eight states it is the policy of the state educational authorities to allocate the preparation of teachers of the special subjects to certain designated institutions. Such a policy is in effect in states of three geographic divisions—New England, Middle States, and East North Central—all located in the northeastern part of the country. Allocations are generally restricted to those subjects or areas in which the total number of teachers required is relatively small, the equipment is relatively expensive, or specialized laboratory facilities are needed.

5. One hundred and twenty-eight institutions list twenty-seven different patterns or combinations of laboratory courses either with one another or with subject-matter courses or other professional courses. The most common pattern is a self-contained course which includes observation, participation, and student-teaching in a single course which is not connected with subject-matter or other professional courses. Almost one-half (45.2 percent) are self-contained courses which combine various aspects of observation, participation, and student-teaching, but are not combined with subject-matter or other professional courses. No decided trend is evident toward greater integration of the laboratory courses with other courses of the curriculum.

6. There is great diversity in the total number of clock-hours of laboratory experience required in different institutions, in both the two-year and the four-year curriculums. The number of

clock-hours required varies with the geographic divisions, being largest in the New England and Middle State Divisions and smallest in the East South Central and South Atlantic Divisions. The median requirement in the four-year curriculums has decreased 20 clock-hours (10.7 percent) in the four years from 1933–34 to 1937–38. Approximately 65 percent of the total laboratory experience is in student-teaching, and 35 percent in observation and participation. Approximately an equal number of clock-hours are required in observation and participation. In the two-year curriculums the median amount of student-teaching is slightly less than the minimum requirement of 90 clock-hours set by the American Association of Teachers Colleges. In the four-year curriculums, the median in the forty-seven institutions exceeds the minimum standard by 33.6 percent, but a number barely meet the standard.

7. Comparatively few institutions allow limited flexibility in the number of clock-hours of laboratory experience which they require, it being more generally the practice to waive a part or all of the requirements than to require them to be exceeded. A relatively small proportion of the students are excused from the minimum requirements. The most common reason for excusing is for prior teaching experience.

8. The total load of the laboratory school per institution has varied at different times over a fourteen-year period. There is a decline in the number of student-teachers in curriculums preparing for service in the one- and two-teacher rural schools. There is a decrease in the proportionate numbers doing student-teaching on the lower grade levels and an increase on the higher levels and in the special subjects. There is a definite shift toward student-teaching in the longer curriculums. Approximately half of the student-teachers are assigned to the campus laboratory schools, a third to off-campus, and the remaining sixth to teaching in both types.

9. Typically, student-teachers receive experience in student-teaching in two elementary grades, two high school subjects, or two special subjects, although approximately one-fifth (1937–38) do student-teaching in a single elementary grade or high school subject. In more than two-thirds of the institutions, teachers in such subjects as art and music, which are commonly taught in

both elementary grades and high school classes, receive experience on both grade levels.

## SECTION C
## THE CAMPUS LABORATORY SCHOOL

Certain aspects of the campus laboratory school are presented in this section: (*a*) the types of laboratory schools; (*b*) advantages of the campus school; (*c*) the use of off-campus schools to supplement and complement the use of the campus school; (*d*) the use of each type of laboratory facility; (*e*) purposes for which the campus school is used; (*f*) the use of campus schools for class demonstrations; (*g*) how pupils are secured; (*h*) enrollment of the school; (*i*) grade levels in the schools; (*j*) the ratio of the number of student-teachers to the enrollment in the laboratory schools; (*k*) a formula for determining the size of the campus school which is adequate for a given teachers college; and (*l*) the ownership and control of the school.

### THE TYPES OF LABORATORY SCHOOL

The types of laboratory school recognized and defined in this study are designated as campus and off-campus laboratory schools. The former is defined as a school which is located on the grounds of the teachers college; the latter, as one not so situated. This distinction is made because, for the purposes of this study, it seems most valuable in terms of the functions which the schools are to serve. A campus school as here defined is conveniently located for its purposes, is controlled by and usually owned by the teachers college, and because of its proximity to the other activities of the teachers college has the possibility of closer integration with the total educational program of the institution than can be established in a school not so located and so controlled.

It is an accepted principle of teacher education that every teachers college shall have sufficient and appropriate laboratory facilities available, in either campus or off-campus schools, to provide for all the types of teaching service for which it seeks to prepare its students. But just as the laboratory school is the heart of the teachers college, so the campus laboratory school is the heart of the laboratory school if it performs the functions which are within its range of possibilities.

### ADVANTAGES OF THE CAMPUS SCHOOL

Advantages of the campus over the off-campus school have been set forth by Mead[65, 66] and Evenden.[67] The advantages which they stated, together with others, are included in the following summary:

I. Advantages relating primarily to the ease and effectiveness of administration:
   (*a*) The campus school avoids divided authority and responsibility for the laboratory school.
   (*b*) The buildings are better planned and have rooms better designed for teaching small groups and for holding conferences than are the public schools.
   (*c*) The time of students and faculty in going from other classes and activities of the teachers college to the laboratory school is economized.
   (*d*) Money is saved for students who must, in many instances, pay their own transportation for teaching in off-campus schools.

II. Advantages relating primarily to the instructional and educational program:
   (*a*) A continuous policy of instruction and consistent educational philosophy can be maintained.
   (*b*) The campus laboratory school can be so organized as to illustrate the *best* theory and practice as an ideal, to present the best type of "model teaching."
   (*c*) There can be demonstrations of superior teaching.
   (*d*) The curriculum, textbooks, and other media of instruction, and techniques of teaching can be controlled by the teachers college.

---

[65] A. R. Mead, "Advantages and Disadvantages of Campus and 'Off-Campus' Laboratory Schools." *Educational Administration and Supervision*, Vol. 16, pp. 196–207, March, 1930.

[66] A. R. Mead, *Supervised Student-Teaching*, pp. 803–804 and 817. 1930.

[67] Evenden, in *National Survey of the Education of Teachers*, Vol. VI, *op. cit.*, p. 175.

(e) Superior practices in conducting extracurricular and extra-school activities can be demonstrated.

(f) The opportunity for gradual induction into teaching by observation and graded participation under skilled supervision is enhanced.

(g) A much better opportunity is given to integrate the laboratory school, the subject-matter departments, and the other professional courses than can be provided in the off-campus laboratory school.

(h) "Long and continuous" contact with the laboratory school can be achieved more readily in the campus school than in the off-campus school.

Certain disadvantages arise if the campus school is used as the sole laboratory school. Costs of maintenance are high; conditions are artificial—the students do not teach under actual normal public school situations; pupils are not typical;[68] and student-teachers fail to develop a helpful attitude toward living of the type found in communities which they will serve, especially if these are non-urban. To ameliorate these unfavorable conditions and compensate for these shortcomings the use of off-campus schools for at least a portion of the laboratory experience is indicated.

## THE RELATION OF THE OFF-CAMPUS SCHOOL TO THE CAMPUS SCHOOL

While a detailed discussion of the off-campus laboratory school must be deferred until Section D of this chapter, it is appropriate at this point to introduce two conceptions which are entertained relative to its purpose, namely: to *supplement* the campus school; and to *complement* the functions of the campus school. Some administrators who hold the first view consider the off-campus school solely as a means of providing release from a crowded condition when the number of student-teachers needing laboratory experience is greater than can be accommodated in the campus school. The functions of both campus and off-campus laboratory

[68] W. D. Armentrout, *The Conduct of Student Teaching in State Teachers Colleges*, p. 147. 1927.

PRESENTATION AND INTERPRETATION OF DATA    107

schools are, according to this conception, considered as approximately identical, the off-campus facilities merely adding to those on the campus. Those whose conception is that the off-campus school should be complementary, on the other hand, believe that although the two types of school have some purposes in common, they also have distinct functions and that, so far as possible, each student-teacher should secure a part of his laboratory experience in each. And so Judd and Parker[69] write of the "somewhat artificial" conditions of the campus laboratory school in which the student may secure his *initial* practice with small groups of children and advocate that student-teaching in such a school be followed by "longer continuous teaching under real public school conditions" in off-campus schools. Wilson[70] agrees that the most satisfactory arrangement is a school located on the college campus which is completely under the control of the college, complemented by the use of the public schools, so that in the latter student-teachers may be confronted with, and be prepared to meet, actual schoolroom conditions in public schools similar to those in which they are preparing to teach. Confirming these points of view, Learned and Bagley assert:

Even where a good sized independent training school is possible, it is extremely desirable for the local school system to be related to the normal school (teachers college) in such a manner as to afford opportunity for extensive observation, participation, and practice under wholly normal conditions.[71]

Higbee[72] senses a desirable trend toward the use of both types of school creating the "ideal" situation, which includes a central campus training school to which are added off-campus facilities "to insure successful service in later full-time employment," the former to permit demonstration, experimentation, and preliminary practice, the latter, final responsible practice. Eubank[73] as

---

[69] Judd and Parker, *op. cit.*, p. 48.
[70] Wilson, *op. cit.*, pp. 20-22.
[71] Learned and Bagley, *op. cit.*, p. 193.
[72] E. C. Higbee, "Twenty Years of Progress in Providing Adequate Training School Facilities, 1907-1927." *Yearbook of the American Association of Teachers Colleges, 1928*, pp. 39-47.
[73] Louis Allen Eubank, *The Organization and Administration of Laboratory Schools in State Teachers Colleges*, p. 73. 1931.

the result of his study of laboratory schools came to the conclusion that there should be a campus laboratory school equipped with a superior teaching staff to serve as a laboratory for observation and demonstration in connection with the professional and subject-matter courses included in the student's curriculum, and an off-campus school to provide a situation in which student-teaching can be done "in a school approaching normal public school conditions."

A plan of organization found in the laboratory schools of the Rhode Island College of Education reveals a situation providing laboratory experience in the off-campus school which complements and is differentiated from that in the campus school:

Since 1893 this state has insisted upon two forms of contact with the public schools as a part of the preparation for teaching. It uses both the laboratory or demonstration school, and the regular classes in the actual public schools. The laboratory or demonstration school is the Henry Barnard School on the college campus. The so-called training schools are now located in approximately one half of all the towns and cities in the state . . . . The Henry Barnard School is a public school under the direct control of the college . . . . Here each college student maintains regular contact through his entire course with school life of the best type that can be secured. This school should give inspiration through the contact with children and with master teachers, and through the quality of the work seen. It serves as a meeting place for theory and practice, and as a source of illustrative material for class discussions. Here new ideals and methods are evaluated, and here are demonstrated possibilities of public school teaching. Here the student is given a most favorable opportunity for his first efforts at class teaching. This school is more than a clinic for demonstrating approved work, it is also a laboratory for the development of better ideals and methods of teaching.[74]

Supplementing this statement, President John L. Alger writes:

In the training school the student becomes a regular and full-time teacher of a standard class in the public schools for an entire half-year, receiving, teaching, and promoting the pupils, but always with the advice and assistance of the critic. This critic is especially prepared for her work, is a paid member of the teaching force of the town or city, with a supplementary payment by the college, and is given charge of two such training rooms if in the lower schools or a single room in the high schools. . . .

[74] Rhode Island College of Education Bulletin, *Bulletin* No. 63, p. 8. January, 1934.

## TABLE XXXIV

*Number and Percent of Normal Schools and Teachers Colleges Using Each Type of Laboratory School Facilities, 1933-34*

| Geographic Division | No. of Institutions Studied | On Campus No. | On Campus % | Off Campus No. | Off Campus % | Both on Campus and Off-Campus No. | Both on Campus and Off-Campus % |
|---|---|---|---|---|---|---|---|
| New England | 7 | | | 2 | 28.6 | 5 | 71.4 |
| Middle Atlantic | 22 | 2 | 9.1 | | | 20 | 90.9 |
| East North Central | 21 | 2 | 9.5 | | | 19 | 90.5 |
| West North Central | 24 | 7 | 29.2 | 3 | 12.5 | 14 | 58.3 |
| South Atlantic | 12 | 2 | 16.7 | 3 | 25.0 | 7 | 58.3 |
| East South Central | 10 | 9 | 90.0 | | | 1 | 10.0 |
| West South Central | 16 | 6 | 37.5 | 3 | 18.8 | 7 | 56.3 |
| Mountain | 8 | 1 | 12.5 | 1 | 12.5 | 6 | 75.0 |
| Pacific | 11 | | | 1 | 9.1 | 10 | 90.9 |
| Total | 131 | 29 | | 13 | | 89 | |
| Percent | 100.0 | | 22.1 | | 9.9 | | 68.0 |

### USE OF EACH TYPE OF LABORATORY FACILITY

How well the teachers colleges approximate the situation in which both campus and off-campus schools are available for the laboratory experience which students receive can be seen from Table XXXIV. Of the institutions reporting, eighty-nine of the 131 (68.0 percent) now use both types. The situation varies with the different geographic divisions. In each of three, the Middle Atlantic, East North Central, and Pacific, more than 90 percent of all the institutions employ both types of facilities. On the other hand, in the East South Central Division only one institution of ten reporting uses both campus and off-campus schools, and in two other divisions in the South less than three-fifths of the institutions use both types.

Of the 131 institutions studied in the questionnaire thirteen (9.9 percent) have no campus school. In the South Atlantic Division a fourth of the institutions have off-campus schools only. Three geographic divisions—Middle Atlantic, East North Central, and East South Central—employ either campus schools or both campus and off-campus schools. None uses only off-campus schools.

Few differences were found when the facilities for 1937-38 were compared with those for three years earlier. One teachers college added a campus laboratory school with grades from the kindergarten through the twelfth. Seven added grades above the sixth, of which one added grades seven and eight; one, grades seven to nine; two, grades seven to twelve; one, grades nine to twelve. Three added nursery schools and two, ungraded classes. On the other hand, one laboratory school for industrial arts and one one-teacher rural school have been discontinued. Three have discontinued grades seven to twelve in the high school; one, grade seven; and three have abandoned the kindergarten.

If the policy of using both campus and off-campus schools is sound, the optimum facilities for the best laboratory school experience are found to be lacking in almost a third of all of the institutions.

### PURPOSES FOR WHICH CAMPUS SCHOOLS ARE USED

In view of the theoretical and practical importance of the campus laboratory school in giving students laboratory experience, it is important to know what purposes it actually is serving. Table XXXV shows its functions in each of the four phases of laboratory experience, observation, participation, class demonstration, and student-teaching. More institutions use the school for student-teaching than for any other purpose (95.4 percent) although almost as large a proportion of the institutions (94.5 percent) use it for observation. The fact that all but 4.6 percent employ it for student-teaching indicates a rather general belief that it should be so used. Only about one in twenty institutions fails to use the school for one or both of these functions. A fifth of the institutions do not use the campus school for participation although most authorities in teacher education advocate such use. A fourth of all of the institutions do not employ the campus laboratory school for demonstration purposes.

A study of 138 laboratory schools used by the same 109 teachers colleges classified in Table XXXV was also made accord-

## TABLE XXXV

*Number of Institutions Using Campus Laboratory Schools for Various Purposes in 109 State Normal Schools and Teachers Colleges, 1934–35*

| Geographic Division | No. of Institutions Studied | Reporting | Observation | Participation | Class Demonstration | Student-Teaching |
|---|---|---|---|---|---|---|
| New England....... | 7 | 4 | 4 | 3 | 3 | 3 |
| Middle Atlantic..... | 22 | 20 | 18 | 15 | 13 | 17 |
| East North Central.. | 21 | 21 | 20 | 15 | 19 | 21 |
| West North Central.. | 24 | 19 | 17 | 14 | 11 | 19 |
| South Atlantic...... | 12 | 8 | 7 | 7 | 6 | 8 |
| East South Central.. | 10 | 9 | 9 | 8 | 8 | 9 |
| West South Central.. | 16 | 13 | 13 | 12 | 11 | 13 |
| Mountain........... | 8 | 7 | 7 | 7 | 7 | 6 |
| Pacific.............. | 11 | 8 | 8 | 5 | 3 | 8 |
| Total............... | 131 | 109 | 103 | 86 | 81 | 104 |
| Percent............ |  |  | 94.5 | 79.1 | 74.3 | 95.4 |

ing to the combination of purposes which each served (not shown in the table). Of these, seventy-seven (55.8 percent) were used for the four purposes, observation, participation, class demonstration, and student-teaching; seventeen (12.3 percent) for observation, participation, and student-teaching; sixteen (11.6 percent) for observation, class demonstration, and student-teaching; twelve (8.7 percent) for student-teaching only; five (3.7 percent) for observation and student-teaching; three (2.2 percent) for observation, participation, and class demonstration; three (2.2 percent) for observation and participation; two (1.4 percent) for observation and class demonstration; two (1.4 percent) for class demonstration and student-teaching; and one (0.7 percent) for participation and student-teaching.

In 1937–38 a similar classification was made of the purposes in 131 institutions. Of 150 laboratory schools, seventy-seven (51.3 percent) were used for the four purposes—observation, participation, class demonstration, and student-teaching; twenty-six (17.3 percent) for observation, participation, and student-teaching; fifteen (10.0 percent) for observation, class demonstration, and student-teaching; seven (4.7 percent) for student-teaching only; seven (4.7 percent) for observation, participation, and class demonstration; four (2.7 percent) for observation, class demonstration, and student-teaching; four (2.7 percent) for class demonstration and student-teaching; four (2.7 percent) for demonstration and student-teaching; three (2.0 percent) for observation and class demonstration; two (1.3 percent) for participation and student-teaching; and one (0.7 percent) for observation and participation.

There was some change in purpose of the campus laboratory schools of the individual institutions. Of eighty-six identical institutions reporting for the two academic years eight added observation and then discontinued it; fifteen added demonstration, a like number discontinued it; eleven added participation, eight dropped it; no institution added student-teaching, two discontinued it.

The purposes for which the schools are used vary with the geographic divisions. In the New England and Pacific Divisions relatively less use is made of the schools for participation. In the East North Central Division twenty of the twenty-one institutions employ them for this purpose. The Pacific and New England Divisions make less than average use of the campus schools for class demonstration while rather general use is made of the schools for this purpose in the East North Central, West South Central and Mountain Divisions.

No investigation of the experimental functions of the laboratory school was made in the present study. Eubank[75] found that, of seventy-six teachers colleges studied, only three used their laboratory school for experimental purposes. Henderson[76] in a later investigation found seven of thirty-seven teachers colleges did so. Armentrout,[77] Learned and Bagley,[78] Mead,[79] and Charters and Waples[80] do not favor general experimentation in the laboratory

---

[75] Eubank, *op. cit.*, p. 25.
[76] Henderson, *op. cit.*, p. 7.
[77] Armentrout, *op. cit.*, p. 72.
[78] Learned and Bagley, *op. cit.*, p. 221.
[79] Arthur R. Mead, *Supervised Student-Teaching*, pp. 554–55. 1930.
[80] Charters and Waples, *op. cit.*, p. 123.

PRESENTATION AND INTERPRETATION OF DATA    113

school. Mead would limit experimental studies to those checking the progress of the school itself. Learned and Bagley believe that the laboratory school should represent *approved* conditions. They are disinclined to favor experimentation because, then, the student-teacher does not see the usual run-of-the-mine school activities, and also there is doubt of the validity of conclusions reached on the basis of schools taught by student-teachers when they are applied to public schools as a whole. Innovations in the schools cannot be made on the basis of judgments formed as the result of data secured under atypical conditions where student-teaching is done. Armentrout sees little need for experiment except on the graduate level, which is not being considered as a part of this study. Evenden[81] expresses his agreement with the other opinions set forth on this point, stating that although in some cases experiments may be conducted in training schools, difficulties are experienced, especially in the school of small enrollment. Charters and Waples fear that in the attempt which experimental-school teachers would quite naturally make to represent the more progressive theories, typical public school conditions would not be maintained. Mead,[82] Henderson,[83] and Mooney[84] agree that the campus laboratory school should be limited in its function to observation (including demonstration), participation, and a limited amount of student-teaching.

THE USE OF CAMPUS SCHOOLS FOR CLASS DEMONSTRATION

In view of the considerable number of teachers colleges which do not make use of their laboratory school for class demonstrations, it is desirable to survey competent opinion on this subject. Barr and Burton suggest that demonstration lessons "involving actual subject matter from the course of study and presented by an expert are of real assistance."[85] Whenever it is possible to make use of off-campus schools for student-teaching, Rugg[86] advocates making the campus school an agency for observation of good

---

[81] Evenden, in *National Survey of the Education of Teachers*, Vol. VI, *op. cit.*, p. 123.
[82] Mead, *loc. cit.*, p. 554.
[83] Henderson, *op. cit.*, p. 111.
[84] Mooney, *op. cit.*, p. 137.
[85] A. S. Barr and W. H. Burton, *The Supervision of Instruction*, p. 428. 1926.
[86] Rugg, *op. cit.*, p. 97.

practice both in individual observations and in class demonstrations. More than seven hundred respondents in teachers colleges agreed "practically without reservation" that there should be many opportunities for prospective teachers to observe good teaching, and affirmed their belief that demonstration plays a valuable role in the professional education of teachers, and they also agreed, although with some reservations, that college instructors should frequently conduct recitations in the laboratory school.[87] In the institutions studied such use of the laboratory schools might well be extended. In Table LVI, Section D (page 160) it is indicated that 71.8 percent of the observation of class demonstrations is done in campus and only 28.2 percent in off-campus schools.

If demonstration teaching is to be effective, definite plans must be made so that it is possible for supervisors in the laboratory school and instructors in subject-matter and professional courses to schedule such teaching conveniently. Haphazard plans in this respect will lessen the use which is made of the facilities which are available. To determine what provision teachers colleges make for class demonstrations, each respondent to the questionnaire was asked whether any classes in the campus laboratory school of his institution were reserved exclusively for a specific period of time (a month, quarter, semester) for class demonstrations and individual observations. If a plan of rotation of classes of different grade levels and subjects was employed, he was asked to describe it. The replies are exhibited and analyzed in Table XXXVI. The various patterns can be included in four general plans. Only a fourth (24.8 percent) of the 113 institutions which replied stated that they reserved classes for class demonstrations and individual observations, and only fifteen (13.2 percent) reported that they rotated classes or subjects according to some definite, prearranged plan. The others arrange for demonstrations at any time when they are requested to do so by the laboratory school supervisors and other members of the faculty. Doubtless considerable flexibility should exist in providing demonstrations, but this is still possible even though certain classes or subjects are reserved especially for demonstration according to a definite plan. The rela-

[87] Rugg, *loc. cit.*, p. 94.

PRESENTATION AND INTERPRETATION OF DATA 115

TABLE XXXVI

*Plans Used in Laboratory Schools of State Normal Schools and Teachers Colleges for Providing Facilities for Class Demonstrations and Observations of Teaching, 1933-34*

Plan I. Training school is available for observation at all times while it is in session.
    1. Demonstration at any time.
    2. Training school always available except when sign "No observers today" is on door.
    3. Certain grades are reserved for a year at a time.

Plan II. Training school is available for observation whenever a request is made by a member of the faculty.
    1. Demonstrations at the request of critic teachers.
    2. Observations and demonstrations are arranged for as requested by the faculty of the college.

Plan III. Training school is available at definite fixed periods only.
    1. The whole afternoon is reserved in all grades.
    2. One primary and one intermediate grade is reserved each quarter.
    3. One room is available for the entire first quarter; all rooms are open for the first week of each quarter.
    4. Each room is available for one hour a week during entire year.
    5. For high school classes, the third period of the school day throughout the year.

Plan IV. Training school classes are rotated on the calendar for observation according to a definite plan.
    1. Each of six grades reserved for a period of six weeks in rotation.
    2. Each of six grades reserved for a period of five weeks in rotation.
    3. The entire group of observers is divided into eight sections. Each section is given observation for one week in each grade from the kindergarten through the ninth grade.
    4. Kindergarten, third, and sixth grades are open during the fall term; first, fourth, and seventh grades during winter term; second, fifth, and eighth grades during the spring term.
    5. There is rotation of grades during the fall term only.

| | |
|---|---|
| Institutions reporting on these items. | 113 |
| Institutions which reserve classes in the campus laboratory schools for class demonstrations and individual observations. | 28 |
| Institutions which do not reserve classes in the campus laboratory schools for class demonstrations and individual observations. | 85 |
| Institutions which rotate classes for demonstrations and observations according to a definite plan. | 15 |
| Institutions which do not rotate classes for demonstrations and observations according to a definite plan. | 43 |

## TABLE XXXVII

*Number of State Normal Schools and Teachers Colleges Having One-Teacher and Two-Teacher Rural Schools as Laboratory Schools for the Preparation of Teachers in Similar Schools, 1934-35*

| Geographic Division | Separate Course for Rural Teachers | Rural Laboratory Schools Campus | Rural Laboratory Schools Off-Campus |
|---|---|---|---|
| New England.................... | | | |
| Middle Atlantic.................. | 7 | 4 | 6 |
| East North Central............... | 12 | | 10 |
| West North Central.............. | 13 | | 7 |
| South Atlantic................... | 1 | | 2 |
| East South Central............... | | | |
| West South Central.............. | 3 | | |
| Mountain....................... | | | 1 |
| Pacific.......................... | | | 2 |
| Total.......................... | 36 | 4 | 28 |

tively small number of schools which make definite reservations seems to affirm other data tending to show that demonstrations are less emphasized in laboratory schools than are the other major functions of the school.

In this connection the campus laboratory school for the preparation of one- and two-teacher rural schools may be considered. Table XXXVII indicates that although thirty-six of the 131 teachers colleges (27.5 percent) give a separate course for rural teachers, only four of them (3.1 percent) maintain a one- or two-teacher rural laboratory school on the campus. All of these are located in institutions in the Middle Atlantic Division. Although, as was shown in Section A of this chapter (see pages 31-32), the education of teachers for such schools is certainly one of the major functions of the teachers college, it is clear that the data shown in the table support the conclusion of that section that there is a marked deficiency in the laboratory facilities which can be used in student-teaching for preparing to teach in such rural schools.

## HOW PUPILS ARE SECURED FOR CAMPUS LABORATORY SCHOOLS

Whether or not the campus laboratory school is composed of pupils typical of the public schools or of a selected group is of importance in determining its functions. For example, if the pupils come from a single district of the city surrounding the teachers college, it can usually be presumed that, on the whole, the pupils are somewhat superior to average pupils. Similarly, if tuition is charged, only the children of the more financially able can attend, a selective factor operating to secure a larger proportion of the higher grade pupils than is found in the usual public school. In Table XXXVIII are shown the sources of pupils enrolled in 106 institutions. In certain institutions, pupils are obtained from more than one source. Since there are a considerable number of different combinations, it seemed desirable to tabulate each laboratory school, or different divisions of the one school, if a different source of pupils was shown for each. For example, if one source was given for the pupils in the campus elementary school, and another one for the campus high school, each was included in the tabulation. In thirty-one (27.6 percent) of the 137 laboratory schools reported, pupils in the laboratory school were charged tuition; in 106 none was charged. The most common plan employed is that in which the laboratory school admits pupils from any source whatever, without tuition charges. This situation includes forty-three institutions (31.4 percent). The next most commonly used plan is admission of pupils from the entire city without tuition charge, which is the situation in twenty-five (18.3 percent) institutions. Totaling the laboratory schools where attendance is from the whole city or a wider area and where pupils attend under a contract with a board of education of a district other than that in which the teachers college is located, eighty-six of the 137 laboratory schools (62.8 percent) secure groups of pupils from areas and sources making them somewhat non-selective, fifty-one (37.2 percent) have selective groups of pupils either because tuition is charged pupils or because they come from a single school district or a limited area. In twenty instances (14.6 percent) the campus school is a school of the city

## TABLE XXXVIII

*Sources from Which Pupils in Campus Laboratory Schools in 106 State Normal Schools and Teachers Colleges Were Secured, 1934-35*

| Geographic Division | No. of Institutions Reporting | A | B | C | D | E | F |
|---|---|---|---|---|---|---|---|
| New England................ | 4 | 2 | | | | 1 | 2 |
| Middle Atlantic.............. | 21 | 4 | 6 | 8 | 3 | 3 | 4 |
| East North Central........... | 20 | 4 | 6 | 9 | 3 | 3 | 1 |
| West North Central.......... | 19 | 3 | 3 | 7 | 1 | 5 | 4 |
| South Atlantic............... | 6 | 3 | 2 | 1 | | 1 | 1 |
| East South Central........... | 9 | | 3 | 3 | 2 | 3 | 4 |
| West South Central.......... | 12 | 2 | 2 | 8 | | 2 | |
| Mountain.................... | 6 | | 1 | 4 | 1 | 1 | 2 |
| Pacific...................... | 9 | 2 | 2 | 3 | 1 | 1 | |
| Total...................... | 106 | 20 | 25 | 43 | 11 | 20 | 18 |

\* A—Campus school is one school of city or town in which teachers college is located.
 B—Pupils from entire city or town of teachers college, tuition free.
 C—Pupils from any source whatever, tuition free to them.
 D—Pupils from entire town or city in which teachers college is located, tuition charged.
 E—Pupils from any source whatever, tuition charged.
 F—Pupils attend by contract with board of education other than that of city in which teachers college is located.

Note: If an institution secures pupils from more than one source, tabulation is made for each source.

or town in which the teachers college is located. For example, at Natchitoches, Louisiana, the laboratory school building was erected on the college campus on a site leased to the college for ninety-nine years by the Parish Board to the college.[88]

### ENROLLMENT OF THE SCHOOLS

If the enrollment of the laboratory school is too small, it is restricted in the complex services which it should render in different phases of the laboratory experience—observation, participation, class demonstration, and student-teaching. On the other hand, if the enrollment is too large, the administration tends to become unwieldy and the school itself is less nearly typical of the usual

[88] Bagley, Alexander, and Foote, *op. cit.*, p. 192.

## TABLE XXXIX

*Enrollments of the Campus Laboratory Schools of State Normal Schools and Teachers Colleges, 1934–35*

| Enrollment | Number of Institutions | Percent |
| --- | --- | --- |
| Less than 100 | 1 | 0.9 |
| 100–199 | 17 | 14.9 |
| 200–299 | 30 | 26.3 |
| 300–399 | 28 | 24.6 |
| 400–499 | 23 | 20.2 |
| 500–599 | 7 | 6.1 |
| 600–699 | 6 | 5.3 |
| 700–799 | 2 | 1.8 |
| Total | 114 | 100.1 |

$Q_1 = 235.0$  Median $= 332.1$  $Q_3 = 441.3$

public school. In Table XXXIX it is indicated that as a rule the enrollment varies from 100 to 500, ninety-eight of the 114 institutions (86.0 percent) coming within this range. The institution which used the laboratory school listed in the table as having an enrollment of less than 100 is the State Teachers College located at Ellendale, North Dakota, which used the school for its laboratory work in industrial arts. The use of this school for this purpose was discontinued in 1937–38. The modal enrollment in the laboratory school lies between 200 and 300 pupils. Though the total enrollment is significant in showing the size of the unit in which the laboratory experience is gained, if taken alone, it does not give a complete picture of the training facilities which are effectively available, because the numbers enrolled in the respective grades do not remain constant.

Table XL shows the mean enrollments for the various divisions of the school by different levels. The table indicates, so far as the mean is concerned, that the institutions have a sufficient number of pupils in each level to care adequately for laboratory activities on that level. In the New England Division the mean enrollment is highest of all the geographic divisions in the enrollment on each

## TABLE XL

Distribution of Mean Enrollments in Different Grade Levels of Campus Laboratory Schools in 111 State Normal Schools and Teachers Colleges, 1934-35

| Geographic Division | No. of Institutions Reporting | Kindergarten No. of Institutions | Kindergarten Mean Enrollment | Primary (Grades 1-3) No. of Institutions | Primary (Grades 1-3) Mean Enrollment | Intermediate (Grades 4-6) No. of Institutions | Intermediate (Grades 4-6) Mean Enrollment | Junior High School No. of Institutions | Junior High School Mean Enrollment | Senior High School No. of Institutions | Senior High School Mean Enrollment |
|---|---|---|---|---|---|---|---|---|---|---|---|
| New England | 5 | 4 | 47.8 | 5 | 154.0 | 5 | 136.5 | 4 | 128.3 | | |
| Middle Atlantic | 20 | 15 | 36.2 | 18 | 104.8 | 18 | 118.8 | 15 | 132.6 | 5 | 155.0 |
| East North Central | 20 | 15 | 39.9 | 20 | 88.0 | 20 | 91.0 | 18 | 88.8 | 11 | 165.5 |
| West North Central | 19 | 14 | 32.5 | 17 | 67.9 | 17 | 67.1 | 17 | 66.3 | 14 | 100.0 |
| South Atlantic | 8 | 2 | 26.5 | 8 | 119.0 | 8 | 130.8 | 3 | 66.7 | 5 | 197.6 |
| East South Central | 11 | 1 | 23.0 | 11 | 104.5 | 11 | 105.9 | 9 | 96.7 | 6 | 67.5 |
| West South Central | 12 | 3 | 20.0 | 11 | 105.1 | 11 | 107.0 | 10 | 99.9 | 9 | 100.7 |
| Mountain | 7 | 6 | 31.5 | 7 | 83.9 | 7 | 88.6 | 7 | 89.1 | 4 | 102.3 |
| Pacific | 9 | 5 | 31.8 | 9 | 92.8 | 9 | 93.9 | 5 | 74.8 | | |
| Total | 111 | 65 | 35.1 | 106 | 96.7 | 106 | 100.4 | 88 | 94.3 | 54 | 105.6 |

level which the laboratory school contains. On the other hand, it is lowest in the East North Central, West North Central, Mountain, and Pacific Divisions, where many of the institutions of greatest college student enrollment are found, showing at least one reason for the wide recourse to off-campus laboratory schools for laboratory experience in institutions of these states. The mean enrollment for each of the three-year divisions of the laboratory school (primary, intermediate, junior high school, and senior high school) is fairly constant.

The pupil enrollment fluctuates slightly from year to year, both in the totals and in the number in each geographic division. However, no marked changes occurred in the general picture during the year 1937–38 as contrasted with 1933–34 except as has been previously noted in the addition or discontinuance of grades or divisions.

## GRADE LEVELS IN THE SCHOOLS

In Table XLI are shown the grade spans of the laboratory schools used by 115 teachers colleges. There are considerable differences among the institutions. Sixty-five institutions (56.5 percent) have kindergartens. An examination of the different geographic divisions reveals that there are relatively few kindergartens in the southeastern part of the United States, i.e., the South Atlantic, East South Central, and West South Central Divisions. The other divisions vary little in the proportion of the institutions having kindergartens. Seven institutions have campus laboratory schools only on the junior or senior high school level. Twenty teachers colleges, located principally in the West North Central and West South Central Divisions, have all grades ranging from the kindergarten through the twelfth. If to this number are added three others, which have a range from kindergarten through the eleventh grade,[89] twenty-three institutions (20 percent) have laboratory schools which cover all grades from the kindergarten through the highest grade of the senior high school. Adding to this sum twenty others having grades ranging from the first to the eleventh or twelfth, there are a total of forty-three

---

[89] A number of southern states are organized with an elementary school of seven grades, followed by a high school of grades eight to eleven, inclusive.

## TABLE XLI

*Grade Span of the Campus Laboratory Schools of 115 State Normal Schools and Teachers Colleges, 1934–35*

| Grades | Number of Institutions | Percent of Institutions |
|---|---|---|
| K | 1 | 0.9 |
| K-4 | 1 | 0.9 |
| K-6 | 8 | 7.0 |
| K-7 | 1 | 0.9 |
| K-8 | 17 | 14.8 |
| K-9 | 14 | 12.2 |
| K-11 | 3 | 2.6 |
| K-12 | 20 | 17.4 |
| 1-6 | 6 | 5.2 |
| 1-7 | 2 | 1.7 |
| 1-8 | 6 | 5.2 |
| 1-9 | 5 | 4.3 |
| 1-10 | 3 | 2.6 |
| 1-11 | 5 | 4.3 |
| 1-12 | 15 | 13.0 |
| 5-12 | 1 | 0.9 |
| 7-9 | 1 | 0.9 |
| 7-12 | 3 | 2.6 |
| 8-11 | 1 | 0.9 |
| 9-12 | 2 | 1.7 |
| Total | 115 | 100.0 |

Key: K = kindergarten; K-4 = grades kindergarten to grade 4; 1-12 = grades 1 to 12, etc.

(37.4 percent) of the teachers colleges reporting which have campus laboratory facilities for the whole range of the usual public school grades. Fifty-three (46.1 percent) of the institutions have laboratory schools on the campus which include one or more grades of the senior high school (grades ten to twelve) and ninety-nine (86.1 percent) of the junior high school (grades seven to nine). In two geographic divisions, the New England and the Pacific, there is no institution which has a campus laboratory school designed to provide laboratory experience on the high school level.

## RATIO OF STUDENT-TEACHER ENROLLMENT TO ENROLLMENT IN THE LABORATORY SCHOOL

Learned and Bagley,[90] Armentrout,[91] and Eubank[92] have presented data, each on a limited number of institutions, to show the ratio between the enrollment of student-teachers in the teachers college and the enrollment in the laboratory school. Learned and Bagley compared seven independent campus laboratory schools in Missouri with six elsewhere which used off-campus schools; Armentrout made a comparison between six institutions with campus laboratory schools and six elsewhere; Eubank compared data for eighteen institutions with the data gathered by Learned and Bagley. Though the number of cases is small in each instance compared with the total number of teachers colleges, the evidence points to a relatively high ratio of student-teachers compared with the pupils in the laboratory schools in those institutions where laboratory work is restricted to the campus school. In all these studies the ratios were found between total teachers college enrollment and enrollment in the laboratory school, except that for eighteen teachers colleges Eubank also presents the ratios between student-teaching enrollment and training school enrollment. It is believed that the latter comparison is the most serviceable, since it is a better index of actual laboratory school adequacy.

In Table XLII, which includes 105 teachers colleges, ratios between the student-teaching enrollment and the enrollment in the campus laboratory schools are given for all institutions whether they use only campus schools or both campus and off-campus schools for laboratory purposes. As a matter of policy for the institution the important information is the amount of supplementation of campus facilities which is necessary. The Standard of the American Association of Teachers Colleges provides:

In the training school there shall be at least one full-time training teacher in charge of at least 30 children for every 18 college students each of whom does during the year a total of 90 clock hours of student teaching or an equivalent load.[93]

---
[90] Learned and Bagley, *op. cit.*, p. 196.
[91] Armentrout, *op. cit.*, p. 151.
[92] Eubank, *op. cit.*, p. 27.
[93] American Association of Teachers Colleges, *loc. cit.*

## TABLE XLII

*Ratio of the Enrollment in Student-Teaching to the Enrollment in the Campus Laboratory Schools in 105 State Normal Schools and Teachers Colleges, 1933-34*

| Ratio | Number of Institutions | Percent of Institutions |
|---|---|---|
| 1 : 0– .49 | 3 | 2.8 |
| 1 : .50– .99 | 15 | 14.3 |
| 1 : 1.00–1.49 | 23 | 21.9 |
| 1 : 1.50–1.99 | 22 | 21.0 |
| 1 : 2.00–2.49 | 18 | 17.1 |
| 1 : 2.50–2.99 | 5 | 4.7 |
| 1 : 3.00–3.49 | 4 | 3.8 |
| 1 : 3.50–3.99 | 3 | 2.9 |
| 1 : 4.00–4.49 | 3 | 2.9 |
| 1 : 4.50–4.99 | 2 | 1.9 |
| 1 : 5.00–5.49 | 2 | 1.9 |
| 1 : 5.50–5.99 | 1 | 1.0 |
| 1 : 6.00 or more | 4 | 3.8 |
| Total | 105 | 100.0 |

$Q_1$ = 1 : 1.18    Median = 1 : 1.76    $Q_3$ = 1 : 2.44

Note: This table should be read as follows: For three of the 105 institutions, 2.8 percent of those for which ratios could be computed, the ratio between the number of student-teachers and the enrollment in the campus laboratory school was one to a range of 0–.49, etc.

This standard assumes a minimum ratio of 1.67 (eighteen to thirty) between student-teachers and laboratory school pupils. Reference to the table indicates that more than 40 percent of all the institutions included fall below this ratio even though a mere minimum of ninety hours of student-teaching is required. In Table XVII (Section B, page 72) it was seen that the total laboratory experience required of the median student-teacher in 1937-38 was 108.1 clock-hours, which is 1.201 times the minimum standard required by the Association. Multiplying 1.67 by 1.201 gives a product of 2.0. In other words, a ratio of 1 : 2 between student-teachers and laboratory school enrollment must be maintained to provide the amount of student-teaching which is the median now required. Reference to Table XLII shows that sixty-three institutions (60.0 percent of the 105 reporting) have not sufficient facilities on the campus alone to meet their need for laboratory experience. If observation and participation are considered a part of student-teaching, the ratio is 3 : 1, and 81.8 percent of the institutions would be found to lack adequate facilities. The need for using off-campus laboratory schools for supplementation of campus facilities is clear. If the off-campus school is used to complement the campus school for purposes of differentiation as well as for supplementation, the need is even more evident. If the amount of laboratory experience required as a criterion in 1933–34 instead of the reduced amount were used in the ratio, the number of institutions needing off-campus facilities would be increased, since the total of all laboratory experience per student is twenty semester hours less in 1937–38 than in 1933–34.

## A FORMULA FOR DETERMINING THE SIZE OF THE CAMPUS SCHOOL NECESSARY TO ACCOMMODATE STUDENT-TEACHERS

Learned and Bagley[94] have proposed the following formula for determining the size of the campus laboratory school needed by a particular institution to supply adequate laboratory facilities:

$$n = 1.30 \left( \frac{15 \, s \, c \, m}{t} \cdot 2 \right)$$

In the formula:
 $n$ = minimal training school enrollment
 $s$ = number of students to whom practice teaching privileges must be available each year
 $c$ = number of recitation units during which each student will be in charge of a section each week
 $m$ = proportion of total year during which practice teaching is required of each student
 $t$ = approximate number of recitation units in the training school each week

The number 1.30 is arrived at by "adding fifteen percent to allow for the margin between enrollment and attendance and another fifteen percent as a margin to ensure sections of at least fifteen pupils." The formula assumes that not more than half of the teaching in the laboratory school will be done by student-teach-

[94] Learned and Bagley, *op. cit.*, p. 195.

ers, the recommendation of Learned and Bagley, hence 2 as a factor.

This formula is based on the assumption that this is the actual load of responsible room teaching and does not include observation and participation. Observation of the teaching of laboratory school supervisors, subject-matter instructors, and instructors in professional courses in the teachers colleges other than those who are supervisors in the laboratory school is not included in student-teaching. If participation is graded, as is considered desirable, it would gradually approach complete charge by the student-teacher at its close and so in reality should be considered in the proportion of teaching which is done by the student-teacher.

The formula does make a 15 percent allowance for the margin between enrollment and attendance and an additional 15 percent for ensuring sections of fifteen pupils each. Ideally some allowance should also be made for less than complete efficiency in the use of the school which results from the following and similar factors: setting aside, on a definite plan, certain rooms for demonstration; allowing for flexibility in the amount of student-teaching done by various students; providing each student practice in the teaching field for which he is preparing to enter; and assuring the student laboratory teaching in not less than two of the grades or subjects which he expects to teach.

Because the standard of the American Association of Teachers Colleges is expressed in clock-hours, it seems advisable to modify the formula. The formula, as revised, may be expressed as follows:

$$n = 1.30 \left( \frac{15\,s\,h}{t\,l} \cdot 2 \right)$$

In this revision:
$n$ = minimal laboratory school enrollment
$s$ = number of student-teachers to whom student-teaching privileges must be made available for each year
$h$ = number of clock-hours of student-teaching required of each student
$t$ = approximate total number of clock-hours contained in the school program of the laboratory school for one week (total clock-hours school is in session, normally thirty per week)
$l$ = length of the academic year in weeks

## PRESENTATION AND INTERPRETATION OF DATA 127

As it is normally advisable for students to secure their laboratory experience in the division of the school or type of school (primary, intermediate, junior high school, senior high school, one- and two-teacher rural, etc.) in which they expect to teach, it is more accurate to apply the formula to each division of the school or type of school, rather than to the laboratory school as a whole. In case the student-teachers do three-fourths of the teaching in the laboratory school, the factor in the formula should be 4/3 instead of 2; if two-thirds, the factor should be 3/2 instead of 2. The following is the recommendation of the American Association of Teachers Colleges:

At least two-fifths of the teaching in the training school should be done by regular teachers of the training school or by other members of the faculty.[95]

To meet this standard the factor 5/3 should be substituted in the formula, making it read:

$$n = 1.30 \left( \frac{15\,s\,h}{t\,l} \cdot \frac{5}{3} \right)$$

Assume that in a given school year each of 100 student-teachers must teach 90 clock-hours in the laboratory school. The school is in session from 9:00 to 11:30 a.m. and 1:00 to 3:30 p.m. for a school year of thirty-six weeks. The school week in this case would consist of 25 clock-hours. After the proper substitutions in the formula above have been made, it reads as follows:

$$n = 1.30 \left( \frac{15 \times 100 \times 90}{25 \times 36} \cdot \frac{5}{3} \right)$$

Solving the formula it is found that a minimum of 325 pupils must be enrolled in the laboratory school to accommodate 100 student-teachers in the elementary school.

Or, given a pupil enrollment of 600 in the campus laboratory school, which is in session thirty-six weeks, five days in the week, five clock-hours a day, in which each student-teacher is to teach a total of 180 clock-hours, let it be assumed that it is desired to determine the number of student-teachers who can secure their

---

[95] American Association of Teachers Colleges, *loc. cit.*

teaching in the school. After substitutions are made the formula becomes

$$600 = 1.30 \left( \frac{15 \times s \times 180}{25 \times 36} \cdot \frac{5}{3} \right)$$

$$= 1.30 \times 5s$$

Transposing:
$$6.5s = 600$$
$$s = 92.3$$

Therefore, the laboratory school under these conditions can accommodate ninety-two student-teachers.

The formula as modified lends itself readily to computing the size of the laboratory school required, whether the school program is organized on the basis of recitation units or on the basis of a freer organization which does not recognize distinct recitation units as in the case of activity schools, and especially on the primary levels of instruction.

The formula applies on the high school level as well as in the elementary grades, provided that the supervision of study is regarded as student-teaching. If not, the size of the laboratory school must be increased above that of the formula. However, it is the opinion of the writer that student-teaching should include all phases of the school's activity, and so the entire school day must be taken as the basis for computation of laboratory experience rather than only that proportion which is devoted to recitation. If the day is shorter, as in the kindergarten or in some high schools, the factor $t$ will be decreased accordingly.

## OWNERSHIP AND CONTROL OF THE CAMPUS SCHOOL

To assure continuous operation and effective use of the campus laboratory school, it is desirable that it be under the exclusive control and ownership of the teachers college. When there is joint control and divided responsibility, there is always a possibility of conflict in judgments and in the exercise of authority. In off-campus laboratory schools this joint control may not always be harmful. But whatever the situation may be in off-campus schools, it is always advisable for an institution to have some part of its laboratory facilities exclusively controlled by the college.

## TABLE XLIII

*Ownership of Campus Laboratory School Buildings in State Normal Schools and Teachers Colleges, 1933–34 and 1937–38*

| Geographic Division | No. of Institutions Reporting 1933–34 | No. of Institutions Reporting 1937–38 | Owning Campus Buildings 1933–34 | Owning Campus Buildings 1937–38 | Not Owning Campus Buildings 1933–34 | Not Owning Campus Buildings 1937–38 |
|---|---|---|---|---|---|---|
| New England....... | 5 | 12 | 3 | 5 | 2 | 7 |
| Middle Atlantic..... | 21 | 26 | 18* | 24 | 3 | 2 |
| East North Central.. | 21 | 20 | 20† | 20 | 1 | |
| West North Central.. | 22 | 18 | 20‡ | 18‡ | 2 | |
| South Atlantic...... | 9 | 10 | 8 | 10 | 1 | |
| East South Central.. | 9 | 9 | 9 | 9 | | |
| West South Central.. | 13 | 9 | 13 | 8 | | 1 |
| Mountain........... | 7 | 4 | 7 | 4 | | |
| Pacific............. | 9 | 9 | 9 | 8 | | 1 |
| Total............... | 116 | 117 | 107 | 106 | 9 | 11 |
| Percent........... | | | 92.2 | 90.6 | 7.8 | 9.4 |

* College owns general campus school, but the local school district owns the campus rural laboratory school in one of the institutions reporting.

† In one of these cases the high school building belongs to the city, the elementary school building to the college.

‡ In one institution the city owns the elementary school building on the campus, the college owns the junior high school building.

Table XLIII presents data concerning the ownership of the laboratory schools in 116 state teachers colleges for 1933–34, and in order to provide a basis for comparison and supplementation it also includes data concerning the situation for a comparable group of 117 institutions in 1937–38. In both years more than 90 percent of the campus laboratory schools were owned by the teachers college. One out of ten institutions do not have their own campus school buildings on their college grounds. In five of the nine geographic divisions, all the institutions reporting own their campus laboratory school buildings. Those institutions which do not own them are located principally in the northeastern part of the country which includes the New England and the Middle Atlantic Divisions.

TABLE XLIV

*Control of Campus Laboratory Schools by State Normal Schools and Teachers Colleges, 1933–34 and 1937–38*

| Geographic Division | No. of Institutions Reporting | | Number of Institutions with Control of Laboratory School | | | |
|---|---|---|---|---|---|---|
| | | | Exclusively by College | | Jointly by College and Local School District | |
| | 1933–34 | 1937–38 | 1933–34 | 1937–38 | 1933–34 | 1937–38 |
| New England | 5 | 12 | 4 | 9 | 1 | 3 |
| Middle Atlantic | 21 | 26 | 19 | 22 | 2 | 4 |
| East North Central | 21 | 20 | 21 | 20 | | |
| West North Central | 22 | 17 | 20 | 17 | 2 | |
| South Atlantic | 9 | 10 | 6 | 8 | 3 | 2 |
| East South Central | 9 | 9 | 9 | 9 | | |
| West South Central | 13 | 9 | 10 | 7 | 3 | 2 |
| Mountain | 7 | 4 | 6 | 3 | 1 | 1 |
| Pacific | 9 | 9 | 9 | 6 | | 3 |
| Total | 116 | 116 | 104 | 101 | 12 | 15 |
| Percent | | | 89.7 | 87.1 | 10.3 | 12.9 |

The situation regarding control of the laboratory school is given in Table XLIV. The percentage of exclusive control for both years is slightly smaller than that given for ownership in the preceding table. With the exception of the East North Central and the East South Central Divisions, each division has one or more institutions which report joint control by the teachers college and the local school district either in 1933–34 or in 1937–38. In 1937–38 a slightly larger percentage of the institutions replying indicated joint control than did so in 1933–34.

## SUMMARY

1. Both campus and off-campus laboratory schools are used quite generally by state normal schools and teachers colleges to provide laboratory school facilities; 68.0 percent of 131 institutions which reported employ both types. Of the remainder 22.1 percent have campus schools only, and 9.9 percent, off-campus schools only. There are differences in the various geographic divi-

sions, institutions using both types being most frequent in the Middle Atlantic, East North Central, and Pacific Divisions, those using campus schools in the East South Central Division, and those using off-campus in the New England and South Atlantic Divisions.

2. The campus laboratory school is employed for observation, participation, demonstration, and student-teaching. More institutions (95.4 percent) use it for student-teaching than for any other function, and almost an equal number for observation. Approximately a fifth of the laboratory schools are not used for participation, and about a fourth are not used for demonstration classes. More than half of the laboratory schools reported serve the four purposes—observation, participation, demonstration teaching, and student-teaching.

3. Only 24.8 percent of the 113 institutions replying on the use of demonstration teaching state that they reserve classes for group demonstration, and only fifteen (13.2 percent) have a definite plan for the rotation of classes which are reserved for class demonstration.

4. Only thirty-six (27.5 percent) of the teachers colleges have one- or two-teacher schools used for laboratory purposes, either as campus or as off-campus schools, and only four (3.1 percent) of them have such a school on the college campus.

5. The most common plan for enrolling pupils in the laboratory school is to admit them from any source whatever, without payment of tuition. This method is employed in forty-three (31.4 percent) of the institutions. In order of their frequency, other sources of pupils are: (1) from the entire city or town in which the teachers college is located, tuition free (twenty-five institutions, 18.3 percent); (2) from any source whatever, tuition charged (twenty institutions, 15.3 percent); (3) from one school of the city or town in which the teachers college is located (twenty institutions, 15.3 percent); (4) from a town or city other than that in which the teachers college is located by contract with the local board of education (eighteen institutions, 13.8 percent); and (5) from the entire town or city in which the teachers college is located, upon payment of a tuition charge (eleven institutions, 8.4 percent).

6. There is considerable variation between institutions in the grade span (i.e., the number of grades included) in the laboratory school. Of the 115 colleges reporting 56.5 percent have kindergartens; 0.9 percent have the junior high school level only; 20 percent have grades one to twelve; 37.4 percent have all grades from the kindergarten or first grade to the eleventh or twelfth, according to the terminal year generally found in the public schools of their respective areas; 46.1 percent include one or more grades of the senior high school (ten to twelve) and 86.1 percent, one or more grades of the junior high school (seven to nine).

7. The modal enrollment of campus laboratory schools is between 300 and 400 pupils. Ninety-eight of the 105 institutions reporting (86.0 percent) have enrollments ranging between 100 and 500, the enrollments being fairly equal in each grade and division of the school.

8. A revised formula for determining the approximate number of pupils which a campus laboratory school must enroll to accommodate the student-teaching required is as follows:

$$n = 1.30 \left( \frac{15\,s\,h}{t\,l} \cdot 2 \right)^*$$

9. More than nine-tenths (92.2 percent) of the campus laboratory schools are owned by and nearly as large a proportion (89.7 percent) are controlled by the teachers college.

10. Few and relatively minor changes have occurred in the aspects of laboratory schools discussed in this chapter between the years 1933–34 and 1937–38.

## SECTION D

## THE OFF-CAMPUS LABORATORY SCHOOL

The purpose of this section is to discuss the use of off-campus laboratory schools by state normal schools and teachers colleges. Data are presented with respect to the following subjects which concern off-campus schools: (*a*) their need as adjuncts to campus schools; (*b*) the populations of the communities in which they are situated; (*c*) their use to supplement and complement the campus

* See pp. 126–127.

# PRESENTATION AND INTERPRETATION OF DATA 133

schools; (*d*) the types of public schools (one- and two-teacher rural, consolidated rural, village and city) which serve as laboratory schools; (*e*) the "cadet" or "interne" plan; (*f*) a formula for determining the size of the community and school enrollment needed to supply the requirements of the teachers colleges; (*g*) the pupil enrollment and its distribution on grade levels; (*h*) the time required to travel from the campus of the teachers college to the off-campus schools; (*i*) the methods of transportation used to reach them; (*j*) the phases of laboratory experience (observation, participation, demonstration, and student-teaching) which the schools provide; (*k*) the kind and amount of compensation which is given to cooperating schools; (*l*) the tuition fees which are charged to pupils enrolled in the schools; (*m*) legal and contractual relationships between the teachers colleges and the off-campus schools; (*n*) agreements and contracts which are made with the off-campus schools; (*o*) the attitudes of individuals and groups toward the use of public schools as laboratory schools; and (*p*) the kind and degree of difficulty which is experienced in using affiliated off-campus schools for laboratory purposes.

## THE NEED FOR OFF-CAMPUS SCHOOLS

Two purposes of the off-campus school were stated in Section C: (*a*) to *supplement* the campus school by providing additional facilities similar in kind and purpose; and (*b*) to *complement* the type of facilities which are available in the campus school and provide for functions differentiated from it. In Table XXXIV of that section it was seen that twenty-nine (22.1 percent) of the 131 institutions studied used only campus schools for laboratory purposes. Either because of practical necessity or theoretical considerations, or both, the remaining 102 (77.9 percent) turned to the use of off-campus schools to provide a part of the facilities which they needed. There it was found that, even when the facilities of the campus school were supplemented by those of the town or city in which the teachers college was located, the facilities often would not meet the laboratory needs of the institution.

When the state normal schools and teachers colleges were founded they were often poorly situated because factors extraneous to the educational purposes of the institution determined their location. The exigencies of political considerations, offers of cash bonuses, donations of building sites, local community demands for "their share" of public funds for maintaining colleges, and acceptance by state legislatures of existing weak and struggling academies or colleges which were then transformed into state normal schools, were primary factors which determined where they were established.[96] Accordingly, a considerable number of them were located in communities which had school enrollments too small to supply sufficient pupils for the laboratory school, even though all the schools of the town or city were made available to the teachers colleges for laboratory purposes. This situation still persists. A study of the population of the communities in which teachers colleges are located makes it clear that many of them have a school population insufficient to provide an adequate number of pupils for the laboratory schools. Humphreys[97] presented data on this point. In constructing his population tables, however, he did not make deductions for the colored population in the southern states in which the races are separated legally in the schools. This is a matter of considerable importance, especially in some cities of the South. For example, Troy, Alabama, has a population of 6,814, of whom 3,115 (45.7 percent) are colored; Greenville, North Carolina, a population of 9,194, of whom 4,233 (47.1 percent) are colored; Natchitoches, Louisiana, a population of 4,547, of whom 1,856 (40.8 percent) are colored; and Valdosta, Georgia, a total population of 13,482, of whom 6,265 (46.5 percent) are colored.

In addition to the racial factor, there are other conditions which limit the number of student-teachers who can be given their laboratory experience in a city of a given size. Some of these are: (*a*) the enrollment in private and parochial schools; (*b*) unevenness in the grade distribution of pupils; (*c*) unequal demands for student-teaching in the different grades and subjects; (*d*) the amount of laboratory experience which is required; and (*e*) the necessity for providing laboratory experience on the grade levels and in the subject areas which the student-teachers expect to teach. How-

[96] Harry C. Humphreys, *The Factors Operating in the Location of State Normal Schools*, pp. 84–88. 1923.
[97] *Ibid.*, p. 95.

## TABLE XLV

*Number and Percent of 160 State Normal Schools and Teachers Colleges Which Were Members of the American Association of Teachers Colleges, 1933–34\**

| Population Range | Number of Institutions | Percent | Cumulative Percent |
|---|---|---|---|
| Less than 500 | 4 | 2.5 | 2.5 |
| 500– 999 | 7 | 4.4 | 6.9 |
| 1,000– 1,999 | 13 | 8.1 | 15.0 |
| 2,000– 2,999 | 21 | 13.1 | 28.1 |
| 3,000– 3,999 | 10 | 6.3 | 34.4 |
| 4,000– 4,999 | 15 | 9.4 | 43.8 |
| 5,000– 5,999 | 12 | 7.5 | 51.3 |
| 6,000– 6,999 | 5 | 3.1 | 54.4 |
| 7,000– 7,999 | 9 | 5.6 | 60.0 |
| 8,000– 8,999 | 10 | 6.3 | 66.3 |
| 9,000– 9,999 | 5 | 3.1 | 69.4 |
| 10,000–10,999 | 2 | 1.2 | 70.6 |
| 11,000–11,999 | 1 | 0.7 | 71.3 |
| 12,000–12,999 | 4 | 2.5 | 73.8 |
| 13,000–13,999 | 1 | 0.6 | 74.4 |
| 14,000–14,999 | 3 | 1.9 | 76.3 |
| 15,000–19,999 | 6 | 3.7 | 80.0 |
| 20,000–24,999 | 6 | 3.8 | 83.8 |
| 25,000–29,999 | 1 | 0.6 | 84.4 |
| 30,000–34,999 | 2 | 1.2 | 85.6 |
| 35,000–39,999 | 2 | 1.3 | 86.9 |
| 40,000–44,999 | 2 | 1.2 | 88.1 |
| 45,000–49,999 |  |  | 88.1 |
| 50,000 or more | 19 | 11.9 | 100.0 |
| Total | 160 | 100.0 | 100.0 |

$Q_1 = 2{,}762$   Median $= 5{,}833$   $Q_3 = 14{,}333$

\* U. S. Census of 1930. Corrected for races other than white, legally segregated in the schools.

ever, while these various conditions must be considered in individual instances in determining the laboratory load which can be carried, they cannot be isolated for the purposes of a general survey.

Data, similar in some respects to those of Humphreys, but based on the figures of the census of 1930 and corrected to exclude the colored population, are presented in Table XLV. This table includes a study of 160 towns and cities in which are located state normal schools and teachers colleges. These institutions are members of the American Association of Teachers Colleges and prepare teachers of the white race. It was Humphreys'[98] conclusion that a town or city of less than 3,000 population is unable to furnish the laboratory school facilities which are necessary and that a minimum population of 5,000 would be much better to guarantee a sufficient pupil enrollment.

If this criterion is correct, a large number of teachers colleges, because of limitations of population in the towns or cities containing them, are compelled to look to other school districts to supplement the facilities available in their own campus school and in the off-campus schools in the towns or cities in which they are located. According to the table, there were in 1933–34 forty-five institutions located in towns or cities with populations of less than 3,000 (census of 1930), and seventy (43.8 percent) in towns or cities with populations of less than 5,000. The situation improved little since the time when Humphreys made his study. Of eleven institutions, not yet founded at the time of his study but in 1933–34 members of the American Association of Teachers Colleges, five were in communities with fewer than 5,000 inhabitants, and only two in communities whose population was more than 10,000. Nearly half of the institutions would have had insufficient laboratory facilities, had they been limited to the schools of their own towns or cities.

In certain states all the teachers colleges are in small communities. For example, in Ohio, four state teachers colleges, each an integral part of a state university, are located in communities which, according to the census of 1930, had populations of 8,375, 7,252, 6,688 and 2,588. Illinois has five state teachers colleges. According to the census of 1930 the largest community containing any of them is a city of 8,545 persons. Iowa has one large teachers college, which supplies the needs of the state; it is located in a city of 7,362. In Pennsylvania, seven of the thirteen teachers colleges are located in communities of fewer than 5,000 persons, and five in communities with fewer than 3,000 persons. In West Virginia,

[98] *Ibid.*, p. 98.

four of the six state teachers colleges are located in villages having fewer than 1,000 inhabitants.

Without doubt it is due in considerable measure to the limited population of the towns and cities containing teachers colleges that in making the present study it was found that of ninety-two teachers colleges which reported that they used the facilities provided in off-campus schools, twenty-six use the schools of their own town or city only; seventeen, the schools of districts other than their own town or city; and forty-nine, the schools both of their own and of other towns and cities. In many instances, it is necessary to supplement the facilities which are available in the town or the city by using the schools of other outlying communities.

In Table XXVI it was revealed that, on the basis of the actual amount of student-teaching, 35.7 percent was done in off-campus schools and an additional 15.2 percent was divided between the campus and off-campus schools. The data confirm the wide use of off-campus schools.*

## THE POPULATION OF COMMUNITIES IN WHICH OFF-CAMPUS LABORATORY SCHOOLS ARE LOCATED

The distribution of collective populations of the towns and cities in which the teachers colleges use off-campus schools for laboratory purposes is indicated in Table XLVI. There are many variations in the composite size of the communities, since some institutions need to supplement their campus schools little; others, much; some need a great variety of laboratory facilities in different special subject areas and on all the grade levels; others require facilities for a single curriculum such as the general elementary or the secondary. Some use the schools of a single town or city; others need the schools of as many as eighty different communities. Some institutions which have special subjects allocated to them must use many off-campus schools in those subjects; others, having a demand for student-teaching relatively balanced between different divisions, can distribute the load of

---

* Student-teaching, as the term is used in this table, indicates the total amount of laboratory experience, whether it is observation, participation, or student-teaching, or any two or all of them combined.

## TABLE XLVI

*Distribution Showing for Each State Normal School and Teachers College the Combined Population of All Communities in Which It Used the Public Schools as Off-Campus Laboratory Schools, 1934-35*

| Combined Population of Communities | Number of Institutions | Percent | Cumulative Percent |
|---|---|---|---|
| Less than 500 | 2 | 2.6 | 2.6 |
| 500-  999 | 1 | 1.3 | 3.9 |
| 1,000- 1,999 | 3 | 3.9 | 7.8 |
| 2,000- 2,999 | 7 | 9.2 | 17.0 |
| 3,000- 3,999 | 4 | 5.3 | 22.3 |
| 4,000- 4,999 | 3 | 3.9 | 26.2 |
| 5,000- 5,999 | 2 | 2.6 | 28.2 |
| 6,000- 6,999 | 4 | 5.3 | 34.1 |
| 7,000- 7,999 | 2 | 2.6 | 36.7 |
| 8,000- 8,999 | 1 | 1.3 | 38.0 |
| 9,000- 9,999 | 3 | 3.9 | 41.9 |
| 10,000-10,999 | 2 | 2.6 | 44.5 |
| 11,000-11,999 | 4 | 5.3 | 49.8 |
| 12,000-12,999 |  |  | 49.8 |
| 13,000-13,999 | 1 | 1.3 | 51.1 |
| 14,000-14,999 |  |  | 51.1 |
| 15,000-19,999 | 6 | 7.9 | 59.0 |
| 20,000-24,999 | 7 | 9.2 | 68.2 |
| 25,000-29,999 | 1 | 1.3 | 69.5 |
| 30,000-34,999 | 2 | 2.6 | 72.1 |
| 35,000-39,999 | 1 | 1.3 | 73.4 |
| 40,000-44,999 | 1 | 1.3 | 74.7 |
| 45,000-49,999 |  |  | 74.7 |
| 50,000 or more | 19 | 25.0 | 99.7 |
| Total | 76 | 99.7 | 99.7 |

$Q_1 = 4,667$    Median $= 12,500$    $Q_3 = 50,000$

Note: This table should be read as follows: There are two state normal schools and teachers colleges, or 2.6 percent, in which the combined population of the communities which include off-campus laboratory schools is less than 500; one, or 1.3 percent, in which the combined population is between 500 and 999; a total of three, or a cumulative percent of 3.9, with a population of less than 999.

the laboratory school well by using the various schools which are located in a single community.

The lower quartile point, which is 4,667 for the group of

seventy-six institutions replying, indicates that, were the off-campus schools used as intensively in proportion to their enrollments as the campus schools are, they would in three-fourths of the instances be able to care for all the laboratory experience which is necessary for the student-teachers. A comparison of Table XLVI with Table XLV indicates that, on the whole, the institutions have increased the possibilities of securing adequate facilities very considerably by using the off-campus schools, since the median size of the combined populations of the communities in which off-campus laboratory schools are located is 12,500, while that of the town or city in which the teachers college is located is 5,833. Reference to Table XXVIII indicates that more of the total student-teaching is done in the campus schools than in the off-campus schools. The three tables indicate that, so far as the use of off-campus schools is concerned, the *intensity* of use is less than in the case of campus schools, and in many institutions the *point of saturation*, i.e., the full or complete use of the off-campus schools so far as it is advisable to employ them, is not usually reached. Of course it must be remembered that, in the off-campus schools, class groups must be larger than in campus schools because the buildings and routine of the school do not adapt themselves to small groups of fifteen pupils, the typical class size in campus schools. Table XLVI indicates that the potentiality of securing sufficient pupils is considerably augmented when the off-campus schools are used to supplement the campus schools.

### THE OFF-CAMPUS SCHOOL AS A SUPPLEMENT AND COMPLEMENT TO THE CAMPUS SCHOOL

The advantages of the campus school were discussed in Section C of this chapter (see pages 105–106). Ideally, the campus school should provide observation in connection with the courses in professional theory and subject matter, and the major portion of the demonstration teaching. It should give opportunity to student-teachers for doing their initial teaching in small groups, exemplify the best theory, and serve as a center to integrate the whole teacher-education program.

Other conditions being equal, the off-campus school can best serve in the following ways:

I. It can *supplement* the facilities of the campus school as follows:
   (*a*) Furnish additional facilities of the same type as already provided in it.
   (*b*) Provide facilities on grade levels and in areas which the campus school lacks.
   (*c*) Make it possible to increase the number of semester-hours of student-teaching for each student.
   (*d*) Make available a variety of types of school, such as rural, village, city, or consolidated rural.

II. It can *complement* the facilities provided on the campus by providing for each student:
   (*a*) Final responsible room teaching under typical conditions as they are found in the public schools, after he has finished his preliminary practice with small groups in the campus laboratory school.
   (*b*) Limited participation and observation of schools which differ from the campus school.
   (*c*) Contact with extracurricular and extra-school life typical of the usual community.
   (*d*) Opportunity for differentiated practice in his field of interest.
   (*e*) Educational experience with a variety of types of pupils.
   (*f*) Training in making adjustments to a community different from the one in which he normally has lived.
   (*g*) Teaching groups of unselected pupils.

As few teachers colleges have rural one- and two-teacher laboratory schools on the campus (see Table XXXVII), off-campus schools must supplement them, and the preliminary student-teaching done in the campus school can well be supplemented by laboratory experience in rural communities under usual rural conditions, particularly for prospective teachers preparing for service in the rural schools. This is an area in which there is marked need for complementing the campus school.

That the off-campus school would fulfill a peculiar function in teacher preparation, even were the institution to have sufficient laboratory facilities without supplementing them with others, is

# PRESENTATION AND INTERPRETATION OF DATA

indicated by the opinions of many who believe that the off-campus school can complement the campus school in furnishing *typical* public school conditions. Jarman[99] found that twenty-nine of thirty jurors approved the principle that the pupils of the laboratory school should be typical of a public school group. Peik[100] learned that more than 90 percent of each of the following groups favored, either fully or with reservations, the proposal that student-teaching should be done under typical conditions: academic instructors, special-subject instructors, presidents, and teachers college instructors.

## THE TYPES OF SCHOOLS USED AS OFF-CAMPUS LABORATORY SCHOOLS

If the teachers college is to have adequate laboratory facilities, it is not sufficient merely to have enough pupils to teach. It is essential to have pupils of the various types which are to be found in the public schools which prospective teachers will enter. For an institution to have rural schools only would handicap the preparation of teachers who are preparing to become teachers in city school systems. Conversely, to prepare all teachers by giving student-teaching in city schools would handicap those who are preparing for service in the rural schools. To furnish *minimum* facilities for laboratory teaching is not sufficient; to furnish a *variety* of facilities is nearly as important if teachers are to be prepared most efficiently. The question of differentiation has already been discussed in connection with the varieties of the curriculum in Section A of the present chapter (see pages 27–32). The curriculum for the preparation of the rural teacher should be different from that designed to prepare the teacher in the city schools, and the student-teaching should likewise be differentiated, at least for a part of the course.

In 1933–34, according to the report of the United States Commissioner of Education,[101] 836,210 teachers were needed in the country, 461,953 (55.2 percent) in rural schools, and 374,257 (44.8 percent) in urban schools. In the Census of the United

---

[99] Jarman, *op. cit.*, p. 112.
[100] Peik, in *National Survey of the Education of Teachers*, Vol. III., *op. cit.*, pp. 270–271.
[101] *Biennial Survey of Education, 1932–34*, Vol. II, Chap. II, p. 40.

States, as well as in the reports of the Office of Education, a city is defined as a community having a population of not less than 2,500. Although more teachers are actually needed for villages, rural consolidated, and rural one- and two-teacher schools than for city schools, the latter type are used more generally for off-campus laboratory schools than those of the former three types. It is shown in Table XLVII that four-fifths of all teachers colleges

TABLE XLVII

*Number of State Normal Schools and Teachers Colleges Using Each Type of Off-Campus Laboratory School, 1934-35*

| Geographic Division | No. of Institutions Reporting | City | Village | Rural Consolidated | Rural One-Teacher and Two-Teacher |
|---|---|---|---|---|---|
| New England | 7 | 5 |  | 4 | 2 |
| Middle Atlantic | 20 | 18 | 8 | 5 | 7 |
| East North Central | 19 | 16 | 6 | 9 | 9 |
| West North Central | 17 | 10 | 5 | 5 | 16 |
| South Atlantic | 9 | 6 | 4 | 3 | 3 |
| East South Central | 1 | 1 |  |  |  |
| West South Central | 10 | 10 | 2 | 2 | 2 |
| Mountain | 7 | 5 | 1 | 2 | 2 |
| Pacific | 11 | 10 | 2 | 1 | 3 |
| Total | 101 | 81 | 28 | 31 | 44 |
| Percent | 100.0 | 80.2 | 27.7 | 30.7 | 43.6 |

utilize city schools as off-campus laboratory schools to supplement the campus school. The disparity between the number of teachers prepared by the teachers college for the smaller communities and the number which should be so prepared is even greater than is at first apparent, because many of the teachers who serve in the metropolitan areas are prepared in state universities and large privately endowed institutions. When considered in this light the number who have secured student-teaching experience in smaller communities seems altogether inadequate.

It is true, to be sure, that many teachers who begin their teaching careers in rural and village schools later find their employment in the cities. Nevertheless, as these teachers move on to the larger population centers, others must be supplied in the rural and village areas, so that the comparative figures remain essentially as stated. Recalling the data presented in Section A of this chapter (see pages 31–32), 138,542 teachers taught in one-teacher rural schools in 1933–34, and another estimated 46,400 in two-teacher rural schools, a total of 184,942. Subtracting this total from the total number who taught in communities having less than 2,500 inhabitants (the minimum for cities), which was 461,953, there were 277,011 who taught in village and consolidated rural schools. Of all teachers (omitting supervisors and principals) in the United States in 1933–34, 44.8 percent taught in city schools, 33.0 percent in village and rural consolidated schools, and 22.2 percent in one- and two-teacher rural schools.

In Table XLVII the number of each type of laboratory school is reported. But the number of schools is only partly indicative of the lack of laboratory facilities in preparing teachers for small communities. Because urban schools of the country average 14.5 teachers per school, whereas the village, consolidated rural, and one- and two-teacher rural schools average 2.2 teachers per school,[102] in order to make the number of classrooms comparable, the number of city schools would have to be multiplied by the ratio of the number of teachers per school in the city to the number per school in the other three types of school district, 6.6 (14.5 divided by 2.2). Computed on this basis, percentages derived from the table would indicate that 83.8 percent of the classrooms used by teachers colleges for student-teaching are in the city schools, 16.2 percent, in village and rural schools combined. When these figures are compared with those of the preceding paragraph, the need for more attention to student-teaching facilities in the smaller communities is clearly evident. The tendency is strong among teachers colleges to give their student-teachers their laboratory experience in city schools, irrespective of the type of school in which they may expect to secure employment as teachers.

In only one geographic division, the West North Central, do a

[102] *Biennial Survey of Education, 1932–34*, Vol. II, *loc. cit.*, Chap. II, pp. 40.

large proportion of the institutions provide for rural one- and two-teacher laboratory schools.

The strong tendency to use city schools is seen also in Table XLVIII. To secure the data, the institutions were asked to state on what date they began to use each off-campus laboratory school which was in use in 1934-35. It was found that fifty-eight of the

TABLE XLVIII

*Type of Off-Campus Laboratory School First Used by 85 State Normal Schools and Teachers Colleges, Together with the Period When Such Use Began, as Reported in 1934-35*

|  | NUMBER OF INSTITUTIONS FIRST USING: | | | | |
| --- | --- | --- | --- | --- | --- |
| Period | City Schools | Village Schools | Rural Consolidated Schools | Rural Schools | Total |
| Prior to 1900....... | 1 | 2 |  |  | 3 |
| 1900-04............ | 1 |  |  |  | 1 |
| 1905-09............ | 3 |  |  |  | 3 |
| 1910-14............ | 4 |  | 1 | 1 | 6 |
| 1915-19............ | 5 | 1 | 3 | 1 | 10 |
| 1920-24............ | 15 |  | 3 | 4 | 22 |
| 1925-29............ | 20 | 1 | 2 | 5 | 28 |
| 1930-34............ | 9 |  | 1 | 2 | 12 |
| Total............... | 58 | 4 | 10 | 13 | 85 |

eighty-five institutions used city schools as the first off-campus school, and only twenty-seven the other three types combined. Inspection of the table shows an increasing trend toward the use of city schools during the period since 1920.

Of the institutions which answered the questionnaire in 1934-35 and again in 1937-38, nine added thirty-one one- and two-teacher rural schools; one, a consolidated rural school; four, eleven village schools; and thirteen, sixteen city schools. Eleven institutions discontinued the use of forty-six one- and two-teacher rural schools; one, two village schools; and seven, twelve city schools. During the period there was a net gain of four city schools serving as laboratory schools and a net loss of four village and rural schools.

## THE USE OF THE "CADET" OR "INTERNE" PLAN

In the questionnaire the "cadet" or "interne" plan is defined as one in which the student-teacher is placed in full charge of a class in a neighboring school system and performs the functions which regular teachers of the systems do, being visited at more or less frequent intervals by a supervisor from the college campus. Of 100 institutions which replied on the use of cadet schools, nineteen (19.0 percent) indicated that they had a cadet system of student-teaching and eighty-one (81.0 percent) that they did not employ this method in preparing teachers. Seventeen of the institutions indicated the frequency of the visits which the supervisor made during the period that the student-teacher was employed as a cadet. The frequencies of the visits were reported as follows:

| | |
|---|---|
| Daily | 2 institutions |
| Semi-weekly | 1 institution |
| Weekly | 8 institutions |
| Two to seven times during the entire period of teaching | 5 institutions |

One gave the rather indefinite reply "as needed." The cadet plan is used most frequently in the Middle Atlantic and Pacific Divisions. No institution in the East North Central or in the East South Central Divisions uses this plan.

In 1937–38 a group of 112 institutions gave replies to the same question. Of these, twenty-six (23.2 percent) stated that they used a cadet system, this being an increase of 4.2 percent over the number which reported such a plan in use in 1933–34. At the earlier date, eleven of the seventeen institutions reported that the supervisors visited cadets at least once a week. In 1937–38, only ten of the twenty institutions reporting indicated that supervisors visited as often as once a week. The tendency is toward less frequent supervisory visits.

In 1933–34 two institutions in the West South Central Division and none in the East South Central used the cadet system, whereas in 1937–38 five in the West South Central and two in the

East South Central Divisions used such a plan of student-teaching.

## FORMULA FOR DETERMINING THE NUMBER OF PUPILS NECESSARY IN OFF-CAMPUS SCHOOLS

In Section C a formula was developed to determine the number of pupils necessary to provide for student-teaching in campus schools. Conditions are different in the public schools which are used as off-campus laboratory schools, and these must be taken into account in determining the number of pupils required for a given number of student-teachers. The construction of public school buildings usually makes it impossible to divide the pupils of a classroom into smaller groups for teaching as is done in campus laboratory schools. For the country as a whole, the number of pupils per teaching position in the urban schools in 1933-34 was 33.2; in the rural schools, 28.0; an average of 30.4 pupils for the two groups combined.[103] This average will, of course, vary with sections of the country, with the composition of the population, with suburban and urban areas, and other factors, and it cannot be used with accuracy to show the situation in the case of a single institution. However, it can well be employed for survey purposes, for the country as a whole, or for a considerable group of institutions, to determine the adequacy of the facilities so far as the whole group is concerned.

During the year 1935-36 the number of pupils enrolled per teaching position was 29.6 for the country as a whole. For the urban schools it was 32.2; for the rural schools, 27.2,[104] the number of pupils per teacher being somewhat smaller than in 1933-34. The average for the two periods is 30.0, which may be used as the class-size for the purpose of formula-making below. The number will fluctuate to some extent from year to year as a result of financial conditions, birth rate, population movements, changes in educational theory, and uneven grade enrollments, but for survey purposes it may be used at the present time.

Of the total population of the country in 1933-34, 20.9 percent were enrolled in the public elementary and secondary schools—

[103] *Biennial Survey of Education, 1932-34*, Vol. II, *loc. cit.*, Chap. II, p. 40.
[104] *Biennial Survey of Education, 1934-36*, Vol. II, *op. cit.*, Chap. II, p. 52.

PRESENTATION AND INTERPRETATION OF DATA 147

16.4 in the former, 4.5 percent in the latter. During 1935–36 the percentages of pupils enrolled in the public elementary and secondary schools were 15.9 and 4.6, respectively, a total of 20.5 percent.[105]

The following may be used as a formula to determine the population needed to provide off-campus teaching for a given number of student-teachers. (Compare formula, Section C, page 126, of this chapter, for the use of campus schools.)

$$P = \frac{30\,s\,h}{.205\,t\,l} \cdot 2 \qquad (1)$$

In the formula:

$P$ = population of the community
$s$ = number of student-teachers to whom student-teaching privileges must be made available for each year
$h$ = number of clock-hours of student-teaching required of each student
$t$ = approximate total number of clock-hours contained in the school program of the laboratory school for one week (total clock-hours school is in session, normally thirty per week)
$l$ = length of the academic year in weeks

The factor, 30, represents the class-size; .205, the fraction that pupils enrolled in elementary and high school are of the total population; 2, the factor introduced because the pupils are to be taught by student-teachers only one-half of the time, necessitating twice as many pupils as would be required otherwise. The formula is based on the assumption that only the white population is counted. Since the factors used are based on public school enrollments, no other correction is necessary; and the factor 1.30 used in the formula for campus schools is omitted.

Suppose that each of 200 student-teachers is required to teach 90 clock-hours, that the school year consists of thirty-six weeks each having five school days, 6 clock-hours long (30 clock-hours a week). By substituting these values in the formula, it becomes:

$$P = \left(\frac{30 \times 200 \times 90}{.205 \times 30 \times 36} \cdot 2\right)$$

$$P = 4{,}878$$

[105] *Ibid.*, p. 56.

Therefore, to support this program of student-teaching, the schools of a single community or a group of communities having a total population of 4,878 is required.

If one substitutes in the formula 90 clock-hours for $h$; 30 clock-hours for $t$; 36 weeks for $l$; 1,000 for $P$; and solves the formula, the number of student-teachers who could be accommodated in a community of 1,000 is found to be 41. That is, for a rather typical school, each 1,000 of population will support a student-teaching program on the basis of the number of hours required by the American Association of Teachers Colleges for forty-one student-teachers.

This formula may be used with accuracy to make a survey of general conditions only in the country as a whole. For the individual institution, the director of training must know how many classrooms he will need to support a given program of student-teaching. Because the conditions are different in the various divisions of the school, such as the primary and intermediate grades and high school, and because student-teachers should be offered laboratory experience on the grade levels and in the subject-matter areas in which they plan to teach, the formula is more serviceable if it is applied to each division of the school. It can then be modified as follows:

$$n = \frac{s\,h}{t\,l} \cdot 2 \qquad (2)$$

where $n$ equals the number of classrooms in the division (kindergarten-primary, intermediate, etc.) and the other letters have the same significance as in formula (1) above. If 200 student-teachers, each teaching 90 clock-hours in schools in session for a school year of thirty-six weeks, each week consisting of a total of 30 clock-hours, are assumed, the formula becomes:

$$n = \frac{200 \times 90}{30 \times 36} \cdot 2$$

$$n = 33\tfrac{1}{3} \ (34) \text{ classrooms}$$

If teachers teach pupils only two-fifths of the time, the factor introduced above would be 5/3 instead of 2.

If student teaching is distributed between campus and off-campus laboratory schools, this formula may be used for the proportionate amount done in the off-campus schools, while the formula on page 126 may be applied to that portion done in the campus schools.

Though the study of laboratory facilities for liberal arts colleges is not within the scope of this study, it may be stated parenthetically that as most of them, lacking campus laboratory schools, are limited to using off-campus laboratory schools for student-teaching, this formula may be advantageously used by them in determining the number of pupils and classrooms required to meet their laboratory school needs.

Arrangements with off-campus schools must be made in terms of the number of classrooms and supervisors rather than in terms of total number of pupils. For this reason it is believed that the formula is most usefully applied in this form. However, if it is wished to determine the total number of pupils required, the 30 may be added as a factor in the numerator, which would give the approximate number required.

It is difficult to provide a formula which will apply accurately to the high school, because, unlike the grades where teachers are usually expected to teach the whole program, subjects are specialized, and it is necessary for student-teachers to teach majors and minors or specific fields of concentration. It is obvious that similar difficulties may be encountered in the case of the special subjects.

THE PUPIL ENROLLMENT AND ITS DISTRIBUTION

The total number of pupils enrolled in the off-campus laboratory schools of sixty-three teachers colleges is distributed in Table XLIX. The median enrollment of the off-campus schools is 787.5 as contrasted with the median enrollment of 332.1 in the campus school (Table XXXIX, page 119). The average combined enrollment of the off-campus schools is greater than that of the campus schools. Whereas the maximum enrollment of any campus school does not exceed 800 in any institution, the enrollment of the off-campus schools in four institutions exceeds 5,000. The two tables are not entirely comparable because the number of institutions represented in them is different. However, in each in-

## TABLE XLIX

*Enrollment of Off-Campus Laboratory Schools in 63 State Normal Schools and Teachers Colleges, 1934-35*

| Enrollment | Number of Institutions | Percent |
|---|---|---|
| Less than 100 | 3 | 4.8 |
| 100– 199 | 4 | 6.3 |
| 200– 299 | 4 | 6.3 |
| 300– 399 | 8 | 12.7 |
| 400– 499 | 5 | 7.9 |
| 500– 599 | 2 | 3.2 |
| 600– 699 | 2 | 3.2 |
| 700– 799 | 4 | 6.3 |
| 800– 899 | 2 | 3.2 |
| 900– 999 | 4 | 6.3 |
| 1,000–1,499 | 11 | 17.5 |
| 1,500–1,999 | 2 | 3.2 |
| 2,000–2,499 | 1 | 1.6 |
| 2,500–2,999 | 2 | 3.2 |
| 3,000–3,999 | 3 | 4.8 |
| 4,000–4,999 | 2 | 3.2 |
| 5,000 or more | 4 | 6.3 |
| Total | 63 | 100.0 |

$Q_1 = 359.4$   Median $= 787.5$   $Q_3 = 1,420.5$

stance, the number is relatively representative and comparisons can be made to show the general situation in the institutions considered as a whole. By adding the medians found in the two tables a total of 1,119.6 is secured, showing the approximate total number of pupils in the training schools, both campus and off-campus, which the median teachers college has available for student-teaching. The comparison shows strikingly to what an extent off-campus schools serve to supplement the facilities provided in those on the campus.

As was suggested in connection with a discussion of the enrollment of the campus laboratory school, it is not sufficient to know the total enrollment, it is important to know its distribution in the different levels of the school. The respondents to the questionnaire indicated the grades which were included in each of the

## TABLE L

*Number of State Normal Schools and Teachers Colleges Having Pupils Enrolled in the Different Grade Levels of Off-Campus Laboratory Schools, 1934–35*\**

| Geographic Division | No. of Institutions Reporting | No. of Laboratory Schools | Kindergarten | 1–3 | 4–6 | 7–9 | 9 or 10– 11 or 12 |
|---|---|---|---|---|---|---|---|
| New England | 3 | 10 | 2 | 2 | 2 | 2 | 1 |
| Middle Atlantic | 15 | 151 | 5 | 12 | 12 | 15 | 12 |
| East North Central | 18 | 75 | 3 | 17 | 18 | 18 | 16 |
| West North Central | 17 | 112 | 3 | 16 | 16 | 17 | 11 |
| South Atlantic | 9 | 29 |  | 6 | 6 | 8 | 7 |
| East South Central |  |  |  |  |  |  |  |
| West South Central | 10 | 19 | 1 | 7 | 7 | 9 | 8 |
| Mountain | 5 | 10 | 1 | 5 | 5 | 5 | 2 |
| Pacific | 10 | 76 | 3 | 9 | 9 | 8 | 5 |
| Total | 87 | 482 | 18 | 74 | 75 | 82 | 62 |
| Percent | 100.0 |  | 20.7 | 85.1 | 86.2 | 94.3 | 71.3 |

Under the heading "Number of Different Institutions Having Each Grade Level".

\* An institution is counted as having enrollment at a given level if it has pupils in one or more grades on that level.

off-campus laboratory schools. From the data received Table L was constructed. Though it is desirable, it is not essential that all grades be included in each division of the laboratory school. But institutions should have pupils enrolled in at least one grade of each division or level of the laboratory school corresponding to those for which they prepare teachers. The table shows that of 482 off-campus schools used by eighty-seven institutions, eighteen (20.7 percent) supplement their campus facilities with off-campus kindergartens. On all grade levels and in all divisions by far the greater number of institutions supplement the facilities of the campus with off-campus schools. The percentage is highest in the number which supplement on the junior high school level. It is to be noted that no institution in the East South Central geographic division uses laboratory schools which are located off the campus to supplement the schools which are located on the campus.

## TIME REQUIRED TO REACH OFF-CAMPUS SCHOOLS FROM THE TEACHERS COLLEGE CAMPUS

How effectively off-campus schools may be used, and the purposes for which they can serve, are determined to a considerable extent by the time it takes to reach them from the campus. If they are far removed it is difficult, perhaps even impossible, for subject-matter instructors, and instructors in professional courses to use them for class demonstrations. It is also difficult for the student-teachers to use the library, equipment, supplies, and other resources of the teachers college to the best advantage if too much time is consumed in reaching them.

Table LI indicates the time taken to travel one way to the off-campus schools by the present method of transportation. Some off-campus schools are located very near the campus, as is indicated by the short time required to reach them. At the other extreme are off-campus schools which are located so far away that it requires twelve hours to reach them. In these extreme cases, of course, it is necessary for student-teachers to live in the communities in which they receive their laboratory experience. Except in

TABLE LI

*Range and Mean Number of Minutes Required to Travel One Way from the Campuses of State Normal Schools and Teachers Colleges to the Off-Campus Laboratory Schools, 1934-35*

| Geographic Division | No. of Institutions Reporting | Minutes Required Range | Mean |
|---|---|---|---|
| New England................ | 2 | 5- 30 | 19.0 |
| Middle Atlantic.............. | 14 | 2-180 | 28.7 |
| East North Central........... | 18 | 3- 60 | 18.0 |
| West North Central.......... | 14 | 5-720 | 40.0 |
| South Atlantic............... | 9 | 5- 35 | 16.4 |
| East South Central........... | | | |
| West South Central.......... | 10 | 2- 55 | 16.2 |
| Mountain.................... | 5 | 5- 30 | 14.8 |
| Pacific...................... | 9 | 5- 50 | 21.1 |
| Total...................... | 81 | 2-720 | 25.0 |

PRESENTATION AND INTERPRETATION OF DATA 153

two divisions, the Middle Atlantic and the West North Central, no institution requires its students to travel a distance consuming more than an hour to reach the off-campus school. In the Middle Atlantic Division the time required to travel to the laboratory school is considerable, because the institutions of New Jersey and New York use a large number of schools as training centers.

A number of the states in the West North Central Division are sparsely populated, the institutions are located in relatively small towns or cities, and their enrollments are usually large. This makes it necessary for them to secure their off-campus laboratory facilities at some distance from the campus. In institutions of the Middle Atlantic and West North Central Divisions the mean time required for student-teachers to reach the off-campus schools is relatively high, being 28.7 minutes and 40.0 minutes respectively. Strikingly enough, the institutions in the Mountain Division are more conveniently located, so far as the time element is concerned, than those of any other division. In all divisions the mean distances to the schools used by the various institutions are so great as to create a serious problem for student-teachers who must travel to them for their laboratory experience. It seems from these data that institutions might well consider using the schools to complement the campus schools by offering a differentiated laboratory experience, rather than as a supplement which merely duplicates the laboratory experience which can be provided on the campus.

### THE METHODS OF TRANSPORTATION TO OFF-CAMPUS SCHOOLS

It was shown in Table LI that in general off-campus schools are so far distant from the campuses of the teachers colleges that an undue amount of time is consumed in reaching them. The time required is conditioned by the transportation which the student-teachers use. In Table LII the methods used by student-teachers in eighty-six institutions having 519 off-campus laboratory schools are shown. Twenty-one institutions arrange to have students live in the community in which they teach, so that no transportation is necessary. Sixty-five others use one or more of the eight methods listed. In many cases one institution used two or three methods. Because the combinations of methods used by individual institutions were so diverse, it seemed best to construct the table to show each method isolated from others, counting an institution each time it used a method.

TABLE LII

*Method of Transportation Used by Student-Teachers in Going from College to Off-Campus Laboratory Schools, 1934–35*

| Method of Transportation | Institutions* Number | Institutions* Percent | Off-Campus Laboratory Schools Number | Off-Campus Laboratory Schools Percent |
| --- | --- | --- | --- | --- |
| Walking | 52 | 35.4 | 98 | 18.9 |
| College bus | 30 | 20.4 | 80 | 15.4 |
| Student's private automobile | 21 | 14.3 | 81 | 15.6 |
| Commercial bus (including taxicab) | 14 | 9.5 | 55 | 10.6 |
| City electric railroad | 6 | 4.1 | 18 | 3.5 |
| Interurban electric railroad | 2 | 1.3 | 3 | 0.6 |
| Public school bus | 1 | 0.7 | 1 | 0.2 |
| Steam railroad | | | | |
| Total requiring transportation | 126 | 85.7 | 336 | 64.8 |
| Total not requiring transportation (Student-teachers live in the community during the period of student-teaching) | 21 | 14.3 | 183 | 35.2 |
| Total | 147 | 100.0 | 519 | 100.0 |
| Total number of institutions reporting | 86 | | | |

* If more than one method of transportation is employed by an institution (e.g., walking and commercial bus), it is counted under each method in this column.

In a third of the off-campus laboratory schools (35.2 percent) students live in the community in which the laboratory school is located while doing their student-teaching. Those living on the campus must have some means of transportation to and from the schools. Students can reach 18.9 percent of the off-campus schools by walking. More institutions use the college bus as a means of transportation than any other method. This is closely followed in frequency by the use of the student's private automobile and the commercial bus. Less than 5 percent of the off-campus schools are reached by transportation by public school bus, steam railroad, and electric interurban railroad combined. The methods are used which are most flexible and which conserve the students' time.

A sixth (15.6 percent) of the institutions whose student-teachers need transportation rely on the student's private automobile. This shifts the burden of expense from the teachers college to the student. Bernard,[106] in a study of 168 students in four teachers colleges of California, who did their student-teaching in off-campus schools, found that the cost of travel caused by teaching off the campus was $18.99 per student. He also found that it cost each student $3.94 more for the period of teaching when he lived in the community in which the teaching was done. These facts would indicate that additional expense incident to off-campus teaching should be borne by the teachers college.

### THE PHASES OF LABORATORY EXPERIENCE PROVIDED IN OFF-CAMPUS SCHOOLS

In Table LIII are shown the purposes for which off-campus laboratory schools are used by ninety teachers colleges, arranged according to geographic divisions. With the exception of one institution in the Middle Atlantic Division and one in the West South Central Division, all institutions reporting employ off-campus schools for student-teaching. About two-thirds employ them for observation (67.8 percent), while about half (52.2 percent) use them for participation and slightly more than a third (34.4 percent) for class demonstration. Thirteen have no campus school and are therefore compelled to use the off-campus school for all laboratory purposes. Another has a kindergarten only on the campus, so that the greater part of the laboratory experience in the institution must be secured in off-campus schools. Of those which must do all laboratory work off the campus ten use the off-campus schools for observation, eight for participation, eight for class demonstration, and thirteen for student-teaching. Were the table adjusted to include only those institutions which have both

---

[106] Lloyd D. Bernard, "Relative Cost and Effectiveness of Campus and Off-Campus Plans of Student-Teaching in California," p. 26. Manuscript. 1935.

campus and off-campus schools, the percentage of those using the off-campus school for observation, participation, and class demonstration, when they have campus facilities which can be used for such purposes, would be still less. The policy of the institutions, taken as a group, is to make extensive use of the off-campus school for student-teaching, and to provide the greater part of the observation, participation, and class demonstration in the campus school.

TABLE LIII

*Number of Institutions Using Off-Campus Laboratory Schools for Various Purposes in 90 State Normal Schools and Teachers Colleges, 1934–35*

| Geographic Division | No. of Institutions Reporting | Observation | Participation | Class Demonstration | Student-Teaching |
|---|---|---|---|---|---|
| New England | 4 | 3 | 3 | 3 | 4 |
| Middle Atlantic | 20 | 13 | 9 | 6 | 19 |
| East North Central | 17 | 9 | 6 | 4 | 17 |
| West North Central | 19 | 15 | 12 | 7 | 19 |
| South Atlantic | 9 | 7 | 4 | 2 | 9 |
| East South Central | | | | | |
| West South Central | 10 | 8 | 7 | 5 | 9 |
| Mountain | 4 | 3 | 4 | 3 | 4 |
| Pacific | 7 | 3 | 2 | 1 | 7 |
| Total | 90 | 61 | 47 | 31 | 88 |
| Percent | | 67.8 | 52.2 | 34.4 | 97.8 |

Contrasting Tables XXXV (see page 111) and LIII, the relative number of institutions providing for each of the four phases of laboratory work done in the campus and off-campus schools is as follows: observation, in campus schools, 94.5 percent; off-campus schools, 67.8 percent; participation, in campus schools, 79.1 percent; off-campus schools, 52.2 percent; class demonstration in campus schools, 74.3 percent; off-campus schools, 34.4 percent; and student-teaching in campus schools, 95.4 percent; off-campus schools, 97.8 percent. In general the prevailing practice tends to confirm the position taken earlier in this section that the off-campus schools should, so far as practicable, complement the campus schools by providing opportunity for student-teaching and giving only minor attention to other phases of laboratory experience, except when they cannot be provided for in the campus schools.

In the three tables which follow are included the percentages of observation, participation, and class demonstration which are furnished students in the campus and off-campus schools respectively, as these have been estimated by the officials of the various institutions which replied to the questionnaire.

In Table LIV the percentages of observation done in campus and off-campus schools are presented. In all curriculums except that for teachers in rural one- and two-teacher schools, the greater portion of the observation is done in the campus schools, 70.3 percent of all observation being done in them. Only 47.4 percent of observation for rural one- and two-teacher schools is done in the campus schools. The proportion of observation done on the campus is greatest in the case of the curriculum for the preparation of kindergarten-primary and intermediate teachers.

There are no marked differences in the various geographic divisions, but there are wide variations in the institutions themselves. One teachers college, for example, which uses thirty-two off-campus schools, states that only 10 percent of the total amount of observation is done in them. Another estimates that 98 percent of the observation in seven special subjects is done in the campus schools. The proportion of observation done in the campus schools ranges from 0 to 100 percent, the institutions included having both campus and off-campus schools.

A study of a similar group of institutions made in 1937–38, four years later, shows a marked tendency toward a greater use of off-campus schools for observation. In the general curriculums changes in the percentages of observation done in campus schools between 1933–34 and 1937–38 were as follows: general elementary, 67.9 to 65.0; kindergarten-primary, 80.7 to 65.9; intermediate, 81.2 to 58.1; junior high school, 63.0 to 56.4; senior high school, 60.3 to 55.0; and rural one- and two-teacher schools, 47.4 to 53.2, the last being the only curriculum in which an increase was shown. In the special subjects there were similar, but less

## TABLE LIV

*Relative Amount of Laboratory Experience in Observation Secured in Campus and Off-Campus Laboratory Schools of State Normal Schools and Teachers Colleges, 1933–34*

| Type of Curriculum | No. of Institutions Reporting | Percent of Observation In Campus Schools | Percent of Observation In Off-Campus Schools |
|---|---|---|---|
| General elementary | 28 | 67.9 | 32.1 |
| Kindergarten-primary | 43 | 80.7 | 19.3 |
| Intermediate | 39 | 81.2 | 18.8 |
| Junior high school | 38 | 63.0 | 37.0 |
| Senior high school | 35 | 60.3 | 39.7 |
| Rural one- and two-teacher schools | 20 | 47.4 | 52.6 |
| Special subjects: | | | |
| Agriculture | 8 | 73.8 | 26.2 |
| Art | 19 | 74.4 | 25.6 |
| Business | 16 | 51.6 | 48.4 |
| Home economics | 18 | 74.4 | 25.6 |
| Industrial arts | 18 | 67.5 | 32.5 |
| Music | 20 | 78.0 | 22.0 |
| Physical education (men) | 19 | 78.2 | 21.8 |
| Physical education (women) | 19 | 77.9 | 22.1 |
| Total | | 70.3 | 29.7 |
| Total number of institutions reporting | 77 | | |

marked, trends. Except in the curriculum for the preparation of teachers of agriculture, all showed a relatively small decrease in the proportion of observation done in the campus school. In agriculture there was a decrease from 73.8 to 48.4 percent.

Fewer institutions require laboratory experience in participation than in observation or student-teaching. For all curriculums and all institutions, taken as a whole, a greater proportionate amount of participation than of observation is done in off-campus schools. Table LV indicates, however, that this is less than half of the whole amount (42.9 percent). If, as is held by some, the off-campus school should be used primarily or solely to complement the work of the campus school by furnishing opportunities for student-teaching after preliminary laboratory experience in cam-

## TABLE LV

*Relative Amount of Laboratory Experience in Participation Secured in Campus and Off-Campus Laboratory Schools of State Normal Schools and Teachers Colleges, 1933–34*

| Type of Curriculum | No. of Institutions Reporting | Percent of Participation In Campus Schools | Percent of Participation In Off-Campus Schools |
|---|---|---|---|
| General elementary | 24 | 56.6 | 43.4 |
| Kindergarten-primary | 35 | 72.3 | 27.7 |
| Intermediate | 32 | 74.0 | 26.0 |
| Junior high school | 33 | 51.3 | 48.7 |
| Senior high school | 30 | 50.0 | 50.0 |
| Rural one- and two-teacher schools | 21 | 35.1 | 64.9 |
| Special subjects: | | | |
| Agriculture | 5 | 58.0 | 42.0 |
| Art | 16 | 65.5 | 34.5 |
| Business | 15 | 34.3 | 65.7 |
| Home economics | 17 | 59.9 | 40.1 |
| Industrial arts | 14 | 70.2 | 29.8 |
| Music | 19 | 68.6 | 31.4 |
| Physical education (men) | 17 | 66.8 | 33.2 |
| Physical education (women) | 18 | 64.2 | 35.8 |
| Total | | 57.1 | 42.9 |
| Total number of institutions reporting | 66 | | |

pus schools, there is a question whether it is not desirable, except in such curriculums as those which prepare teachers of agriculture and for service in the rural one- and two-teacher schools, to have a larger portion of the experience in participation secured in the campus school.

In the case of general curriculums, the greater proportion of participation in off-campus schools is found in the curriculum for rural one- and two-teacher schools, where almost two-thirds (64.9 percent) is off-campus participation. Among the curriculums for preparing teachers in the special subjects a similar situation is found in those designed to prepare teachers for business or the commercial subjects, where 65.7 percent of the laboratory experience is provided in off-campus schools.

In participation, as in observation, the trend during the years between 1933–34 and 1937–38 is toward a greater proportionate use of the off-campus schools. The trend is particularly noticeable in the curriculums which prepare teachers for rural one- and two-teacher schools and for teaching agriculture, in both of which approximately two-thirds, 68.8 percent and 61.6 percent respectively, is done in off-campus schools.

A comparison of the data in Tables LVI and LIV indicates that observation and class demonstration correspond closely in the relative amounts of laboratory experience secured in each in campus and off-campus schools.

On the whole it seems desirable that the greater portion of the class demonstrations be provided in the campus laboratory

TABLE LVI

*Relative Amount of Laboratory Experience in Class Demonstration Secured in Campus and Off-Campus Laboratory Schools of State Normal Schools and Teachers Colleges, 1933–34*

| Type of Curriculum | No. of Institutions Reporting | Percent of Class Demonstration In Campus Schools | In Off-Campus Schools |
|---|---|---|---|
| General elementary | 23 | 68.3 | 31.7 |
| Kindergarten-primary | 38 | 85.2 | 14.8 |
| Intermediate | 35 | 84.1 | 15.9 |
| Junior high school | 37 | 70.8 | 29.2 |
| Senior high school | 34 | 62.6 | 37.4 |
| Rural one- and two-teacher schools | 18 | 41.3 | 58.7 |
| Special subjects: | | | |
| Agriculture | 6 | 81.7 | 18.3 |
| Art | 16 | 75.3 | 24.7 |
| Business | 15 | 65.1 | 34.9 |
| Home economics | 17 | 69.1 | 30.9 |
| Industrial arts | 17 | 72.5 | 27.5 |
| Music | 18 | 75.0 | 25.0 |
| Physical education (men) | 15 | 71.7 | 28.3 |
| Physical education (women) | 15 | 72.7 | 27.3 |
| Total | | 71.8 | 28.2 |
| Total number of institutions reporting | 73 | | |

schools, which are peculiarly adapted for this purpose. Among the advantages (see Section C, p. 105) of the campus school over the off-campus is its availability for class demonstrations by supervisors and subject-matter instructors. That more than two-thirds (71.8 percent) of all class demonstrations are given in campus schools indicates a desirable situation.

It was found from the data in Table XXXVII that few teachers colleges maintain campus laboratory schools specifically adapted to the needs of rural teachers. For this reason it is desirable that class demonstrations for teachers preparing for service in rural schools be provided in off-campus schools in rural situations. The data show that 58.7 percent of the class demonstrations in curriculums for rural one- and two-teacher schools are so provided. In view of the small number of teachers colleges which provide campus facilities of suitable type, this is a practice which might well be extended to more institutions.

There are decided variations in the practices of the different institutions. In some of them, all observation and participation is provided in off-campus schools, and the campus classes are reserved exclusively for class demonstrations. In a few, class demonstrations are available only in off-campus schools, this being the case particularly in institutions which have had special subjects allocated to them.

During the four years following 1933–34 a trend is seen toward providing a greater proportionate number of class demonstrations in off-campus schools, although this tendency is not so marked in general as it was found to be in the case of observation and participation.

Though the three tables are based on estimates rather than on actual records of school officials, they present a reasonably accurate record of the relative use of the two types of schools in providing laboratory experience in observation, participation, and class demonstration. A common factor is found in the three. Generally speaking, the greater part of the laboratory experience was provided in campus, rather than in off-campus, schools. The trend during a four-year period was toward greater use of the off-campus schools. The off-campus schools were used more frequently for all these purposes in the case of the rural curriculums which prepared teachers for service in one-teacher and two-teacher schools than for any other curriculum.

## KIND AND AMOUNT OF COMPENSATION TO COOPERATING SCHOOLS

The cooperation of off-campus schools is secured most effectively if the teachers college pays a financial consideration either directly to the cooperating school or to the supervisors of student-teaching. It is usually necessary to subsidize the local schools to meet the increased expenses incurred in using the schools for laboratory purposes, to employ superior supervisors, and to maintain a spirit of cordiality and cooperation.

The officials who replied to the questionnaire gave data regarding the forms and amounts of compensation which are given. Of 131 institutions which participated in this study, 102 use off-campus schools (Table XXXIV). Ninety of these reported the compensation which is given to cooperating schools, as shown in Table LVII. Eighty-six (95.6 percent) give compensation in one

TABLE LVII

*Number of State Normal Schools and Teachers Colleges Compensating Off-Campus Laboratory Schools in Money or Services, 1934–35*

| Geographic Division | No. of Institutions Reporting | No. Giving Compensation | No. Paying Partial Expense | No. Furnishing Substitute Teachers | No. Waiving Fees for Supervisors |
|---|---|---|---|---|---|
| New England........ | 4 | 4 | 4 | | |
| Middle Atlantic..... | 16 | 15 | 10 | 3 | 4 |
| East North Central.. | 17 | 17 | 17 | 5 | |
| West North Central.. | 17 | 17 | 17 | 5 | |
| South Atlantic...... | 9 | 8 | 8 | 2 | 1 |
| East South Central.. | 1 | 1 | 1 | | |
| West South Central.. | 9 | 9 | 9 | 3 | |
| Mountain........... | 6 | 5 | 4 | 1 | 2 |
| Pacific............. | 11 | 10 | 8 | 2 | |
| Total.............. | 90 | 86 | 78 | 21 | 7 |
| Percent........... | 100.0 | 95.6 | 86.7 | 23.3 | 7.8 |

or more of three forms: (*a*) by paying a part of the expenses involved in conducting the school; (*b*) by furnishing substitute teachers who, without college credit and without pay, serve as substitutes for regular teachers when they are absent; and (*c*) by waiving tuition fees to supervisors who take courses in college for credit. It is the most common practice to pay a portion of the expense of conducting the laboratory school, seventy-eight institutions making payment in this manner. Less than a fourth (23.3 percent) provide substitute teachers for the cooperating schools and only about one in thirteen (7.8 percent) waive tuition fees to supervisors who take college courses for credit. Waiving tuition fees is more commonly the practice in the institutions of the Middle Atlantic Division than in other sections of the country.

Of the twenty-one institutions which provide substitute teachers, thirteen furnish all substitute teachers needed by the cooperating schools without definite limits for each student-teacher or each supervisor or critic teacher; four, for a period not to exceed ten half-days; two, "occasionally only"; one, "not exceeding two days at a time"; and one, for the "supervisor to whom assigned."

Few institutions waive tuition fees as compensation. Of the seven institutions which do waive them, four are in the State of New Jersey, each of which waives the fees for a maximum of four credit hours per year. Another waives a fee of $5.00, which pays for two semester-hours of credit. One waives a fee of $10.00 on extension courses only; and one a fee of $10.00 for three semester-hours of college credit.

To discover the extent to which off-campus schools are subsidized financially, officials of the teachers colleges were asked to estimate the percentage—whether 0, 25, 50, 75, or 100 respectively—of certain items of expense which their institutions pay. Table LVIII exhibits a summary of the replies. Sixty-one of the sixty-nine institutions paid some part of one or more items which are listed in the table. Eight of the remaining nine paid a part of the expense but did not express it in terms of percentages, so that sixty-eight of the sixty-nine institutions contributed financially to the support of the cooperating off-campus schools.

An examination of the table indicates that payments are more often made for instructional expense than for buildings, equip-

## TABLE LVIII

*Number of Institutions Paying Percent of Various Items of Expense as Compensation to Off-Campus Laboratory Schools, as Estimated by Officials of the Institutions, 1934–35*

| Item of Expense | 0% | 25% | 50% | 75% | 100% | Total Number |
|---|---|---|---|---|---|---|
| Buildings | 5 | 2 | 1 | | | 8 |
| Grounds | 5 | | 1 | 1 | | 7 |
| Equipment | 5 | 5 | 3 | 1 | 1 | 15 |
| Supplies | 5 | 6 | 2 | 3 | 1 | 17 |
| Textbooks | 5 | 6 | | 1 | | 12 |
| Light and power | 5 | 1 | 1 | | | 7 |
| Heat | 5 | 1 | 1 | | | 7 |
| Salary of: | | | | | | |
| Janitor | 5 | 2 | 1 | 1 | 1 | 10 |
| Superintendent | 7 | 9 | 2 | 1 | 4 | 23 |
| Principal | 8 | 5 | 3 | 2 | 5 | 23 |
| Transportation of training school pupils | 5 | 1 | 2 | | 4 | 12 |
| Salaries of critics | 9 | 26 | 9 | 7 | 6 | 57 |

| | |
|---|---|
| Number of institutions studied | 131 |
| Number of institutions having off-campus schools | 102 |
| Number of institutions reporting on this section | 69 |

ment, and maintenance. The item of expense paid most frequently, either in part or in full, is the salary of the supervisor. More than two-thirds (69.6 percent) of the institutions subsidized the school for this item. Next in order of frequency are the salaries of the principal and of the superintendent of schools. Seventeen institutions paid for supplies, and twelve for textbooks.

The percentage of the supervisor's or critic's salary which is paid by the teachers college is shown in Table LVIII, but not the method of making the payment. Four plans of payment are followed:

1. The college pays a flat lump sum to the cooperating school. Five institutions use this method, paying yearly sums of $25, $480, $700, $1,000, and $10,000 respectively. The last is in a large city where the student-teaching load is heavy.

2. The college pays a stated percentage of the salary of each critic or supervisor. Seventeen institutions employ this method, and the portion paid ranges from 5 to 100 percent. (This is to be distinguished from the sum given in Table LVIII, which is an estimate of the percentage paid, irrespective of whether the supervisor or the college is paid.) Five teachers colleges vary the percentages paid to supervisors in the different affiliated schools which they use.

3. The college pays each critic or supervisor a flat sum irrespective of the number of student-teachers which are supervised. Twenty-nine use this plan. The amount sometimes varies in elementary schools and high schools. One institution pays each elementary teacher $200, and each high school teacher $400. Another compensates the elementary teachers with $150, the high school teachers with $500. Still another pays the critic teachers in the classrooms $1,400, and the supervisors of the school $1,920. The sums range from $75 to $4,500.

4. The college pays the critic or supervisor on a per capita basis for each student-teacher supervised. Nineteen institutions employ this plan, paying from $1.00 a week to $400 a year per student. Eleven compensate on a yearly basis, paying from $15 to $100 per student. One pays $50 to $75 a semester; two, from $15 to $33 a quarter; two, $5.00 to $20 a month; and three, $1.00 to $2.00 a week.

In certain instances a single institution may employ more than one plan of payment within the institution. For example, one teachers college pays a fixed amount to each critic in the elementary schools, depending on the training and experience of the supervisor; a fixed amount per semester for each student-teacher securing his laboratory experience in the high school classes; and a flexible amount on an adjusted scale which depends on the number of student-teachers and the student's practice load in public elementary schools with a flexible program.

The compilations in Table LIX exhibit the relative expenditures of the teachers college for salaries of supervisors or critic teachers in campus and off-campus laboratory schools. The payments in seventy-six teachers colleges which use both campus and off-campus schools are given. For this group of institutions, 79.8 percent of the total salaries of the supervisors were paid in the campus schools and 20.2 percent for the supervisors in the off-campus schools.

TABLE LIX

*Total Expenditures for Salaries of Critics or Supervisors in State Normal Schools and Teachers Colleges Having Both On-Campus and Off-Campus Laboratory Schools, 1933–34*

| Geographic Division | No. of Institutions | | Expenditures | | |
|---|---|---|---|---|---|
| | Studied | Having Both Types of Schools | Campus Schools | Off-Campus Schools | Total |
| New England....... | 7 | 3 | $ 63,000.00 | $ 10,000.00 | $ 73,000.00 |
| Middle Atlantic..... | 22 | 18 | 347,354.71 | 79,219.57 | 426,574.28 |
| East North Central.. | 21 | 16 | 527,513.19 | 177,439.95 | 704,953.14 |
| West North Central.. | 24 | 14 | 282,219.76 | 60,147.26 | 342,367.02 |
| South Atlantic...... | 12 | 8 | 75,734.36 | 14,193.00 | 89,927.36 |
| East South Central.. | 10 | | | | |
| West South Central.. | 16 | 6 | 41,295.74 | 22,711.63 | 64,007.37 |
| Mountain........... | 8 | 4 | 75,843.92 | 1,000.00 | 76,843.92 |
| Pacific.............. | 11 | 7 | 121,171.13 | 23,646.66 | 144,817.79 |
| Total............... | 131 | 76 | $1,534,132.81 | $388,358.07 | $1,922,490.88 |
| Percent............ | 100.0 | 58.0 | 79.8 | 20.2 | 100.0 |

Reference to Table XXVI (see page 85), which shows the relative amounts of teaching done in campus and off-campus schools and comparison of this table with Table LIX, indicate that student-teaching is furnished in off-campus schools at considerable saving in cost per student, so far as the salaries of supervisors are concerned. Table XXVI shows that some students do a part of their student-teaching in campus schools, and the remainder in off-campus schools. Assuming that the amount is equal in each, one-half of 15.2 percent, 7.6 percent, should be added to 33.7 percent, the relative number doing student-teaching in off-campus schools, making 41.3 percent of the total laboratory experience which is provided in the off-campus schools, whereas the cost

(Table LIX) is only 20.2 percent of the total cost for supervisors. Of course the campus laboratory school performs some other services which are not possible in the off-campus school, but with all due allowance for these factors, it is probable that there is still a considerable saving made by using the off-campus school for laboratory teaching.

A comparison of these tables (XXVI and LIX) for the different geographic divisions reveals marked differences between different sections. For example, in the Mountain Division $75,843.92 is paid to critics in campus schools, $1,000.00 (1.3 percent) to critics in off-campus schools, and in that same division 49.1 percent of all student-teaching is done in off-campus schools and 19.3 percent is done by students each of whom receives a part of his experience in each type. In the South Atlantic Division, where a negligible number of students divide their experience between campus and off-campus schools, 48.2 percent of the student-teaching is furnished in off-campus schools, whereas the salaries of the supervisors in them are 15.7 percent of the total for all supervisors. The differentials in cost are less in the East North Central and West South Central Divisions, in the latter the cost being approximately equal in both types of school on the basis of the service which is rendered.

Similar comparisons can be made for the year 1937–38. Table LX shows the relative payments which were made. The salaries of supervisors in the campus schools were 76.0 percent of the total; in off-campus schools, 24.0 percent. Reference to Table XXVII indicates that 52.8 percent of the students did their student-teaching in campus schools, 35.0 percent in off-campus schools, and 12.2 percent partly in each. In the institutions in the South Atlantic Division 52.5 percent of the student-teaching was done in campus schools, and 5.2 percent was divided between the campus and off-campus schools. The payments to supervisors in off-campus schools were 17.8 percent of the total amount paid to supervisors in all laboratory schools. During the four years from 1933–34 to 1937–38 there was some tendency to pay more adequately for the service in off-campus schools in proportion to the amount of laboratory experience they furnished, the proportionate amount paid to the off-campus supervisors being increased.

There was, however, a small decrease in the amount of service they rendered, as measured by the number of students who completed a course in student-teaching under their direction.

TABLE LX

*Total Expenditures for Salaries of Critics or Supervisors in State Normal Schools and Teachers Colleges Having Both On-Campus and Off-Campus Laboratory Schools, 1937–38*

| Geographic Division | No. of Institutions Studied | Having Both Types of Schools | Expenditures Campus Schools | Off-Campus Schools | Total |
|---|---|---|---|---|---|
| New England....... | 15 | 7 | $ 181,236.00 | $ 19,839.00 | $ 201,075.00 |
| Middle Atlantic..... | 27 | 20 | 451,907.78 | 104,520.90 | 556,428.68 |
| East North Central.. | 20 | 18 | 634,117.22 | 291,542.52 | 925,659.74 |
| West North Central.. | 23 | 9 | 186,778.76 | 57,181.69 | 243,960.45 |
| South Atlantic...... | 15 | 7 | 89,481.00 | 19,369.00 | 108,850.00 |
| East South Central.. | 10 | 3 | 23,541.86 | 5,200.00 | 28,741.86 |
| West South Central.. | 12 | 5 | 88,192.27 | 27,535.96 | 115,728.23 |
| Mountain........... | 6 | | | | |
| Pacific............. | 9 | 8 | 126,718.34 | 36,105.05 | 162,823.39 |
| Total.............. | 137 | 77 | $1,781,973.23 | $561,294.12 | $2,343,267.35 |
| Percent........... | 100.0 | 56.2 | 76.0 | 24.0 | 100.0 |

TUITION FEES PAID BY PUPILS IN THE LABORATORY SCHOOLS

A portion of the expense of the campus laboratory school is met by receipts from tuition charged to pupils who attend. Table LXI exhibits amounts which were collected from this source. Of the seventy-five institutions which replied to this item in the questionnaire, twenty-five make a tuition charge to pupils in campus schools, one to pupils in off-campus schools. In only one institution in the Middle Atlantic Division is a tuition charge made. Considering the number of institutions and student-teachers involved, the charges are higher in New England than in other sections of the country, the average total tuition received by each of the five institutions being $12,283.20. One institution stated that it received $50,000 in tuition. In two divisions, the East South Central and West South Central, no institution made tuition

TABLE LXI

*Total Tuition Fees Paid by Pupils in Laboratory Schools in State Normal Schools and Teachers Colleges Having Both On-Campus and Off-Campus Laboratory Schools, 1933–34*

| Geographic Division | No. of Institutions Studied | No. of Institutions Having Both Types of Schools | Tuition Fees Campus Schools | Tuition Fees Off-Campus Schools | Tuition Fees Total |
|---|---|---|---|---|---|
| New England....... | 7 | 5 | $ 61,416.00 | | $ 61,416.00 |
| Middle Atlantic..... | 22 | 17 | 41,513.19 | $5,725.00 | 47,238.19 |
| East North Central.. | 21 | 17 | 33,105.24 | | 33,105.24 |
| West North Central.. | 24 | 14 | 23,453.79 | | 23,453.79 |
| South Atlantic...... | 12 | 7 | 9,251.34 | | 9,251.34 |
| East South Central.. | 10 | 1 | | | |
| West South Central.. | 16 | 4 | | | |
| Mountain........... | 8 | 5 | 21,733.60 | | 21,733.60 |
| Pacific............. | 11 | 5 | 1,500.00 | | 1,500.00 |
| Total.............. | 131 | 75 | $191,973.16 | $5,725.00 | $197,698.16 |
| Percent........... | 100.0 | 57.3 | 97.1 | 2.9 | 100.0 |

charges to pupils. Only one institution in the Pacific Division charges tuition, the amount collected being $1,500.

Table LXII indicates the amount of tuition which was received in 1937–38. No institution made any charge of tuition to pupils in off-campus schools, the institution which did so in 1933–34 having discontinued the practice. Thirty-three institutions of the 77 replying made a tuition charge in the campus school in 1937–38. Two received more than $50,000 each in tuition, one located in the New England Division and one in the East North Central Division. The total amounts received by institutions from this source range from $133.00 to $52,677.39. All geographic divisions

## TABLE LXII

*Total Tuition Fees Paid by Pupils in Laboratory Schools in State Normal Schools and Teachers Colleges Having Both On-Campus and Off-Campus Laboratory Schools, 1937–38*

| Geographic Division | No. of Institutions Studied | Having Both Types of Schools | Campus Schools | Off-Campus Schools* | Total |
|---|---|---|---|---|---|
| New England | 15 | 6 | $ 59,477.39 | | $ 59,477.39 |
| Middle Atlantic | 27 | 19 | 28,829.50 | | 28,829.50 |
| East North Central | 20 | 17 | 120,902.34 | | 120,902.34 |
| West North Central | 23 | 11 | 22,392.04 | | 22,392.04 |
| South Atlantic | 15 | 8 | 5,735.00 | | 5,735.00 |
| East South Central | 10 | 3 | 2,524.95 | | 2,524.95 |
| West South Central | 12 | 5 | 4,644.00 | | 4,644.00 |
| Mountain | 6 | 2 | 6,179.00 | | 6,179.00 |
| Pacific | 9 | 6 | 2,930.00 | | 2,930.00 |
| Total | 137 | 77 | $253,614.22 | | $253,614.22 |
| Percent | 100.0 | 56.2 | 100.0 | | 100.0 |

* No institution made any charge.

include one or more institutions which charge pupils tuition, and there seems to be no greater tendency to charge tuition in one division than in another. The total sum collected in the East North Central Division increased greatly (265.2 percent) over that of 1933–34, but $78,060.00 of this is received by two institutions which reported tuition received in 1937–38 but did not do so in 1933–34. Thirty-six institutions reported for each of the two periods. Of these, fourteen which charged tuition in 1933–34 did so in 1937–38; seven discontinued the tuition charges; fifteen which charged no tuition in 1933–34 did so in 1937–38. There is a trend in the direction of charging a tuition fee. Institutions establishing a charge during the four years are found in six of the nine geographic divisions. The policy of charging tuition in laboratory schools is undesirable, as it tends to make them selective institutions. Because a policy of charging tuition is being begun at a time when the general movement in the country is toward democratizing educational opportunity by giving free tuition and by awarding scholarships and grants-in-aid, it seems particularly undesirable. This condition may be a temporary one which can perhaps be attributed to financial stringency during the period studied.

## LEGAL AND CONTRACTUAL RELATIONSHIPS BETWEEN THE TEACHERS COLLEGE AND OFF-CAMPUS SCHOOLS

To prepare teachers effectively it is necessary for the normal school or teachers college to have at its disposal sufficient off-campus laboratory schools to supplement and complement the campus schools, if the latter alone cannot provide facilities adequate for the institution's needs. So important this is, that Learned and Bagley[107] declare that communities which include teachers colleges should be required to allow the teachers college to use the public schools for laboratory purposes as a condition of retaining the institution.

The problem involved is shown by the legislation which is found on the statute books of a considerable number of states. Some typical laws are quoted in Appendix B (p. 248), to show the range and diversity of the laws and the main items which they include. In general they relate to the following subjects: authority to contract for the use of laboratory schools; provisions for making laboratory schools mandatory for the teachers college and making it mandatory for communities to furnish them; establishing laboratory schools as a part of the public school system; the financial obligations of the teachers college and the school districts; the question of joint administration and control between the teachers college and the boards of education; the transportation of student-teachers; and the authorization of student-teachers to instruct without holding legal teachers' certificates.

Various aspects of legislation have been studied by Mead,[108] Good,[109] and Edwards.[110] Judicial decisions affecting student-

---
[107] Learned and Bagley, op. cit., p. 193.
[108] A. R. Mead, Supervised Student-Teaching, pp. 681–753. 1930.
[109] H. G. Good, "The Legal Status of Practice Teaching." National Society of College Teachers of Education, Educational Monographs, No. IX, pp. 13–17. 1920.
[110] Newton Edwards, The Courts and the Public Schools, pp. 124–131. 1933.

teaching have been made in the states of New York, Arizona, Illinois, Iowa, North Dakota, Washington, and West Virginia. They have covered various aspects of the use of public schools as laboratory schools. Edwards concludes that, as a result of his study of the decisions, certain facts stand out:

Where a board of education is vested by statute with broad powers and discretion in the conduct and management of schools, it may, as an exercise of its authority to determine the course of study, maintain a model school for the use of normal-school students. Students doing practice teaching in the public schools are not required to have teachers' certificates. Employment of practice teachers is merely a variation in the mode of instruction, a matter which falls wholly within the discretion of the school authorities.[111]

The decisions further show that a board of education may not delegate its authority to control the practice-school facilities. It cannot, therefore, delegate its authority to the teachers college to select the teachers of the training school, determine the course of study or mode of instruction, or decide the time when the school term shall begin and end. It is permissible, however, for the school board and the normal school to pay the salaries of supervisors in whose rooms student-teaching is done.

It is not the purpose of the writer to make an elaborate study of the legal aspects of student-teaching. The situation in particular states is determined by the provisions of the state constitution, the legislation establishing the public schools, the powers granted to state boards of education, and other limiting factors. The decisions of the courts in the different states are dependent upon the whole legal and constitutional structure of the state. Too few decisions have been made on the different aspects of contractual relationships to be a sure guide for action. Lacking definite judicial decisions, the teachers colleges are free to follow the provisions of the state laws, on the assumption that they are constitutional until judicial decisions indicate otherwise.

Of considerable importance to the whole structure of laboratory schools, and the power of voluntary non-state associations such as the American Association of Teachers Colleges, is a decision of the United States Circuit Court of Appeals in a suit brought by

[111] *Ibid.*, p. 125.

Governor Langer of North Dakota to restrain the North Central Association from dropping the North Dakota Agricultural College from the accredited list of the Association. The decision of the court was that it was within the power of the Association to fix its own conditions of membership and promulgate regulations for such membership, especially in view of the fact that the opportunity for review and appeal is provided by means of the administrative machinery within the Association itself and an institution which believes it is unjustly treated can find recourse by appeal within the Association.[112] Applying the terms of this decision to the teachers college field, it is within the power of the American Association of Teachers Colleges to determine the standards for the laboratory school, and a member of the Association has no recourse at law if the Association should decide to withdraw accrediting from it, provided the Association gives in its administrative procedures an opportunity for appeal within the Association itself. In view of this decision it would be wise for the Association to provide definite machinery for an institution to appeal from the decision of its Committee on Standards.

Within the limits permitted by the legal structure of the states concerned, it is desirable for the teachers college to exercise considerable control over the laboratory schools, and particularly over those aspects which determine the success of student-teaching. Learned and Bagley[113] suggest that the teachers college should have definite control of the training school facilities since a plan of dual control by the teachers college and board of education is difficult to administer. Others approve a policy of joint control by the teachers college and the board. Evenden[114] recommends that institutions have enough control "to assign and supervise the work of student teachers." Foster[115] thinks that the teachers colleges should have sufficient control of the laboratory schools "to approve the teachers with whom students are placed, determine

---

[112] A. W. Clevenger, "A Review of the Governor Langer Suit." *The North Central Association Quarterly*, Vol. 13, pp. 505–517, April, 1939.

[113] Learned and Bagley, *loc. cit.*, p. 193.

[114] E. S. Evenden, "Findings of the National Survey of the Education of Teachers: Implications for the Improvement of Current Practice." *Twelfth Yearbook of the American Association of Teachers Colleges*, p. 114. 1933.

[115] Foster, *loc. cit.*, p. 400.

the assignments of students, and modify the curriculum and the methods of instruction in the schools."

In view of the legislation and court decisions in the various states, a policy of cooperation and joint control is indicated. Actually, few teachers colleges exercise exclusive control over the public schools which are affiliated with them for laboratory purposes. Table LXIII contains the replies from teachers colleges at two different periods. It is indicated that few teachers colleges

TABLE LXIII

*Number of State Normal Schools and Teachers Colleges Having Exclusive Control of Some Off-Campus Laboratory School, 1933–34 and 1937–38*

|  | 1933–34 | 1937–38 |
|---|---|---|
| Number of institutions reporting. | 82 | 80 |
| Number having exclusive control. | 5 | 8 |
| Number not having exclusive control. | 77 | 72 |

have entire control of the off-campus laboratory schools. A study of the different geographic divisions indicates no regional trend in this respect. There are several marked exceptions. In one instance an institution has complete control of a rural consolidated school for a period of twenty-five years, according to the terms of a written contract entered into between the institution and the board of education of the school district.

AGREEMENTS AND CONTRACTS WITH OFF-CAMPUS SCHOOLS

An analysis of the types of agreement which are in effect between teachers colleges and off-campus schools was made from replies to the questionnaire used as a basis for this study. There are three general types: verbal agreement, written memorandum of minutes of the board of education, and formal written contract.

To learn to what extent the institutions represented had written contracts with cooperating schools the direct question was asked: "Do you have a written contract with the boards of education of cooperating schools?" A similar question was asked regarding a memorandum from the board of education. Two tables

## TABLE LXIV

*Number of State Normal Schools and Teachers Colleges Having Written Agreements with Boards of Education of Off-Campus Laboratory Schools, 1934-35*

| Geographic Divisions | No. of Institutions Studied | No. of Institutions Reporting | Written Contract | Memorandum from Board | Written Contract or Memorandum* | Total |
|---|---|---|---|---|---|---|
| New England.......  | 7 | 7 | 5 | | | 5 |
| Middle Atlantic..... | 22 | 20 | 7 | 1 | | 8 |
| East North Central.. | 21 | 20 | 5 | 4 | 2 | 11 |
| West North Central.. | 24 | 16 | 7 | 3 | | 10 |
| South Atlantic...... | 12 | 11 | 3 | | | 3 |
| East South Central.. | 10 | 2 | | | | |
| West South Central.. | 16 | 9 | 6 | 1 | | 7 |
| Mountain........... | 8 | 6 | 1 | | | 1 |
| Pacific............. | 11 | 11 | 3 | 3 | | 6 |
| Total.............. | 131 | 102 | 37 | 12 | 2 | 51 |

* Institutions reported in this column have written contracts with some schools, memoranda with others.

were constructed from the replies which were received, Table LXIV for the year 1934-35 and Table LXV covering the year 1937-38. In the former table it is indicated that fifty-one institutions, exactly half of those replying, had either written contracts or memoranda from the board of education. Thirty-seven had formal written contracts and two additional had written contracts with certain of their off-campus schools, a total of thirty-nine which had written contracts with one or more schools. The differences in the various geographic divisions are indicated in the table. In 1937-38 (Table LXV) the total number having some form of written agreement decreased from 50 percent to 46.6 percent. Thirty-six institutions employed written contracts with all of the off-campus schools, four with part of them, a total of forty, each of which employed written contracts in their relationships with one or more cooperating schools. In 1924-25 and 1929-30

## TABLE LXV

*Number of State Normal Schools and Teachers Colleges Having Written Agreements with Boards of Education of Off-Campus Laboratory Schools, 1937-38*

| Geographic Division | No. of Institutions Studied | Reporting | Written Contract | Memorandum from Board | Written Contract or Memorandum* | Total |
|---|---|---|---|---|---|---|
| New England....... | 15 | 10 | 5 | 1 | | 6 |
| Middle Atlantic..... | 27 | 25 | 5 | 1 | 1 | 7 |
| East North Central.. | 20 | 17 | 7 | 1 | 1 | 9 |
| West North Central.. | 23 | 14 | 8 | | | 8 |
| South Atlantic...... | 15 | 12 | 3 | | 1 | 4 |
| East South Central.. | 10 | 4 | 1 | | | 1 |
| West South Central.. | 12 | 7 | 2 | 2 | 1 | 5 |
| Mountain........... | 6 | 5 | 3 | 1 | | 4 |
| Pacific............. | 9 | 9 | 2 | 2 | | 4 |
| Total.............. | 137 | 103 | 36 | 8 | 4 | 48 |

* Institutions reported in this column have written contracts with some schools, memoranda with others.

data were secured by the writer to show the number of institutions which then used formal written contracts. Table LXVI indicates that there was a trend through a period of fourteen years toward employing a written contract as a form of agreement with cooperating schools.

In addition to stating whether they entered into a formal written contract with the board of education or had a written memorandum from the board, institutions were asked to make a detailed analysis of the type of agreement they had with each of their off-campus laboratory schools. Fewer institutions replied to this more detailed statement, but still there were eighty-seven which gave data in 1934-35 and eighty-four in 1937-38. A compilation of the answers for both academic years is presented in Table LXVII. Here the analysis is made in terms of the number of individual off-campus laboratory schools concerned instead of by institutions. Accordingly, the percentages of this table do not agree with those of Tables LXIV to LXVI. One teachers college may use ten or more off-campus schools, with which it has various types of agreement; another, a single off-campus school. When an informal verbal agreement is made, it is usually with the superintendent of schools of the town or city rather than with the board of education or other school officials. This table corre-

TABLE LXVI

*Number and Percent of Schools Making Formal Contracts in State Normal Schools and Teachers Colleges, 1924–38*

| Academic Year | Number of Institutions | Number with Formal Contracts | Percent with Formal Contracts |
|---|---|---|---|
| 1924–25 | 117 | 29 | 24.8 |
| 1929–30 | 112 | 32 | 28.6 |
| 1934–35 | 102 | 39* | 32.8 |
| 1937–38 | 103 | 40* | 38.8 |

* In 1934–35 two, and in 1937–38 four of the teachers colleges, had written contracts with some off-campus schools, written memoranda from others.

sponds with those preceding in showing that the relative number of agreements by written memoranda or minutes of the board of education is becoming fewer, having decreased almost 50 percent in the three-year interval indicated. On the other hand, the relative number both of verbal agreements and of formal written contracts has increased. The usual parties to the contract are the board of education and the teachers college, although in a number of instances the contracting parties are the state board of education or state department of education and the school board of the district. In Table LXVI it is indicated that the number of institutions which make written contracts with the authorities in charge of off-campus schools is increasing. When the individual off-campus schools rather than institutions are considered, the same trend is evident.

The trend toward definite written contracts is in accord with the opinion of a number of students of the problems of the labora-

## TABLE LXVII

*Type of Agreement Between State Normal Schools and Teachers Colleges and Local School Authorities for Use of Off-Campus Laboratory Schools, 1934–35 and 1937–38**

| Type of Agreement | Number of Laboratory Schools 1934–35 | Number of Laboratory Schools 1937–38 | Percent of Laboratory Schools 1934–35 | Percent of Laboratory Schools 1937–38 |
|---|---|---|---|---|
| **Verbal, with:** | | | | |
| Board of education | | 8 | | 1.9 |
| Superintendent of schools | 154 | 198 | 42.5 | 45.7 |
| Principal of school | 17 | 17 | 4.7 | 3.9 |
| Teachers | 5 | 13 | 1.4 | 3.0 |
| Total | 176 | 236 | 48.6 | 54.5 |
| **Written memorandum or minutes of the board of education** | 88 | 54 | 24.3 | 12.5 |
| Total | 88 | 54 | 24.3 | 12.5 |
| **Written contract:** | | | | |
| Teachers college with local board of education | 75 | 111 | 20.7 | 25.6 |
| State office of education with local board of education | 22 | 32 | 6.1 | 7.4 |
| Teachers college with state welfare department | 1 | | .3 | |
| Total | 98 | 143 | 27.1 | 33.0 |
| Grand total | 362 | 433 | 100.0 | 100.0 |
| Number of teachers colleges reporting—1934–35 | | | | 87 |
| Number of teachers colleges reporting—1937–38 | | | | 84 |

* Each off-campus school is considered a separate unit in compiling this table.

tory school. Baugher,[116] Jarman,[117] Henderson,[118] and Peik[119] agree in recommending formal written agreements. On the other hand, the president of a teachers college who has had long and varied contact with the problems involved in teacher education believes

[116] Jacob I. Baugher, *Organization and Administration of Practice-Teaching in Privately Endowed Colleges of Liberal Arts*, p. 92. 1931.
[117] Jarman, *op. cit.*, p. 129.
[118] Henderson, *op. cit.*, p. 111.
[119] Peik, in *National Survey of the Education of Teachers*, Vol. III, *op. cit.*, p. 270.

that a simple resolution of the board of education which leaves the administrative details in the hands of executive officers is preferable because it allows greater freedom of action. He finds that definite contracts "are almost certain to cause trouble." On the whole, however, sentiment favors the more formal agreement. Whether or not a written contract is restrictive and inflexible, and thereby works a hardship on either party, will depend upon its terms and the spirit in which it is enforced.

The written contract has the following advantages:

1. It provides an agreement binding on both parties.
2. It clarifies and defines the functions and powers of the teachers college and the cooperating schools.
3. It assures that facilities will be available for a definite period, and that a program of student-teaching will not be disrupted suddenly and, perhaps, with little warning.
4. It enables the institution to plan the curriculum, equipment, and supervisory personnel over a relatively long period, thereby making it possible to have a continuous, long-range program.
5. It removes the dangers of upheavals due to political campaigns.
6. It prevents community interference under the stress of temporary emotional excitement in the community.
7. It gives *status* to the cooperating school and to the supervisors in it.
8. It gives an opportunity to build superior school morale, since the program can be planned more definitely and for a longer period of time.
9. It provides conditions which make for ease of administration, and make unnecessary frequent disrupting changes in administrative routine.

While these advantages may be secured through informal agreements, it is less likely that they will be. For these reasons the trend toward greater use of the written contract seems desirable and one which should be extended. Too few institutions have the stabilization which would result from a more definite and better clarified contractual relationship.

A cooperative attitude will be more likely if the terms of the contract are mutually helpful to the teachers college and the cooperating schools, if there is sufficient time given to discussion and consideration of its terms, if the cooperation of the administrative and teaching staff is secured in advance, if the contract is not entered upon unless it has strong support in the community, if the parents are encouraged to learn to know the student-teachers, if the schools secure better teachers and supervisors and higher class instruction as a result of the cooperative arrangement, if the student-teaching load is not too large, if student-teachers who are incapable are withdrawn from teaching, if there is careful selection of student-teachers, if the teachers in the local schools who serve as supervisors are compensated for their service, and if it is shown by tests and otherwise that the opportunities of pupils are not impaired by the arrangement.

In 1937–38 twenty-five of the forty institutions which stated that they had written contracts with one or more cooperating schools furnished copies which have been analyzed to discover the items which they contained, the results being shown in Table LXVIII. Thirty-five main items are included, of which only six are found in 50 percent or more of the contracts. They are: the effective date of the contract, its duration, the delegation of administrative and supervisory responsibility, the quality of the instruction, the methods by which supervisors are chosen, and the compensation which supervisors receive.

Mead[120] advocates a short-term contract. Because it gives an opportunity to have the matter thoroughly considered before the agreement is renewed, he thinks it is better to make a contract of only one or two years' duration. Peik,[121] on the other hand, expresses the opinion that, because it helps to stabilize the situation, a long-term contract covering five years or more is desirable, in which "the obligations, responsibilities, and duties of each party are specified and provisions for superior critic teachers and adequate supervision are specifically drawn up."

There is a great variety in almost all provisions. In none is this more marked than in the duration of the agreements, and the provisions for terminating them. Eleven contracts are for a single

---

[120] A. R. Mead, *Supervised Student-Teaching*, p. 805. 1930.
[121] Peik, in *National Survey of the Education of Teachers*, Vol. III, *loc. cit.*, p. 270.

## TABLE LXVIII

*Analysis of Twenty-five Written Contracts Providing for the Use of Laboratory Schools by State Normal Schools and Teachers Colleges*

|  | No. of Institutions |
|---|---|
| I. The Contract | |
|     1. Date when effective | 25 |
|     2. Duration | 25 |
|     3. Method of termination | 10 |
|     4. Reference to legal authority for contracting | 6 |
|     5. Protection of state official signing from personal liability | 1 |
| II. Calendar of schools identical with that of the teachers college | 6 |
| III. Definitions and boundaries of school districts containing laboratory schools | 3 |
| IV. Administration and Supervision | |
|     1. Administrative and supervisory control and responsibility | 15 |
|     2. Rules and regulations | 6 |
|     3. Curriculum | 6 |
|     4. Selection of textbooks | 4 |
|     5. Quality of instruction | 13 |
|     6. Special subjects of instruction such as music and art | 3 |
|     7. Critics and supervisors | |
|         *a*. Qualifications | 6 |
|         *b*. Method of selection and employing | 16 |
|         *c*. Promotion | 1 |
|         *d*. Dismissal | 2 |
|         *e*. Compensation | 13 |
|     8. Student teachers | |
|         *a*. Qualifications | 1 |
|         *b*. Restrictions on numbers | 8 |
|         *c*. Compensation | 1 |
| V. Financial Provisions | |
|     1. Subsidies for salaries for administration | 6 |
|     2. Subsidies for salaries of critics and supervisors | 5 |
|     3. Housing | 8 |
|     4. Maintenance of buildings | 11 |
|     5. Equipment | 7 |
|     6. Supplies for student-teachers | 4 |
|     7. Supplies for pupils | 7 |
|     8. Janitorial service | 8 |
|     9. Transportation of pupils | 1 |
|     10. Transportation of student-teachers | 2 |
|     11. Tuition charges to pupils | 2 |
|     12. Compensation to school district by college | 8 |
|     13. Compensation to college by school district | 3 |
| VI. Summer Session | 4 |

year, four for two years, one for ten years; and nine are indefinite in duration. No provision is made for cancellation or termination of the contract when it is made for a single year. Of the two-year contracts two have no provisions for cancellation, but look toward renewal, one making it "subject to an annual renewal thereafter at the discretion of the two parties concerned," the other "with full intent to and purpose to renew the contract at the time of expiration for a period of two years with such alterations and additions as experience may indicate as advisable." Two others in force for two years are subject to cancellation, in one case by written notice five months before its expiration date, in the other by notice at any time. The ten-year contract cannot be revoked prior to two years from its effective date and then only on notice given before April 10th of the year in which the change is to be made.

In nine of the contracts the terms are indefinite. Two communities which have teachers colleges located in them are required by the state laws to provide laboratory schools for the teachers colleges. The schools of one of these have been used for laboratory purposes continuously since 1896. The other requires a two-year notice for abrogation of the contract, although it may be terminated at any time by mutual agreement. Of the remaining seven contracts, one provides for termination upon six months' notice; one upon a notice of nine months; two, one year; one, two years; and another, three years, although the last may be abrogated at any time by mutual consent of the contracting parties. One institution has a contract of indefinite duration which has no provision for discontinuing it.

Six contracts provide that the calendar of the off-campus school shall coincide, as nearly as possible, with the calendar of the teachers college. The definition of administrative and supervisory control and responsibility is a major concern, and a number of the contracts have this responsibility clearly defined. Four specifically fix the responsibility for the selection of textbooks, two stating that they shall be the same as in other schools of the district; one, that they shall be equal in quality to others; and one, that the board of education and the state board of education jointly shall determine the textbooks which shall be used.

In eleven of the sixteen contracts which provide for the method of selecting and employing supervisors, eight make provision for joint action by the teachers college and the officials of the local public schools; three, for election by the teachers college. In one of the latter the stipulation is made that the teachers who act as supervisors must fully meet the requirements for the supervisors in the campus school of the teachers college. The method of determining the compensation is stated in thirteen of the twenty-five contracts, sometimes on a fixed basis, sometimes on a percentage basis.

From the data the conclusion can be drawn that the contractual relationships are on a temporary and unstable basis, and that long-range planning is impossible in developing a superior curriculum, securing skilled and properly prepared supervisors, furnishing adequate library facilities and equipment, and developing creative community spirit conducive to the most effective student-teaching until such time as a more permanent policy can be placed in operation.

Table LXVIII identifies the elements which may well be considered by the administrators of teachers colleges in drawing up contracts with boards of education for the use of laboratory schools. In Appendix C (p. 252) a group of six typical contracts executed by teachers colleges are printed. They represent varying forms, subject matter, and complexity.

## THE ATTITUDES OF INDIVIDUALS AND GROUPS TOWARD THE USE OF PUBLIC SCHOOLS AS LABORATORY SCHOOLS

In 1933–34 the institutions of thirty-four states reported that the state departments of education were favorable to the use of public schools as laboratory schools; in two the state departments took no definite stand on the matter. There were no replies to the question in the other states which maintain teachers colleges. In 1937–38, ninety-six institutions reported thirty-six state departments favorable, two taking no definite stand, and one not favorable to their use for this purpose.

The institutions were asked to check the attitudes of certain persons in the communities toward the use of the public schools as off-campus laboratory schools, whether hostile, indifferent, or favorable. The replies are set forth in Table LXIX. By far the greater percentage of the six groups represented in the answers had a favorable attitude. The superintendents, principals, and teachers were generally favorable; the boards of education less so; and the pupils and parents were either indifferent or hostile in 20.2 percent and 24.3 percent, respectively, of the cases reported. This is a considerable percentage. Steps should be taken by the institutions to modify this attitude which interferes with the most favorable operation of the schools.

TABLE LXIX

*Number of Institutions Reporting Attitudes of Certain Individuals and Groups Toward the Use of Cooperating Laboratory Schools by State Normal Schools and Teachers Colleges, 1933–34*

| Individual or Group | No. of Institutions Reporting | Hostile No. | % | Indifferent No. | % | Favorable No. | % |
|---|---|---|---|---|---|---|---|
| Superintendents of schools............ | 96 | 1 | 1.0 | 3 | 3.1 | 92 | 95.8 |
| Principals of schools... | 97 | | | 4 | 4.1 | 93 | 95.9 |
| Teachers of schools.... | 95 | | | 5 | 5.3 | 90 | 94.7 |
| Parents of pupils..... | 99 | 5 | 5.1 | 19 | 19.2 | 75 | 75.7 |
| Pupils of the schools... | 94 | 2 | 2.1 | 17 | 18.1 | 75 | 79.8 |
| Boards of education... | 98 | 1 | 1.0 | 12 | 12.3 | 85 | 86.7 |

KIND AND DEGREE OF DIFFICULTY ENCOUNTERED IN THE USE OF OFF-CAMPUS SCHOOLS

The officials of the teachers colleges were asked to indicate the type and amount of difficulty which were encountered in employing the off-campus schools as laboratory schools. Tables LXX and LXXI summarize the results for 1933–34 and 1937–38 respectively. Any analysis of the last two columns of Table LXX shows that conflicts with college schedules are the most frequent source of difficulty, only 31.3 percent reporting that there was no difficulty here. In 1937–38 an even greater number of institutions report difficulty of this type. When the off-campus school is so far removed that it requires considerable time to reach it, and when the daily schedule of the college and the off-campus laboratory schools do not synchronize, especially in the instance of high school classes, difficulties often arise. It improves the situation greatly if the student-teachers can have their schedules arranged

TABLE LXX

*Number and Percent of Institutions Reporting Degree and Kind of Difficulty Encountered in Using Off-Campus Schools as Laboratory Schools, 1933–34*

| Kind of Difficulty | No. of Replies on Each Item | Institutions Reporting Difficulty |||||
|---|---|---|---|---|---|---|---|
| | | Much ||  Little || None ||
| | | No. | % | No. | % | No. | % |
| Inadequate school buildings.......... | 95 | 17 | 17.9 | 32 | 33.7 | 46 | 48.4 |
| Local teachers are poorly prepared as supervisors......... | 91 | 16 | 17.6 | 42 | 46.1 | 33 | 36.3 |
| Difficulty of supervision by college teachers and supervisors.. | 99 | 15 | 15.2 | 41 | 41.4 | 43 | 43.4 |
| Time consumed by student-teachers in travel............. | 97 | 12 | 12.3 | 49 | 50.5 | 36 | 37.1 |
| Insufficient control by teachers college..... | 95 | 12 | 12.6 | 42 | 44.2 | 41 | 43.2 |
| Conflicts with the college schedule....... | 99 | 10 | 10.1 | 58 | 58.6 | 31 | 31.3 |
| Securing means of transportation for student-teachers.... | 96 | 10 | 10.4 | 26 | 27.1 | 60 | 62.5 |
| Poor cooperation of local school administrators............. | 92 | 3 | 3.3 | 23 | 25.0 | 66 | 71.7 |
| Objections of the community............ | 97 | 2 | 2.1 | 43 | 44.3 | 52 | 53.6 |
| Legal difficulties...... | 95 | 2 | 2.1 | 5 | 5.3 | 88 | 92.6 |
| Objections of student-teachers........... | 96 | 2 | 2.1 | 22 | 22.9 | 72 | 75.0 |
| Number of institutions to which questionnaire was sent...... | 131 | | | | | | |

so that at least one-half of the day is free for their student-teaching.

In 1933–34 almost two-thirds (63.7 percent) of the institutions had more or less difficulty in securing effective supervision of

### TABLE LXXI
*Number and Percent of Institutions Reporting Degree and Kind of Difficulty Encountered in Using Off-Campus Schools as Laboratory Schools, 1937–38*

| Kind of Difficulty | No. of Replies on Each Item | Much No. | Much % | Little No. | Little % | None No. | None % |
|---|---|---|---|---|---|---|---|
| Local teachers are poorly prepared as supervisors............ | 94 | 16 | 17.0 | 39 | 41.5 | 39 | 41.5 |
| Difficulty of supervision by college teachers and supervisors.. | 100 | 15 | 15.0 | 44 | 44.0 | 41 | 41.0 |
| Conflicts with college schedule............ | 101 | 12 | 11.9 | 59 | 58.4 | 30 | 29.7 |
| Insufficient control by teachers college..... | 98 | 12 | 12.2 | 46 | 46.9 | 40 | 40.8 |
| Time consumed by student-teachers in travel............... | 97 | 10 | 10.3 | 45 | 46.4 | 42 | 43.3 |
| Inadequate school buildings........... | 96 | 8 | 8.3 | 30 | 31.3 | 58 | 60.4 |
| Securing means of transportation for student-teachers.... | 99 | 7 | 7.1 | 24 | 24.2 | 68 | 68.7 |
| Poor cooperation of local school administrators............ | 97 | 2 | 2.0 | 22 | 22.7 | 73 | 75.3 |
| Objections of student-teachers............ | 98 | 2 | 2.0 | 19 | 19.4 | 77 | 78.6 |
| Objections of the community............ | 101 | 1 | 1.0 | 49 | 48.5 | 51 | 50.5 |
| Legal difficulties...... | 99 | 1 | 1.0 | 2 | 2.0 | 96 | 97.0 |
| Number of institutions to which questionnaire was sent...... | 137 | | | | | | |

student-teaching because the local teachers were poorly prepared as supervisors. It is probable that at least a part of the difficulty is traceable to the fact that in a considerable number of cases the compensation is poor and the supervisors lack proper professional status in the teachers college.

In only five of the eleven kinds of difficulty which are listed do more than half of the institutions replying report no difficulty: objections of student-teachers, legal difficulties, objections of the community, poor cooperation of local school administrators, and securing means of transportation for student-teachers. With the exception of transportation few report the difficulty to be great. Legal difficulties are rarely experienced, and only two report them to be great.

The situation as regards control of the laboratory school was discussed earlier in this section. There it was found that there is a considerable difficulty because the teachers college lacks control. The tables confirm the fact that there is such difficulty existing in a significant number of institutions.

Some differences between the two periods are shown when Table LXXI is compared with Table LXX. Fewer institutions report the lack of adequate school buildings to house the off-campus schools in 1937–38 than in 1933–34; while more than half (51.6 percent) stated that they had a certain degree of difficulty in 1933–34, only two-fifths (39.6 percent) did so in 1937–38. As in 1933–34, there was considerable difficulty in securing qualified supervisors, in conflicts with the college schedule, and in insufficient control by the teachers college, each of these being a difficulty found in some degree in more than half of the institutions.

The respondents to the questionnaire were asked not only to indicate the degree of difficulty which existed in the selected items shown in Tables LXX and LXXI but to rank those which they had indicated as causing much difficulty in order of the amount of difficulty which had been experienced. In Table LXXII an exhibit of the replies is shown. Forty-three institutions made rankings for 1933–34, and a group of forty-four institutions in 1937–38. The incidence of greatest difficulty is found to be somewhat different in the two periods, but it remains in the same general fields. In neither year is the greatest difficulty found by the larger number of institutions in objections of the student-teachers or community, in poor cooperation of local school administrators, in securing transportation for student-teachers, or in time consumed in going to the off-campus schools. It is found, rather, in inadequate school buildings, poor supervision, insufficient control of the teachers college, difficulty of supervision by college teachers or supervisors, and conflicts with the college schedule. This table agrees with Tables LXX and LXXI in showing improvement in the school buildings, in better supervision, but shows more difficulty because of conflicts with the college schedule and because the teachers college does not exercise sufficient control over the off-campus schools.

TABLE LXXII

*Greatest Difficulties Experienced in Using Off-Campus Laboratory Schools in State Normal Schools and Teachers Colleges, 1933-34 and 1937-38*

| Nature of Difficulty | Number of Institutions Judging Most Difficult | |
|---|---|---|
| | 1933-34 | 1937-38 |
| Inadequate school buildings.......................... | 9 | 4 |
| Local teachers are poorly prepared as supervisors........ | 8 | 6 |
| Insufficient control by the teachers college............. | 6 | 9 |
| Difficulty of supervision by college teachers and supervisors | 6 | 5 |
| Conflicts with the college schedules.................... | 5 | 9 |
| Time consumed by student-teachers in travel............ | 3 | 5 |
| Securing means of transportation for student-teachers.... | 3 | 3 |
| Objections of student-teachers........................ | 2 | 1 |
| Poor cooperation of local administrators............... | 1 | 1 |
| Objections of the community.......................... |   | 1 |
| Number of institutions................................ | 43 | 44 |

One of the most persistent and frequent difficulties relates to the inadequate preparation of local teachers as supervisors or critic teachers. This is not an isolated problem but is related to other of the difficulties, such as insufficient control of facilities by the teachers college and inadequate school buildings. At least three main remedies for the situation may be indicated: more definite agreement between the teachers college and the off-campus school, authorizing the teachers college to participate more fully in selecting and assigning supervisors; recognition of their status; and supplementing their salaries. Discussing the problem involved, Engleman concludes: "Public-school teachers serving as critic teachers should be selected on the basis of their preparation, should not be required to serve against their will, and should receive extra compensation for their added duties."[122]

In the vote of a jury of thirty deans, directors of student-teaching, and principals of university high schools canvassed by Jarman,[123] twenty-nine favored as an administrative guide that "recognition and regards of the supervising (critic) teachers should be great enough to attract the best teachers." Peik[124] holds to the opinion that differentials in salary are legitimate, and when the salary schedule of the teachers who serve as supervisors exceeds the usual schedule for other teachers the difference ought to be deemed a legitimate subsidy for the institution or the board of education in return for the special services which are rendered. One president who replied to the questionnaire stated that the institution which he represented was finding difficulty because the teachers, formerly paid a subsidy, no longer received additional compensation because of economy which was enforced by the financial depression. The teachers, who had formerly been cooperative, became less so, and it was increasingly difficult to select superior supervisors from the teachers in the off-campus schools. If supervisors' salaries are supplemented, it becomes a motive to superior work and operates to secure supervisors who are better prepared.

### SUMMARY

1. Normal schools and teachers colleges are often poorly located in communities too small to supply an adequate number of pupils for the laboratory school, even if all the schools of the town or city containing the institution are available for student-teaching purposes.

2. The *intensity* of use or *point of saturation* of use in the off-

---

[122] J. O. Engleman, "A Study of Student Teaching in State Normal Schools and Teachers Colleges." *The Elementary School Journal*, Vol. 26, p. 262, December, 1925.
[123] Jarman, *op. cit.*, p. 113.
[124] Peik, in *National Survey of the Education of Teachers*, Vol. III, *op. cit.*, p. 362.

campus schools of the town or city is usually less than in the campus school.

3. The off-campus school can supplement the campus school by furnishing additional facilities and by providing a variety of situations; it can complement the experience of the student-teacher in the campus school by providing opportunities to secure experience under typical public school conditions. It can also provide final responsible student-teaching.

4. Off-campus laboratory schools are one- and two-teacher rural schools, rural consolidated, village, and city. The tendency is strong to furnish teachers their student-teaching in city schools even though a large proportion of the students are preparing to enter rural service.

5. The "cadet" or "interne" plan of student-teaching is employed by 19 percent of the institutions studied. The modal number of supervisory visits is one per week.

6. A formula can be devised for the purpose of surveying the adequacy of the populations of towns and cities to provide pupils sufficient for the needs of the teachers college. But a more serviceable formula determines the number of classrooms which are needed for each division of the school. Such a formula has been developed as follows:

$$n = \frac{s\,h}{t\,l} \cdot 2$$

7. A study of the pupil enrollment and its grade distribution indicates that off-campus schools supplement the campus schools to a marked degree.

8. Much time is required to travel from the campus to the off-campus schools, the range being 2 to 720 minutes, the mean, 25.0 minutes.

9. Almost a fifth (18.9 percent) of the student-teachers reach the off-campus school by walking, a sixth (15.6 percent) by using their own automobiles. In most other cases college or commercial buses are used.

10. A smaller percentage of observation, participation, and class demonstration is provided in the off-campus schools than in the campus schools, and a smaller number of institutions use off-campus schools for these purposes.

11. Institutions generally compensate the cooperating schools or the supervisors of student-teaching by paying a financial consideration, furnishing substitute teachers, or waiving college tuition fees for supervisors who take college courses. Ninety-five and six tenths percent of the institutions replying compensate in one or more of the three ways. The cost for supervisory service in the campus schools in 1937–38 was 24 percent of the total cost of all supervision in campus and off-campus schools.

12. There is a trend toward charging pupils in the laboratory school a tuition fee. Of thirty-six institutions which submitted data for both 1933–34 and 1937–38, twenty-one made a charge for tuition in the former year, twenty-nine in the latter.

13. Few teachers colleges exercise exclusive control over off-campus laboratory schools.

14. Three methods of agreement for the use of laboratory schools are found: verbal agreements, written memoranda or minutes of the board of education, and written contracts. During a period of eighteen years there is a tendency toward formal written contracts.

15. Superintendents of schools, principals, teachers, and boards of education have more favorable attitudes toward using public schools for laboratory purposes than do pupils of the schools and their parents.

16. The chief difficulties experienced in using public schools as laboratory schools are: inadequate school buildings, ineffective supervision, time consumed by student-teachers in traveling to them, insufficient control by the teachers college, conflicts with the students' college schedule, and objections of the community.

17. Differentials in salary are indicated as a remedy for ineffective supervision.

## SECTION E

### OFF-CAMPUS LABORATORY SCHOOLS NEEDED AND THOSE POTENTIALLY AVAILABLE

The final section in this chapter is concerned with the following subjects: (*a*) the institutions which are in need of additional laboratory facilities; (*b*) the proposals made for securing the facilities which are needed; (c) the distance and time required to reach schools which are potentially available as laboratory schools if public schools nearest the institution are used; (d) the types of school which are potentially available within a radius of ten miles of the campus of the teachers college; (e) the rural one-teacher and two-teacher schools within radii of five and ten miles, respectively, of the campus; (f) comparison of the enrollments of campus and off-campus laboratory schools with those of other public schools which are potentially available within ten miles of the campus; and (g) private schools as laboratory schools.

## INSTITUTIONS NEEDING ADDITIONAL LABORATORY FACILITIES

In Section D, Table XLVII (page 142), the number of state normal schools and teachers colleges which used each type of school to supplement their campus laboratory facilities was shown. It is important to know not only the number and type of schools in use but also the additional number which are needed. The writer made a survey of the number of institutions which needed additional facilities for laboratory experience in four academic years, 1924-25, 1929-30, 1934-35, and 1937-38. The data secured from this survey are exhibited in Table LXXIII. For the first two of these academic years, the institutions were asked whether they needed additional facilities in observation and stu-

TABLE LXXIII

*Number of State Normal Schools and Teachers Colleges Needing Additional Laboratory School Facilities in Different Academic Years from 1924-25 to 1937-38*

| Academic Year | No. of Institutions Studied | Institutions Needing Facilities No. | % |
|---|---|---|---|
| 1924-25 | 117 | 87 | 74.4 |
| 1929-30 | 112 | 74 | 66.1 |
| 1934-35 | 131 | 46 | 35.1 |
| 1937-38 | 137 | 51 | 37.2 |

dent-teaching; for the last two, in observation, participation, and student-teaching. However, it is not believed that the inclusion of participation in the earlier reports would have changed the results to any marked degree, since in 1924-25 and 1929-30 when the data were assembled relatively few institutions had a definite program of participation, and accordingly, laboratory experience now classified as participation was included either under observation or under student-teaching. In the first two periods for which data were collected, the need was much greater than during the last two when the facilities more nearly approached the demand for them. In each instance the need was expressed, of course, in terms of the program which the institution deemed best for its purposes considering the amount of laboratory experience which it required, rather than on the basis of any fixed, determinate standard.

PLANS FOR SECURING ADDITIONAL FACILITIES NEEDED

At four intervals covering in all a period of sixteen years, data were secured about the type of facilities (campus, off-campus, or both) which the institutions proposed to use to supply their needs for additional off-campus schools for laboratory experience. Table LXXIV presents data for the four academic years, 1924-25, 1929-30, 1934-35, and 1937-38. The trend is definitely toward greater

TABLE LXXIV

*Number and Percent of Institutions Reporting Need for Various Types of Facilities in Different Academic Years from 1924-25 to 1937-38*

| Academic Year | No. of Institutions Studied | Needing Facilities | On Campus No. | On Campus % | Off Campus No. | Off Campus % | Both On Campus and Off Campus No. | Both On Campus and Off Campus % |
|---|---|---|---|---|---|---|---|---|
| 1924-25 | 117 | 81 | 31 | 38.2 | 13 | 16.0 | 37 | 45.8 |
| 1929-30 | 112 | 74 | 25 | 33.8 | 22 | 29.7 | 27 | 36.5 |
| 1934-35 | 131 | 46 | 8 | 17.4 | 14 | 30.4 | 24 | 52.2 |
| 1937-38 | 137 | 51 | 10 | 19.6 | 16 | 31.4 | 25 | 49.0 |

## TABLE LXXV

*Number of State Normal Schools and Teachers Colleges Proposing to Use Additional Laboratory Facilities for Various Curriculums and Types of Laboratory Experience, 1934-35*

| Type of Curriculum | Observation |  |  |  | Participation |  |  |  | Student-Teaching |  |  |  |
|---|---|---|---|---|---|---|---|---|---|---|---|---|
|  | C* | OC† | B‡ | Total | C | OC | B | Total | C | OC | B | Total |
| General elementary | 2 | 2 | 6 | 10 | 2 | 2 | 6 | 10 | 1 | 3 | 7 | 11 |
| Kindergarten-primary | 2 | 3 | 8 | 13 | 2 | 3 | 5 | 10 | 3 | 4 | 10 | 17 |
| Intermediate | 2 | 3 | 7 | 12 | 2 | 3 | 4 | 9 | 2 | 4 | 9 | 15 |
| Junior high school | 2 | 2 | 6 | 10 | 1 | 2 | 3 | 6 | 3 | 4 | 8 | 15 |
| Senior high school | 2 | 2 | 11 | 15 | 1 | 4 | 9 | 14 | 3 | 5 | 14 | 22 |
| Rural one-teacher and two-teacher schools |  | 10 | 3 | 13 |  | 8 | 5 | 13 |  | 10 | 5 | 15 |
| Special subjects: |  |  |  |  |  |  |  |  |  |  |  |  |
| Agriculture | 2 | 1 | 2 | 5 | 1 | 1 | 2 | 4 | 3 | 1 | 3 | 7 |
| Art | 2 | 1 | 3 | 6 | 2 | 2 | 2 | 6 | 3 | 2 | 4 | 9 |
| Business | 2 | 1 | 3 | 6 | 1 | 1 | 3 | 5 | 2 | 1 | 5 | 8 |
| Home economics | 2 | 1 | 4 | 7 | 1 | 2 | 3 | 6 | 2 | 2 | 6 | 10 |
| Industrial arts | 2 | 2 | 2 | 6 | 2 | 2 | 2 | 6 | 3 | 3 | 5 | 11 |
| Music | 2 | 1 | 2 | 5 | 1 | 2 | 3 | 6 | 2 | 2 | 5 | 9 |
| Physical education (men) | 2 | 1 | 2 | 5 | 1 | 3 | 3 | 7 | 2 | 4 | 5 | 11 |
| Physical education (women) | 2 | 2 | 2 | 6 | 1 | 2 | 1 | 4 | 2 | 2 | 3 | 7 |
| Number of institutions replying |  |  |  |  |  |  |  |  |  |  |  | 46 |

\* C—Campus school † OC—off-campus school
‡ B—both campus and off-campus school

use of off-campus schools in supplying the facilities for the additional student-teaching needed. An increasing number of institutions expressed their intention of using both campus and off-campus schools in the last two of the four years.

Though it is important to know in general whether an institution has sufficient schools for laboratory purposes, it is still more necessary for planning to know in what areas the needs exist. In Table LXXV an analysis is made of the number of institutions

## TABLE LXXVI

*Number of State Normal Schools and Teachers Colleges Proposing to Use Additional Laboratory Facilities for Various Curriculums and Types of Laboratory Experience, 1937–38*

| Type of Curriculum | \multicolumn{4}{c}{Observation} | | | | \multicolumn{4}{c}{Participation} | | | | \multicolumn{4}{c}{Student-Teaching} | | | |
|---|---|---|---|---|---|---|---|---|---|---|---|---|
| | C* | OC† | B‡ | Total | C | OC | B | Total | C | OC | B | Total |
| General elementary | 4 | 2 | 9 | 15 | 4 | 2 | 7 | 13 | 6 | 2 | 9 | 17 |
| Kindergarten-primary | 6 | 4 | 7 | 17 | 6 | 3 | 7 | 16 | 6 | 4 | 6 | 16 |
| Intermediate | 6 | 2 | 5 | 13 | 6 | 2 | 6 | 14 | 4 | 3 | 2 | 9 |
| Junior high school | 7 | 3 | 3 | 13 | 8 | 3 | 1 | 12 | 10 | 4 | 1 | 15 |
| Senior high school | 7 | 6 | 3 | 16 | 8 | 6 | 2 | 16 | 7 | 9 | 4 | 20 |
| Rural one-teacher and two-teacher schools | | 8 | 2 | 10 | | 7 | 2 | 9 | | 10 | 3 | 13 |
| Special subjects: | | | | | | | | | | | | |
| Agriculture | | 1 | 1 | 2 | | 1 | | 1 | | 1 | | 1 |
| Art | 2 | | 3 | 5 | 2 | | 2 | 4 | 3 | 1 | 2 | 6 |
| Business | 4 | 1 | 2 | 7 | 4 | | 1 | 5 | 2 | 3 | 2 | 7 |
| Home economics | 2 | 3 | 3 | 8 | 2 | 3 | 2 | 7 | 1 | 6 | 2 | 9 |
| Industrial arts | 3 | 1 | 2 | 6 | 3 | 1 | 2 | 6 | 2 | 3 | 2 | 7 |
| Music | 5 | 3 | 3 | 11 | 5 | 4 | 2 | 11 | 4 | 7 | 2 | 13 |
| Physical education (men) | 5 | 3 | 4 | 12 | 5 | 3 | 3 | 11 | 4 | 5 | 3 | 12 |
| Physical education (women) | 5 | 3 | 4 | 12 | 5 | 3 | 3 | 11 | 4 | 5 | 3 | 12 |
| Number of institutions replying | | | | | | | | | | | | 51 |

\* C—campus school     † OC—off-campus school
‡ B—both campus and off-campus school

which need additional facilities in each type of curriculum and for each of the three types of laboratory experience, observation, participation, and student-teaching. The table reveals clearly that the needs are specific rather than general. The greatest area of need for additional facilities is in the senior high school; the next, in the curriculum for teachers in the kindergarten-primary division of the schools. The need is greater for student-teaching than for observation and participation. It is proposed by the greater number of institutions to meet the need for student-teaching for rural teachers by utilizing off-campus schools, a decision which is wise because of the differentiated environmental conditions which obtain in the rural setting. The trend shown here, as in other tables related to the subject, is definitely toward making more extensive use of off-campus schools.

Table LXXVI shows the corresponding data for fifty-one institutions for the academic year 1937–38. While there are differences in detail, the total situation does not show great variation from that of three years earlier. There is somewhat greater need for facilities in music and physical education, somewhat less in home economics and industrial arts. The need is also somewhat greater in the general elementary curriculum in 1937–38 than at the earlier period. There is some trend toward securing additional facilities on the campus rather than in off-campus schools.

In the foregoing analysis, answers are given by institutions in terms of their present practices and ideals, which vary more or less from the criteria which are desirable for an optimum program. Six of these criteria which would increase the enrollments and the number of classrooms necessary for laboratory purposes are the following:

1. Student-teaching should be done under typical conditions. This implies that varying types of schools—city, village, and rural—should be included in the laboratory facilities.
2. Student-teaching should be specialized and differentiated according to the grade divisions and special subject areas for which the prospective teachers are preparing.
3. Differentiated student-teaching should be provided for prospective teachers who are preparing for service in rural one- and two-teacher schools.
4. Student-teaching should include all phases of curricular, extracurricular, school, and extra-school activities which teachers normally perform.
5. The amount of student-teaching should, in many instances, be increased to assure initial competence in teaching in the first teaching position.
6. The total classroom teaching done by student-teachers should not exceed one-half of the total for the school.

The off-campus school should be typical of conditions which the teacher will later encounter in the size of the community and school, the composition of the population, the character of the community, whether rural or urban, the textbooks, curriculum, and school organization. Contrasting such a situation with the "cloistered, campus, laboratory, hot-house school" Hunt[125] declares that "The contact with a high school or elementary school which has all the difficulties of race, intelligence, and mixed vocational choice is much better."

Evenden[126] found that instructors in colleges, universities, normal schools, and teachers colleges united in voting "very positively" in favor of the criterion that provision for practice teaching should be given in situations typical of surrounding regions. This subject has already been discussed in Section D.

Student-teaching in the high school should be provided in the major and minor subject-matter fields. In special subjects there should be opportunity for student-teaching in the field of subject-matter specialization. In the elementary teaching fields, student-teaching should be specialized for the curriculums such as kindergarten-primary, intermediate, and upper grades. Preferably, the teachers preparing to teach in the junior high school should be given an opportunity for laboratory experience in the junior high school grades.[127]

Differentiated student-teaching should be provided for those students who plan to teach in the rural schools. Carney[128] advocates both general and specialized student-teaching for the preparation of teachers for rural schools, the former so that "habits fundamental to all good teaching may be fixed," the latter, that there may be given "specific practice designed to meet actual rural conditions, and done in one-teacher, two-teacher, and consolidated schools." She also recommends that not only rural teachers but all elementary teachers who are likely to secure initial appointments in one- and two-teacher rural schools have the

---

[125] Charles W. Hunt, "Practice, A Control for the Selection of Subject-Matter." *Educational Administration and Supervision*, Vol. 16, p. 362, May, 1930.
[126] Evenden, in *National Survey of the Education of Teachers*, Vol. VI, *op. cit.*, p. 121.
[127] Learned and Bagley, *op. cit.*, pp. 153-156.
[128] Carney, in *National Survey of the Education of Teachers*, Vol. V, *op. cit.*, p. 377.

opportunity of a limited number of observations of skillful teaching in such schools.[129] Brim[130] advocates that the teachers college furnish those wishing to prepare as rural teachers the common general features found in all curriculums and "specific preparation for those who wish to teach in rural fields equal *in every respect* to that provided for prospective urban teachers."

It is not sufficient that student-teachers be given opportunity for developing skill in classroom teaching and management; it is quite as important that their experience include all other factors of the teacher's work such as extracurricular and extra-school activities. It is agreed by Alexander,[131] Stratemeyer,[132] Schorling,[133] Nelson,[134] and Mooney[135] that the prospective teacher should have laboratory experience in all the principal activities in which he will engage as a teacher.

Even the preparation for classroom teaching is often narrowly conceived and practiced. Charters and Waples[136] found that the activities of student-teachers were confined more to classroom teaching and less to school and classroom management and teaching pupils how to study than were those of regular teachers of the school. Nelson[137] states that 95 percent of the student-teachers in the elementary grades received actual practice in such mechanical features of the teacher's work as school housekeeping, while less than 5 percent were given practice in making professional contacts, and in participating in the social, civic, and welfare organizations of the community. She also discovered that although less than a fifth of the student-teachers secured experience in establishing relationships with the community there was a greater variety of contacts when both campus and off-campus laboratory schools were used.

---

[129] *Ibid.*, p. 375.
[130] Orville G. Brim, "Guiding Principles in Rural Education." *Thirtieth Yearbook* of the National Society for the Study of Education, Part I, p. 268. 1931.
[131] Thomas Alexander, "A Wider Extension of the Content of Student-Teaching." *Educational Administration and Supervision*, Vol. 16, p. 352, May, 1930.
[132] Florence B. Stratemeyer, "A Proposed Experiment in Teacher-Training." *Educational Administration and Supervision*, Vol. 18, p. 357, May, 1932.
[133] Schorling, *op. cit.*, pp. 138–139.
[134] Nelson, *op. cit.*, p. 292.
[135] Mooney, *op. cit.*, p. 148.
[136] Charters and Waples, *op. cit.*, pp. 31–32.
[137] Nelson, *op. cit.*, pp. 124–125.

Bernard,[138] in a study of four teachers colleges in California, shows that the greatest weaknesses in the activities of student-teachers have to do with the extra-classroom activities of pupils and community and parent relationships. He also found, however, that the activities of campus student-teachers are more like those of regular teachers in these respects than are those of off-campus student-teachers in these fields.

Mooney[139] expresses the opinion that cooperating off-campus schools are superior to campus schools in providing opportunity for supervising the pupils' extracurricular activities and making contacts with professional, social, and recreational organizations in the community, basing his judgment in part on a survey of the opinions of 392 student-teachers who indicated that the off-campus teaching was the most valuable experience which they had during their courses in student-teaching.

The conflict in the findings of Bernard and Mooney may be due to a difference in the skillfulness of the supervision, to the small number of institutions from which the conclusions were drawn, or to differences in local situations. On the whole, it seems clear that the off-campus schools as well as campus schools must be used for experience in extracurricular and extra-school activities if these are to be secured under conditions typical of those which teachers find in the actual teaching situation in the public schools.

If the teachers college plans to give student-teachers experience in these factors, it is clear that it will be necessary to employ off-campus schools for a considerable portion of the training, if it is to be secured under normal conditions, thus adding to the necessity of a sufficient number of affiliated off-campus schools.

## DISTANCE AND TIME OF TRAVEL TO POTENTIAL OFF-CAMPUS SCHOOLS NEAREST TO CAMPUS

Two views prevail regarding the general plan for using public schools as off-campus laboratory schools. One group of teachers college administrators favors a situation where student-teaching is concentrated in one or at most a few schools. Another group

[138] Bernard, *op. cit.*, p. 60.
[139] Mooney, *op. cit.*, pp. 138-139.

prefers to use only a few classrooms in any one school system, sending students to a great number and variety of schools. The former plan is the more frequently used. The latter is employed primarily in a few states including New Jersey, New York, and Rhode Island. One institution operating under this plan describes it as follows:

Our student teaching is done entirely off-campus. The supervisor of student teaching, upon the recommendation of supervising principals, city superintendents, and county superintendents, visits teachers and selects those whose work proves satisfactory. Our student teaching may be done in any public school in the state. . . . In a single term, we generally use about thirty different school districts. . . . The communities vary in population from purely rural areas to cities of 100,000 people. The schools may be small rural or large rural consolidated ones; departmentalized or straight grade buildings of the elementary level. . . . The schools are used for observing or for student teaching. . . . The agreement between the college and the local schools is purely verbal and informal, and operates for a period of nine weeks. . . . Students furnish their own transportation, or, in the case of mass observations, pay a proportionate share of a hired bus transportation.

Another executive describes the preparation of high school teachers in the institution's off-campus schools as follows:

We appoint a headmistress in each of four schools and send our seniors to them for eighteen weeks of practice. Some seniors stay two nine-week periods, others stay eighteen weeks straight. These students do about three-fifths of the teaching, while the headmistress does the rest. . . . These students prepare for lessons at night under the eye of the headmistress and their lesson plans are gone over by her. She observes their teaching during the next day as far as possible and criticizes them at the end of the day. This is extremely close supervision, the teachers and students living together in the same house.

Under usual conditions it is difficult to maintain a satisfactory program of supervision far distant from the campus, and the student loses much by being removed from, and more or less isolated from, the campus and its opportunities.

The following question was proposed to institutions to discover the nearness or remoteness of adequate facilities: "Assuming that you now need additional laboratory school facilities, that all public schools in the area near your teachers college are available for

## TABLE LXXVII

*Distance to, and Time Required to Reach, the Farthest Public School Which a Teachers College Needing Additional Facilities Must Use as a Laboratory School, 1934-35*

| Geographic Division | No. of Institutions Reporting | Distance in Miles Range | Distance in Miles Median | Time in Minutes Range | Time in Minutes Median |
|---|---|---|---|---|---|
| New England†......... | | | | | |
| Middle Atlantic........ | 9 | 1.2–30 | 10.0 | 10–50 | 20.0 |
| East North Central..... | 11 | 1.0–30 | 10.0 | 15–60 | 25.0 |
| West North Central..... | 11 | 2.0–20 | 9.0 | 10–60 | 20.0 |
| South Atlantic......... | 4 | 1.0–25 | 18.0 | 10–50 | 30.0 |
| East South Central..... | 3 | 1.0– 5 | 3.0 | 10–20 | 10.0 |
| West South Central..... | 7 | 1.0–32 | 10.0 | 10–75 | 20.0 |
| Mountain.............. | 6 | 2.0–18 | 5.0 | 20–45 | 30.0 |
| Pacific................ | 5 | 1.5–20 | 3.0 | 10–60 | 25.0 |
| Total................. | 56 | 1.0–32 | 10.5 | 10–75 | 28.2 |

\* It is assumed that all public schools in the area of the teachers colleges are available for laboratory purposes and that each student will secure his student-teaching in the grades or subjects which he is preparing to teach.

† No institution in New England reported data for this table.

student-teaching, and that you would use the schools nearest your college, what is the farthest distance that any student-teacher would have to travel from the campus to secure student-teaching in the grades or subjects he is preparing to teach?" It was indicated that the distance and time should be given by using as a basis the usual method of travel. Table LXXVII summarizes the replies of fifty-six institutions which responded to the question. The range, both in distance and time, varied much with the institutions. Some could easily accommodate all their students in schools not more than a mile from the campus; others were compelled to send their students as far as thirty-two miles away. The time consumed ranged from ten to seventy-five minutes. Except for the East South Central Division there is little difference in different sections of the country.

The table indicates that it is possible for all, or nearly all, of the institutions to secure laboratory school facilities near enough

## TABLE LXXVIII

*Types of Off-Campus Facilities Within a Radius of Ten Miles of the Campus Potentially Available to State Normal Schools and Teachers Colleges Needing Additional Laboratory Schools, 1934-35*

| Geographic Division | No. of Institutions Reporting | City Schools | Village Schools | Rural Consolidated Schools | Rural Schools |
|---|---|---|---|---|---|
| New England....... | | | | | |
| Middle Atlantic..... | 3 | 1 | 3 | 1 | 1 |
| East North Central.. | 8 | 3 | 5 | 3 | 7 |
| West North Central.. | 8 | 5 | 2 | 1 | 8 |
| South Atlantic...... | 3 | 2 | 1 | 1 | 1 |
| East South Central.. | 2 | 1 | | | 1 |
| West South Central.. | 6 | 4 | 3 | 4 | 4 |
| Mountain........... | 3 | 1 | | | 2 |
| Pacific............. | 4 | 1 | 2 | 3 | 4 |
| Total.............. | 37 | 18 | 16 | 13 | 28 |
| Percent........... | | 48.7 | 43.3 | 35.1 | 75.7 |

so that student-teachers may live on the campus during their period of practice, provided all public schools are available as off-campus laboratory schools, particularly if the schedule of classes is so arranged that students are free from other college classes for half a day during the period of student-teaching.

### THE TYPES OF SCHOOL POTENTIALLY AVAILABLE WITHIN A RADIUS OF TEN MILES FROM THE CAMPUS

The types of off-campus laboratory facilities potentially available, i.e., those which are not used by the teachers college but which might be available for student-teaching if the cooperation of local school authorities were secured, are shown in Table LXXVIII. This table includes only institutions which need additional facilities. That there are real difficulties encountered in providing student-teaching in schools of the type students will enter for their initial teaching experience is evident. Fewer than half of the institutions have city schools or village schools, not in

## TABLE LXXIX

*Number of Institutions Having Various Types of Off-Campus Facilities Within a Radius of Ten Miles of the Campus Potentially Available and Not Needing Additional Laboratory Schools, 1934-35*

| Geographic Division | No. of Institutions Reporting | City Schools | Village Schools | Rural Consolidated Schools | Rural Schools |
|---|---|---|---|---|---|
| New England....... | 1 | 1 | | 1 | 1 |
| Middle Atlantic..... | 11 | 4 | 9 | 7 | 10 |
| East North Central.. | 7 | 4 | 5 | 3 | 5 |
| West North Central.. | 10 | 5 | 6 | 3 | 9 |
| South Atlantic...... | 5 | 5 | 2 | 2 | 4 |
| East South Central.. | 1 | 1 | 1 | 1 | 1 |
| West South Central.. | 4 | 2 | 3 | 1 | 3 |
| Mountain........... | 3 | 2 | 1 | | 1 |
| Pacific............. | 4 | 3 | 2 | 2 | 3 |
| Total............... | 46 | 27 | 29 | 20 | 37 |
| Percent........... | | 58.7 | 63.0 | 43.5 | 80.4 |

use as laboratory schools, within ten miles of the campus. Two-thirds lack rural consolidated schools; a fourth, rural one- and two-teacher schools.

An analysis of the data on which the table is based indicates that of thirty-seven institutions only two have all of the four types of school (city, village, consolidated rural, and rural one- and two-teacher schools) available; eight have city, one- and two-teacher rural, and either village or rural consolidated schools; one has city and one- and two-teacher rural; and one has city and village schools only. Seventeen have no city schools available; seven, no rural schools. Three have city schools only available; two, village schools only; one, consolidated rural schools only; and eight, rural one- and two-teacher schools only.

Table LXXIX gives similar data for a group of forty-six institutions which have sufficient laboratory facilities. Although they now need no additional facilities, a larger percentage of them as

TABLE LXXX

*Number of Rural One-Teacher and Two-Teacher Schools Within a Radius of Ten Miles from the Campus Not Used but Potentially Available as Laboratory Schools, 1934–35*

| Geographic Division | No. of Institutions Reporting | One-Teacher Less than Five Miles | One-Teacher Five to Ten Miles | Two-Teacher Less than Five Miles | Two-Teacher Five to Ten Miles |
|---|---|---|---|---|---|
| New England....... | 1 | 1 | 6 | | |
| Middle Atlantic..... | 13 | 103 | 44 | 10 | 16 |
| East North Central.. | 11 | 81 | 152 | 11 | 4 |
| West North Central.. | 16 | 82 | 188 | 7 | 9 |
| South Atlantic...... | 6 | 13 | 40 | 11 | 25 |
| East South Central.. | 1 | 1 | | 3 | |
| West South Central.. | 7 | 23 | 15 | 11 | 11 |
| Mountain........... | 2 | 5 | 2 | 2 | 5 |
| Pacific............. | 5 | 14 | 22 | 12 | 7 |
| Total.............. | 62 | 323 | 469 | 67 | 77 |

a group have each of the four types of school potentially available than the institutions which now lack sufficient facilities.

### RURAL ONE-TEACHER AND TWO-TEACHER SCHOOLS POTENTIALLY AVAILABLE NEAR THE CAMPUS

Throughout this study the inadequacy of the facilities for preparing teachers for rural service has been evident. To discover whether this lack is due to the impossibility of securing the necessary facilities or to other causes, data have been secured separately for the rural school. The institutions were asked to state the number of one-teacher and two-teacher rural schools not used for laboratory purposes located within a radius of five and ten miles respectively from the campus. Table LXXX was constructed on the basis of the data received. The range of the number of rural one-teacher schools potentially available within a radius of five miles for each of the sixty-two teachers colleges reporting is zero to twenty-five; within five to ten miles, zero to forty-four.

The number of rural two-teacher schools is smaller. Each teachers college has a mean number of 6.3 classrooms available in rural one- and two-teacher schools, within a radius of five miles or less; 8.8 additional within a radius of five to ten miles; a total of 15.1 within a radius of ten miles or less from the institution.

Six of the teachers colleges have no rural one- and two-teacher schools within the ten-mile limit. Comments from them are as follows: "Now use all schools within ten miles"; "Facilities within thirty miles seem to be adequate"; "Located in a sparse neighborhood"; "Not available"; "It is a problem to provide participation, practice teaching, and Americanization work with Spanish-speaking children."

The data shown in Table LXXX indicate that the lack of proper facilities for student-teaching in rural schools is not due, in most instances, to insufficient schools within a reasonable distance of the teachers college, but rather either to indifference to the need for using them or to inability to make desirable arrangements with local school boards and school officials for their use.

## COMPARISON OF PUPIL ENROLLMENTS OF CAMPUS AND OFF-CAMPUS LABORATORY SCHOOLS WITH THOSE OF SCHOOLS POTENTIALLY AVAILABLE WITHIN TEN MILES OF COLLEGE CAMPUS

Table LXXXI is based on data concerning the enrollments of the campus and off-campus laboratory schools and those of other public schools not used, but potentially available, within ten miles of the college campus. Thirty-four teachers colleges, located in seventeen states, representing seven of the nine geographic divisions, contributed data which made comparisons of the three enrollments possible. Table LXXXI portrays the situation for all public schools with the exception of rural one- and two-teacher schools, the data for the latter being presented separately in Table LXXXII.

In interpreting the data, it should be observed that the enrollment in off-campus schools is that included in schools which are used in any way and to any degree for student-teaching. No attempt was made to learn how many of the schools' total number of classes were taught by student-teachers. The comparisons,

## TABLE LXXXI

*The Enrollment of Campus and Off-Campus Laboratory Schools and That of Public Schools Within Ten Miles of the Teachers College Campus Potentially Available But Not Used as Laboratory Schools, 1934-35*

| Geographic Division | Institution | \multicolumn{2}{c}{Campus Schools} | | \multicolumn{2}{c}{Off-Campus Schools} | | \multicolumn{2}{c}{Public Schools Potentially Available} | |
|---|---|---|---|---|---|---|---|
| | | No. | % | No. | % | No. | % |
| New England | None | | | | | | |
| Middle Atlantic | A....... | 440 | 8.0 | 2,500 | 45.1 | 2,600 | 46.9 |
| | B....... | 397 | 7.1 | 4,875 | 87.7 | 285 | 5.1 |
| | C....... | 253 | 2.7 | 5,303 | 56.2 | 3,873 | 41.1 |
| | D...... | 306 | 5.4 | 3,437 | 60.6 | 1,924 | 34.0 |
| | E....... | 307 | 6.9 | 3,402 | 77.0 | 712 | 16.1 |
| | F....... | 292 | 15.2 | 830 | 43.1 | 805 | 41.7 |
| | G....... | 156 | 6.5 | 1,221 | 51.0 | 1,019 | 42.5 |
| | H...... | 527 | 2.2 | 22,799 | 96.1 | 395 | 1.7 |
| | I....... | 190 | 0.8 | 22,460 | 96.5 | 620 | 2.7 |
| East North Central | J....... | 226 | 4.9 | 542 | 11.7 | 3,857 | 83.4 |
| | K..... | 343 | 32.5 | 124 | 11.7 | 590 | 55.8 |
| | L....... | 639 | 3.6 | 13,937 | 79.3 | 3,012 | 17.1 |
| | M...... | 367 | 6.2 | 650 | 11.0 | 4,905 | 82.8 |
| | N...... | 576 | 4.3 | 1,250 | 9.3 | 11,600 | 86.4 |
| | O...... | 235 | 24.8 | 489 | 51.8 | 220 | 23.3 |
| | P....... | 259 | 5.6 | 1,318 | 28.7 | 3,011 | 65.6 |
| | Q....... | 219 | 6.7 | 990 | 30.4 | 2,047 | 62.9 |
| | R...... | 613 | 6.0 | 1,167 | 11.4 | 8,427 | 82.6 |
| | S....... | 495 | 24.9 | 886 | 44.5 | 609 | 30.6 |
| | T....... | 383 | 4.2 | 3,579 | 39.5 | 5,109 | 56.3 |
| | U...... | 275 | 6.2 | 4,036 | 90.7 | 140 | 3.1 |
| West North Central | V....... | 409 | 2.4 | 14,899 | 87.5 | 1,713 | 10.1 |
| | W...... | 376 | 8.8 | 1,277 | 29.7 | 2,643 | 61.5 |
| | X...... | 329 | 13.7 | 55 | 2.3 | 2,012 | 84.0 |
| | Y...... | 485 | 29.4 | 716 | 43.5 | 448 | 27.1 |
| | Z....... | 147 | 13.0 | 305 | 27.1 | 675 | 59.9 |
| South Atlantic | AA..... | 522 | 21.5 | 477 | 19.7 | 1,424 | 58.8 |
| | BB..... | 345 | 23.8 | 385 | 26.7 | 715 | 49.5 |
| East South Central | None | | | | | | |
| West South Central | CC..... | 240 | 26.8 | 383 | 42.7 | 274 | 30.5 |
| | DD..... | 638 | 53.5 | 310 | 26.0 | 244 | 20.5 |
| Mountain | EE..... | 204 | 1.0 | 4,900 | 23.1 | 16,050 | 75.9 |
| Pacific | FF..... | 140 | 1.1 | 10,157 | 77.0 | 2,900 | 21.9 |
| | GG..... | 287 | 5.5 | 2,395 | 46.2 | 2,507 | 48.3 |
| | HH..... | 260 | 14.9 | 1,031 | 58.9 | 458 | 26.2 |
| Total................. | | 11,880 | | 133,085 | | 87,823 | |
| Percent............... | | | 5.1 | | 57.2 | | 37.7 |
| Mean................. | | 347.1 | | 3,914.3 | | 2,583 | |

## TABLE LXXXII

*The Number of Campus and Off-Campus Rural One- and Two-Teacher Laboratory Schools and the Number Potentially Available Within Ten Miles of the Teachers College Campus but Not Used as Laboratory Schools, 1934–35*

| Geographic Division | Institution | Campus Laboratory Schools | Off-Campus Laboratory Schools | Potentially Available | Total Used and Potentially Available |
|---|---|---|---|---|---|
| New England | None | | | | |
| Middle Atlantic | A......... | | | | |
| | B......... | | 8 | 6 | 14 |
| | C......... | | 2 | | 2 |
| | D......... | | | 19 | 19 |
| | E......... | | | 6 | 6 |
| | F......... | | 1 | 22 | 23 |
| | G......... | 1 | | 2 | 3 |
| | H......... | | 1 | 26 | 27 |
| | I......... | | | 19 | 19 |
| East North Central | J......... | | 1 | 56 | 57 |
| | K......... | | 4 | 55 | 59 |
| | L......... | | | | |
| | M......... | | | 8 | 8 |
| | N......... | | 1 | 5 | 6 |
| | O......... | | 2 | 18 | 20 |
| | P......... | | | 2 | 2 |
| | Q......... | | | 4 | 4 |
| | R......... | | | | |
| | S......... | | | | |
| | T......... | | | 5 | 5 |
| | U......... | | 1 | 7 | 8 |
| West North Central | V......... | | 1 | 33 | 34 |
| | W......... | | 4 | 20 | 24 |
| | X......... | | 5 | 20 | 25 |
| | Y......... | | 1 | 32 | 33 |
| | Z......... | | 4 | 2 | 6 |
| South Atlantic | AA...... | | | | |
| | BB...... | | | | |
| East South Central | None | | | | |
| West South Central | CC...... | | | 12 | 12 |
| | DD...... | | | | |
| Mountain | EE...... | | | | |
| Pacific | FF...... | | | | |
| | GG...... | | | 4 | 4 |
| | HH...... | | 1 | 9 | 10 |
| Total................... | | 1 | 37 | 392 | 430 |
| Percent................ | | 0.20 | 8.60 | 91.20 | 100.00 |
| Mean.................. | | 0.03 | 1.08 | 11.53 | 12.64 |

207

however, present a fairly accurate picture of the possibilities of providing facilities additional to those in use. It should be noted that, in so far as off-campus schools are not used up to the point of saturation (i.e., the greatest number of student-teachers who can be accommodated), they can be utilized for additional student-teaching. The data indicate that the off-campus schools which are used for laboratory purposes have more than ten times the pupil enrollment of the campus schools although, as was seen in Tables XXVI and XXVII, more than half of the student-teaching is done in the campus schools. These facts indicate that, were all the off-campus schools used to the point of saturation, they would accommodate about five times as many student-teachers as at present. The expansion possible in the off-campus schools when combined with the facilities which are potentially available in public schools within ten miles of the campus, indicates that there are at present sufficient facilities available for student-teaching in most institutions which, if used to the full, would make it unnecessary to utilize schools far distant from the campus. If the enrollments are segregated by elementary and high school grades, enough pupils are enrolled in each to satisfy future needs.

Ten teachers colleges located in nine states of seven of the nine geographic divisions replied in 1937–38 which did not respond in 1934–35. The proportionate enrollments in campus schools, off-campus schools, and schools potentially available were 8.3 percent, 47.9 percent and 43.8 percent respectively. The corresponding means were 309.6, 1,779, and 1696.6. These figures indicate no great variation from the facts shown in the tables for the thirty-four institutions which reported in 1934–35.

In Table LXXXII the data were assembled for rural one- and two-teacher schools for the same group of thirty-four institutions which were listed in Table LXXXI. In this table the report is by number of schools rather than enrollments. The data show how few rural schools within ten miles of the campus are used for laboratory purposes. Only one institution has a campus rural laboratory school and only thirty-seven have off-campus schools. Within ten miles of the campus, however, 392 schools are available, of which forty-one are two-teacher schools. Only 8.6 percent of the resources available to the teachers colleges are used. In view of the need for student-teaching in rural schools, as shown by the number of teachers preparing for rural teaching, it is evident that here is a point at which laboratory facilities can well be expanded.

Ten institutions which did not respond to the questionnaire in 1934-35 did so in 1937-38. None of them utilized campus rural schools, and five of them reported using a total of seven rural one- and two-teacher off-campus schools. There were 167 schools potentially available within a radius of ten miles from the campus, of which 154 were one-teacher and thirteen, two-teacher schools.

## PRIVATE SCHOOLS AS LABORATORY SCHOOLS

The questionnaire sought information relative to private schools in use and those ten miles or less from the campus which might be used. The institutions were asked to exclude parochial and certain other schools from the report.

Of forty-two institutions only two reported that they used other than public schools. However, in both cases though the schools utilized are not public schools in the usual sense, they are publicly supported. The State Normal School at Geneseo, New York, utilizes the Craig Colony Demonstration School, a state institution for epileptics, as a practice center for student-teachers in special classes, for which teacher-preparation is allocated to this institution by the State Department of Education. At Illinois State Normal University, Normal, Illinois, a written contract has been made with the State Welfare Department whereby the state school for the children of soldiers and sailors is made available for laboratory purposes.

Only three of the forty-two teachers colleges reported that there were private schools which were potentially available as laboratory schools within ten miles of the campus. One listed a small kindergarten; another, a county children's home enrolling sixty pupils; a third, located in a metropolitan area where many public schools are available, two private secondary schools.

From the foregoing facts it is evident that few private schools are available for laboratory purposes and that to utilize them would assist very little in providing the facilities needed. Several reasons may be given why it is undesirable to use them: (*a*) they are usually not typical of the public schools in which students will later teach; (*b*) there is a question about the legality of subsidizing the salaries of teachers in private schools with public funds; (*c*) the pupils as a rule are selected groups; (*d*) there is a danger of restrictions on teaching; (*e*) cooperative arrangements may be temporary and transitory; and (*f*) conflicts in administrative control are more likely to arise than in the case of public schools. The schools may themselves be quite laudable in their purposes and activities as schools, but they should not be employed for use as laboratory schools if public schools are available.

## SUMMARY

1. The relative number of normal schools and teachers colleges needing additional laboratory facilities decreased from 74.4 percent to 35.1 percent during the ten-year period between 1924-25 and 1934-35. There is a slight increase in the relative number which needed additional off-campus schools between 1934-35 and 1937-38.

2. For the period beginning in 1924-25 and ending in 1937-38 there was a continuous trend toward the provision of additional laboratory facilities by the utilization of off-campus public schools.

3. Institutions which need additional facilities report that need is found in specific areas rather than in all types of curriculums and laboratory experience. The need is greatest in the senior high school and kindergarten-primary curriculums. The need is greater for facilities in student-teaching than in observation and participation.

4. The median of the maximum one-way distances which it would be necessary for any students to travel to reach the off-campus schools in the vicinity of the several teachers colleges, provided all were available for laboratory school purposes, is 10.5 miles; the median time needed to travel the distance is 28.2 minutes. The corresponding ranges are one to thirty-two miles and ten to seventy-five minutes, respectively.

5. For some institutions there is difficulty in providing all types of schools (city, village, rural consolidated, and rural one- and

two-teacher schools) within ten miles of the teachers college campus.

6. Few rural one- and two-teacher schools are utilized as laboratory schools. However, there are ample facilities of this type potentially available to most of the institutions within a short distance of the campus. The mean number of classrooms is 6.3 within five miles, and 15.1 within ten miles of the teachers college campus.

7. A comparison of the enrollments of the campus and off-campus laboratory schools now utilized with those of off-campus schools not used but potentially available for laboratory purposes shows that, so far as the number of pupils enrolled is concerned, few of the teachers colleges lack actual or potential laboratory facilities adequate for their needs within a distance of ten miles from the campus.

8. Of forty-two teachers colleges only two utilize off-campus laboratory schools which are not public schools, and both of these are publicly supported. Only three others have private schools potentially available. On both theoretical and practical grounds it is inadvisable to utilize such schools for laboratory purposes.

## CHAPTER III

## SUMMARY, CONCLUSIONS, AND RECOMMENDATIONS

FROM a period more than one and a half centuries ago, student-teaching has increasingly become an essential activity in teacher education. This is the result of long experience rather than of scientific proof that student-teachers gain in skill from the experiences which they have in the laboratory school. It is only in recent years that serious attempts have been made to establish the validity of various aspects of student-teaching through experimental procedures, and such attempts are still in their early phases.

In the social studies, to which category the study of education belongs, it is impossible to present proof which has the exactitude to be found in the physical sciences. Obviously, the factors involved are less stable, more complex, and more difficult to isolate. Therefore recourse must be had to competent opinion on the issues involved. Though it is rarely possible to secure unanimity of view on educational matters, it is possible to determine the weight of well-informed opinion. The mere fact that a large number of persons hold an opinion is not proof of its validity, but all else being equal, when a preponderant number agree on a principle which is derived from the experience of the judges, this agreement may be accepted in lieu of demonstrated proof until such is forthcoming. Similarly, the fact that a certain practice is found does not establish its validity as a criterion. But if under conditions which make change easily possible the practice is accepted as valid by professional workers in the areas involved, for practical purposes it may become the criterion pending experimental proof or disproof of its validity, and may be used as a basis for action.

The purpose of this chapter is both a theoretical and a practical one. It aims to present a summary of the data given in previous chapters, and on this basis to make recommendations concerning the problems involved in the administration of laboratory facilities. It consists of four parts: (*a*) a description of the method which was used in the investigation, (*b*) a summary of the findings and the conclusions which may be drawn from them, (*c*) recommendations which may be made on the basis of the findings, and (*d*) suggestions for further studies and additional research.

## *METHOD*

The data for the study were secured principally from replies to a questionnaire which were received from 131 of the 160 members of the American Association of Teachers Colleges in 1933–34. A similar questionnaire was submitted in 1937–38, to which 137 institutions replied. Thus there was furnished a basis for determining any changes which had occurred during the interval and for discovering trends. In addition supplementary sources of information were used, including state school laws, interviews, copies of contracts, and letters from educational authorities. The institutions studied are located in forty-one states representing all geographic sections of the country. The replies have been interpreted in terms of the opinions of competent workers in the field of teacher education.

## *SUMMARY AND CONCLUSIONS*

### THE CALENDAR YEAR AND CURRICULUMS

In the academic year 1933–34, 53.4 percent of the institutions which are represented in the study were organized on the semester plan. The percentage increased to 59.1 in 1937–38.

The curriculums vary in length from one to four years. They are differentiated for prospective teachers in the various subject-matter fields and on the different grade levels. They range from a single general curriculum in the elementary field in one institution to eighteen specialized curriculums in another. There are no marked variations characteristic of particular geographic divisions of the country. In proportion to the number of prospective teachers needed in each curriculum to supply the needs of the teaching service, too few students are enrolled in curriculums which are designed to prepare teachers for the elementary schools, the deficiency being especially notable in the case of the curriculums which are designed to prepare teachers for rural one- and two-teacher schools. The type of curriculum most universally offered by the institutions is one that prepares for teaching in the kindergarten-primary grades, followed in order by curriculums for intermediate grades, general elementary grades, senior high school, and junior high school. Approximately two-fifths of the teachers colleges offer a curriculum for teachers in rural one- and two-teacher schools.

A fifth of the teachers colleges offer no curriculum shorter than four years, but another fifth offer a curriculum as short as one year. Two-thirds of all the students enrolled are registered in four-year curriculums; only one-twenty-fifth, in one-year curriculums. Seventy-six percent of all students are enrolled in curriculums not less than two years long. The trend in enrollment is toward the longer curriculums.

The one-year curriculums remaining are designed almost exclusively for students who plan to teach in the general elementary field and the rural one- and two-teacher schools. More than 95 percent of the curriculums in the special subjects are four years in length. The consensus of informed educational opinion indicates that at an early date the length of the curriculums should be increased to a minimum of four years.

## LABORATORY COURSES IN THE TRAINING SCHOOL

The greater number of institutions have their curriculums so arranged that the student-teacher begins his laboratory experience with the initial quarter of the final year, irrespective of the length of the curriculum. In three-fourths of the curriculums four years in length, including those which prepare teachers for the junior and senior high schools, the laboratory experience begins with the third year. The laboratory experience in curriculums which prepare for teaching in the special subject fields is begun most often at the beginning of the fourth year. Except in the New England, the Middle Atlantic, and the East North Central Divisions, it is the prevailing practice to postpone the laboratory experience to the opening of the last year of the curriculum. Though there are wide variations, approximately four-fifths of the institutions have placed student-teaching in the final year of the two-year, three-year, and four-year curriculums. During the four-year period from 1933–34 to 1937–38 there was a definite tendency to defer the beginning of the laboratory experience to a later point in both the two-year and the four-year curriculums. The initial laboratory experience in curriculums for the preparation of kindergarten-primary teachers is usually placed early in the course.

The time span during which the laboratory experience is given varies from a single quarter to twelve quarters (1933–34). It increases with the length of the curriculum, but in no curriculums does the median time equal a full academic year. The data reveal that "long and continuous" contact with the laboratory school is an ideal rather than an actuality in many institutions. The median is 3.5 quarters for sixty-one institutions in the two-year curriculum and 4.5 quarters for 118 institutions in the four-year curriculum. This is a larger time span than was found four years earlier.

For more than a quarter of a century, educational writers have urged that the state should allocate the preparation of teachers in special subjects to *one*, or at most *two*, of the regular normal schools or teachers colleges. While the principle has been accepted in theory, only eight states apply it in practice, allocating one or more special subjects to each of forty-five institutions. There was some tendency during the four-year period ending in 1937–38 to make new allocations, and those which were in effect have been continued. This is a policy which might with profit be extended to other institutions in other states. The most frequent allocations in each subject are: art, seven; business, nine; home economics, nine; industrial arts, eleven; music, eight; and health and physical education, nine. Allocations are more general in the northeastern part of the country than elsewhere.

Sixty-five jurors cooperating in two former studies almost unanimously agreed that the theory and practice departments of the teachers college should be coordinated. In the present study 128 institutions stated that they employ twenty-seven different patterns or combinations of laboratory courses. Most commonly employed is a self-contained course composed of observation, participation, and student-teaching in a single course. Forty-five and two-tenths percent of all the laboratory courses are not combined with other courses but are self-contained, while the remaining 54.8 percent are combined with other professional courses, subject-matter courses, or both. From the data the evidence is clear that there is lack of integration of the laboratory school courses with others in the institution.

Gradual induction into the work of student-teaching is advocated by educational writers, the plan being to begin with the simpler elements of teaching and proceed through observation and participation to responsible room teaching. The amount of laboratory experience which should be required has not been experimentally determined, but it should be sufficient to prepare the prospective teacher effectively for his first teaching position. In both the two-year and the four-year curriculums the institutions show great diversity in the amount required. The median for the two-year curriculum is 131.6 clock-hours; for the four-year curriculum, 159.9 clock-hours. In the four-year curriculums, there was a decrease of 20 clock-hours in the amount during the period between 1933–34 and 1937–38. The amount is greatest in the New England and Middle Atlantic Divisions of the country. Of the total, 35.9 percent was in observation and participation, 64.1 percent in student-teaching. There was no marked change in the proportionate amounts for a four-year interval, 1933–34 to 1937–38.

The majority of the teachers colleges favor a flexible requirement in the amount of laboratory experience. The tendency in the New England Division is to maintain rigid requirements; in the Pacific Division, to accept the principle of flexible requirements. However, in the country as a whole, relatively few actually practice the principle. It is more usual to waive a part or all of the requirements than to demand that they be exceeded. The total number of students excused is small; in 1937–38 it was less than 5 percent of each of the phases of laboratory experience—observation, participation and student-teaching—and fewer students were excused than for the period four years earlier. Teaching experience is the most common reason for waiving the requirements.

During a fourteen-year period, 1923–24 to 1937–38, the total amount of laboratory experience required in the laboratory schools varied. There were decreases in the number of student-teachers enrolled in curriculums for rural one- and two-teacher schools and on the lower levels, and an increase on the upper-grade levels and in the special subjects. More and more of the student-teaching was done in connection with the longer curriculums. Approximately a half of the student-teachers completed their work entirely in campus schools, a third entirely in off-campus schools, and a sixth divided the teaching between the two.

The most common practice is to require student-teaching in two elementary grades, two high school subjects, or two special subjects, but an increasing number of institutions require experience in three grades or subjects. Approximately a fourth of all student-teachers, whether in the elementary grades, high schools, or special subjects, do their student-teaching in a single subject.

## THE CAMPUS LABORATORY SCHOOL

Sixty-eight percent of the 131 teachers colleges replying use both campus and off-campus laboratory schools. Of the remainder, 22.1 percent employ campus schools only, 9.9 percent, off-campus schools only. The number of institutions which utilize both types is greatest in the Middle Atlantic, East North Central, and Pacific Divisions. Those using only campus schools are most frequent in the East South Central Division; those using off-campus, in the New England and South Atlantic Divisions.

The campus school is used to provide all types of laboratory experience. Few institutions use it for experimental purposes. More institutions, 95.4 percent, use it for student-teaching than for any other single purpose and almost an equal percentage, 94.5, for observation. More than half the schools serve the four purposes—observation, participation, class demonstration, and student-teaching. Only thirty-six, 27.5 percent, include rural one- and two-teacher schools as a part of the laboratory facilities, of which only four, 3.0 percent, are on the campus.

Twenty-eight of 113 teachers colleges reserve classes for group demonstrations, and only 13.2 percent of them have a definite plan for the rotation of classes for this purpose in the demonstration school.

Many plans are employed for obtaining pupils for the laboratory schools, the most common being to admit them from any source, tuition free. In 23.7 percent of the teachers colleges which maintain campus schools, tuition is charged pupils in the schools.

The grade spans which include the pupils enrolled in the laboratory schools vary widely with institutions. The laboratory schools are fairly representative of public schools in the grades included, although only one-fourth of them enroll pupils in all grades.

The typical laboratory school enrolls between three and four hundred pupils. Eighty-six percent of the 105 institutions have an enrollment ranging between one and five hundred, the enrollment being rather well distributed among the different grades and divisions of the school.

The grade combinations most commonly included in the laboratory schools are: kindergarten-twelve, 17.4 percent of the institutions; kindergarten-eight, 14.8 percent; one-twelve, 13.0 percent.

The ratio of enrollment of student-teachers to that of pupils in the laboratory school varies from 1 : 0–.49 to 1 : 6.00 or above. The median is 1 : 1.76. (See Table XLII)

A formula for determining the number of pupils which a laboratory school must enroll to accommodate a given number of student-teachers in the campus school is as follows:

$$n = 1.30 \left( \frac{15\,sh}{tl} \cdot 2 \right)^1$$

In 1933–34, 116 of the teachers colleges owned 92.2 percent of the campus laboratory schools and exclusively controlled 89.7 percent of them. In 1937–38, 117 owned 90.6 percent, and 116 exclusively controlled 87.1 percent of them.

Few important changes occurred in the facilities provided by the campus laboratory schools during the four years between 1933–34 and 1937–38.

[1] See pp. 126–127.

## THE OFF-CAMPUS LABORATORY SCHOOL

Often normal schools and teachers colleges are located in communities with small populations and must resort to the use of off-campus schools, either in their own city or in other cities and school districts. Whereas the median size of the town or city which includes the teachers college is 5,833, the median combined population of the communities providing off-campus laboratory schools is 12,500, showing that the *intensity of use* is much greater in the case of the campus school than it is in off-campus schools.

The off-campus school can supplement the campus school by providing a variety of situations; it can complement it by furnishing the student-teacher opportunity to secure his experience under typical public school situations. It can also provide for final responsible student-teaching with classes of usual public school size. There is a definite failure in many of the institutions to provide sufficient facilities for the preparation of rural one- and two-teacher schools. The data indicate that many institutions should utilize the off-campus schools as complements as well as supplements to the campus schools in order to provide a richer, more efficient, and varied laboratory experience.

The "cadet" plan of student-teaching is utilized by 19 percent of the institutions. Supervisory visits to these schools are too infrequent to secure the optimum results, the modal number being one per week.

An analysis of the pupil enrollment indicates that the off-campus school not only furnishes more pupils in the same grades than the campus school, but supplements it with grades not included in it.

Travel to the off-campus schools consumes an undue amount of time, the mean time taken to reach them being twenty-five minutes. In 18.9 percent of the cases the student-teachers walk to the school; in 15.6 percent they use their own automobiles.

Campus schools provide the major portion of the laboratory experience in observation, participation, and demonstration teaching offered by the teachers college, the percentages being 70.3, 57.1, and 71.8 respectively.

Eighty-six of ninety teachers colleges, 95.6 percent, compensate the off-campus schools by paying a financial consideration, providing substitute teachers, or waiving tuition fees. In 1937–38, $2,343,267.35 was expended for the salaries of supervisors, 24 percent of which was paid to supervisors in the off-campus schools. The service is provided at a lower cost per student-teacher in the off-campus schools than in the campus schools.

The data indicate a growing trend toward charging a tuition fee in the laboratory schools; a total of $253,614.22 was collected from pupils in the campus schools in 1937–38, no institution charging tuition in the off-campus schools.

Fifty percent of the teachers colleges have either a written contract or a written memorandum from the board of education. There was a trend toward formal contracts during the period between the academic years 1924–25 and 1937–38.

Usually superintendents, principals, and teachers have favorable attitudes toward granting the use of the public schools for laboratory school purposes. There is, however, often an unfavorable attitude on the part of the parents and pupils. The principal difficulties encountered in using the off-campus laboratory schools are inadequate school buildings, ineffective supervision, loss of time in going to the school, insufficient control, and conflicts with the college schedule.

## OFF-CAMPUS LABORATORY SCHOOLS NEEDED AND THOSE POTENTIALLY AVAILABLE

A study was made of the facilities which are needed and those which are potentially available for laboratory school purposes. The data indicate that, granting full use is made of those which are now available, few institutions need to send student-teachers to live in communities other than those in which the teachers colleges are located. In 1934–35 only 37.2 percent of the institutions expressed a need for additional facilities. The percentage increased slightly during the following four-year period. Off-campus schools are steadily growing in favor and more institutions are utilizing them. The need for additional facilities is in specific rather than general areas, and it is greater in student-teaching than in the other phases of laboratory work.

Were the teachers colleges to use all their potential laboratory resources, the maximum distance it would be necessary for any students to travel to reach the off-campus schools would vary from one to thirty-two miles in the different institutions; the time expenditure would be from ten to seventy-five minutes. The means of the distance and time for all teachers colleges are 10.5 miles and 28.2 minutes respectively. Some institutions would encounter difficulty in providing all the types of schools, city, rural, and village, within a radius of ten miles of the campus. Few rural one- and two-teacher schools are now utilized as laboratory schools, although there are adequate resources of this type potentially available within reasonable distances—7.4 classrooms within five miles, and 17.4 within ten miles of the campus.

When an analysis is made of the data relating to the laboratory schools utilized, and those potentially available, it is indicated that there are few teachers colleges which lack laboratory resources sufficient for their needs within ten miles of the campus. Only two teachers colleges use private schools as laboratory schools, and only three have others available (which it is desirable to use) within ten miles.

## RECOMMENDATIONS

In the light of the data which have been presented, interpreted in terms of the views of leading workers in the field of teacher education, the following recommendations are made:

1. The teachers college, according to the preponderant opinion of instructors and administrative officers in institutions which prepare teachers, should offer specialized curriculums, differentiated for grade levels and subject-matter areas for all of the major fields in which it prepares teachers (pp. 36-37). Specialized curriculums imply specialized laboratory school experience. It is possible to specialize the curriculums too highly; yet there should be differentiation enough in the major fields in both theory and laboratory experience to assure the distinctive understandings and skills necessary in at least the following areas: kindergarten-primary, intermediate, junior high school, senior high school, rural one- and two-teacher schools, and the special subjects such as art and home economics.

2. In accordance with the data in Table III which indicate that a considerable majority of teachers now have preparation in a four-year curriculum, it is recommended that all curriculums for the preparation of teachers for the elementary schools, including rural schools, should cover four years, and if the curriculums are lengthened, the amount of laboratory experience required may and probably should be increased. Institutions should eliminate curriculums less than four years in length as rapidly as possible.

3. The period of contact with the laboratory school should be lengthened beginning when the student enters upon the curriculum designed to prepare him for teaching and continuing until his graduation. In the four-year curriculum the graded laboratory experience should be distributed over a minimum period of two years, but four years are preferable. In those institutions which fail to provide for curricular specialization directed toward teaching within the first year of the course and defer it until the last two years, the contact with the laboratory school should begin as soon as the student enters upon the portion of the curriculum designed specifically to prepare him as a teacher.

4. In Table XI it is revealed that eight states allocate the preparation of teachers for the special subjects to particular specified institutions. This policy might well be extended to other states. Where the laboratory equipment and student-teaching facilities must be highly specialized, the state should allocate the preparation of teachers to one or more designated institutions in the state, which have or may readily acquire the special facilities needed. The needs of the teaching service rather than institutional ambition or student convenience should govern the allocations.

5. Investigations have shown (pp. 57–58) that a preponderance of informed opinion is in favor of the principle that the curriculums should be so organized and the laboratory school should so function as to facilitate the integration of the student's laboratory experience in observation, participation, class demonstration, and student-teaching with subject-matter courses and other professional courses. This implies frequent contacts on the part of the subject-matter and education instructors with the laboratory

schools and with their students who are engaged in laboratory work, and an arrangement or pattern of organization in which the laboratory courses are integrated with other courses. It is recommended that the application of this principle be extended to the end that the student's experience in preparation for teaching be integrated.

6. The curriculum should provide for inducting the student into the teaching process by a gradation in difficulty from the simpler to the more complex activities of the teacher, beginning with observation, and continuing through participation to the culmination of his preparation in responsible classroom teaching.

7. The amount of laboratory school experience required of the prospective teacher should be sufficient to ensure the student's competency and success in his initial teaching position after graduation. In view of present practice (Tables XIII–XVII), and considering the potential facilities which are available (Tables LXXXI and LXXXII), the standard amount of student-teaching in all curriculums might well be raised to 120 clock-hours of responsible room teaching.

8. The amount of laboratory experience should vary with the ability, experience, and needs of the individual student, and with the needs of the teaching service but, whatever the amount, the outcome of the laboratory experience should result in a teacher product of superior quality. The student's prior teaching experience (Table XXI) should be considered in determining what the desirable minimum is. The effectiveness of the student's preparation rather than ease in administering the program must be the criterion which will govern the application of this principle. The institution should determine the minimum necessary on the basis of the student's demonstrated skill as indicated by a teaching test in the laboratory school rather than by recommendations of employers, though only a third now do so. Some teachers should be required to exceed the usual minimum standards. (Table XXIII.) The flexibility should be in quantity, not in quality. Each student-teacher admitted to teaching on a proper basis of selection should be required to continue his activities in the laboratory school until such time as he has demonstrated unquestioned ability as a teacher.

9. Just as curriculums should be specialized for different levels and areas, so student-teaching (pp. 36–37 and 195–198), at least in part, should be differentiated according to the curriculums. It should be specialized to meet the varied interests, abilities, and needs of students, and to prepare them for the types of teaching service which they expect to enter. It is particularly desirable to provide differentiated student-teaching in the curriculums for the preparation of rural teachers. Institutions should not undertake to prepare teachers in fields in which they lack laboratory facilities reasonably convenient of access and adequate in quantity and quality. Facilities should be available in each of the division levels and special subjects in which teachers are prepared.

10. In accordance with the data (Table XXXIII) and the summaries of current practice (pp. 100–101) it may be concluded that students should have the opportunity to do student-teaching in more than one grade if they are preparing for teaching in the elementary grades, and in at least two teaching subjects if they are preparing to teach in high schools. Student-teaching in three grades for elementary teachers and three subjects in high schools is desirable. If they are preparing to teach a special subject, such as music or art, which is usually taught on both the elementary and high school levels, they should have opportunity for laboratory experience on both levels.

11. The campus school should serve as a laboratory for observation, participation, class demonstration, and for initial classroom teaching of small groups. It should present the best school practices in terms of the best educational theory. Little emphasis should be placed upon experimentation, and such as there is should be primarily to improve the effectiveness of the school, *as a school*. Not more than one-half of the teaching in the laboratory school should be done by student-teachers.

12. A definite plan for class demonstrations in the laboratory school by supervisors and by college instructors in education and subject-matter courses is recommended. It is usually desirable to arrange for class demonstrations on the basis of a definite plan of rotation.

13. Except in special classes and special schools, pupils should be secured for the campus laboratory school in such a way as to

# SUMMARY, CONCLUSIONS, RECOMMENDATIONS

provide pupils typical of those in the public schools, thus providing student-teachers their laboratory teaching experience under normal school conditions. So far as possible the selective factor should be eliminated. However, even though working under usual conditions, student-teachers should be encouraged to standards of excellence superior to those customarily found in such schools, and should have superior standards brought to their attention as goals for improvement.

14. The enrollment in the campus school should include pupils sufficient in numbers and distributed according to grade levels, subject-matter fields, and special subjects in order that an adequate number and kind of classes may be provided.[2]

15. The teachers college should either own its campus laboratory school, or should exercise enough control to determine the curricular and instructional policy. Otherwise there is no assurance that it will be able to demonstrate the superior teaching which is indispensable in a campus school.

16. No teachers college should in the future be established in any community where the population is too small to guarantee a sufficient number of pupils for the campus laboratory school. Those which are already located in such small communities should use the schools of their own town or city and other nearby schools for the same purposes as the campus school.

17. The off-campus school should supplement the campus school by providing additional facilities and should complement it by furnishing the student-teacher additional types of opportunity to have laboratory experience under normal public school conditions (pp. 139-141 and Table XLVI). It should provide the student-teacher with his final laboratory experience in responsible room teaching. The complementary aspects of the off-campus school should receive greater emphasis than is common at present.

18. The off-campus laboratory school should contain sufficient grade levels and subject-matter areas and should be located in the types of communities in which the student-teachers will probably be employed later so that they may secure laboratory experience

[2] To determine the number of pupils required to accommodate a given number of student-teachers in the campus school see formula, pp. 126-127.

specifically designed to prepare them for their respective initial teaching positions. It is recommended that greater use be made of rural and village schools.

19. If the "cadet" or "interne" plan of preparing teachers is used, weekly or more frequent supervisory visits should be made.

20. To determine the number of classrooms needed for student-teaching in off-campus schools, the following formula may be used:

$$n = \left(\frac{s\,h}{t\,l} \cdot 2\right)^3$$

The formula is based on the assumption that half of the classes of pupils will be taught by student-teachers. Proper change must be made if this proportion of time is increased or decreased.

21. Off-campus schools should be reasonably accessible to the campus. It is preferable that the student-teachers live in the teachers college community as students while they are securing their laboratory school experience, except possibly in final responsible room teaching. If transportation must be provided, the college should bear the cost, if necessary charging student-teachers a uniform laboratory fee to equalize the expense to the students.

22. While off-campus laboratory schools serve for observation, participation, and class demonstrations, their major function is to provide student-teaching. This is in accord with the principle that these schools should complement the campus schools, and the practice is to be encouraged and extended.

23. Off-campus schools should be compensated for the service they render to the teachers college, preferably by the payment of supplementary salaries to the supervisors. This should be in addition to the salaries which the supervisors regularly receive as teachers in the public schools, and as compensation for additional duties which they perform. It should not serve merely as a device to save money for the local school district.

24. In general, it is recommended that teachers colleges do not charge tuition for pupils in the laboratory school because this procedure creates a selected, atypical group which is not representative of the public schools.

[3] See p. 147.

25. Though court decisions suggest that a policy of cooperation and joint control by the local boards of education and the teachers college may be exercised, the states should enact legislation which will assure the teachers colleges the use of sufficient laboratory facilities. Student-teaching should be given undoubted legal status either by definite legislative act or, better, by regulations of the state departments of education promulgated under broad powers which have been granted to them by the legislature.

26. In view of a court decision on the power of voluntary non-state associations to set standards mandatory for their members (pp. 172-173), and because the standards for student-teaching in teachers colleges of the country are maintained primarily by standards which are set by the American Association of Teachers Colleges, and a minimum of 90 clock-hours of student-teaching is required as a condition of approval by that Association, it is recommended that the Association provide means within its administrative machinery by which an appeal may be taken from the decision of its Committee on Accrediting and Classification. This is to remove any possibility of successful legal attack against decisions of the Committee regarding the accrediting of an institution.

27. Teachers colleges should enter into written contracts with off-campus schools used for laboratory purposes. The provisions should be definite and specific. So that the institution will be assured of sufficient continuous control to inaugurate and maintain a consistent program of laboratory experience comparable to that in the campus school, the term should be from three to five years, with provision for renewal. The rights and duties of the contracting parties should be defined clearly.

28. Steps should be taken to secure the effective cooperation of school officials and especially of parents and pupils, to the end that desirable harmony may prevail to assure good educational spirit. Means to this end are effective supervision, school visits by parents, school publicity, and careful selection of student-teachers.

29. Although the subject of providing experience in conducting extracurricular and extra-school activities was not studied in this

investigation, the need for even more additional laboratory facilities is indicated, if such experience is to be arranged for students.

30. The total laboratory facilities of each teachers college should encompass a variety of schools, differing in size and type, and should include city, village, and rural schools. It is particularly important that rural one- and two-teacher schools and small high schools which enroll one hundred or less be included in the facilities, as well as city schools which now provide an undue proportion of the laboratory experience for students irrespective of their future teaching positions. Tables LXXVII to LXXXII show that resources are available, if they are used, to implement this recommendation in the teachers colleges.

31. It is recommended that public schools only should be used as off-campus laboratory schools, except possibly for such students as are preparing for teaching in private schools.

32. Other things being equal, it is desirable for the teachers college to utilize the facilities immediately surrounding the institution as off-campus schools, using those within ten miles of the campus if it is possible to do so.

## SUGGESTED ADDITIONAL STUDIES

Additional areas in which it is desirable that studies be made are listed below. Although, at the present time, at least in some of the areas, it is difficult to arrive at valid conclusions, their importance warrants that they be suggested as fields for future studies.

1. The relative use and effectiveness of campus and off-campus schools in providing extracurricular and extra-school laboratory experiences for student-teachers.

2. The relative contribution made to the student-teacher's teaching efficiency by "cadet" or "interne" teaching, and student-teaching in closely affiliated and closely supervised laboratory schools.

3. Determination of the amount of laboratory experience which is necessary to assure the student's competency in the initial teaching position.

4. The relative value of observation and responsible room teaching to the student-teacher in the laboratory schools.

5. The relative cost of campus and off-campus student-teaching, both to the teachers college and the student-teacher.

6. The differences in the teaching activities of student-teachers who receive their laboratory experience in campus and off-campus schools.

7. A comparison of the effectiveness of teachers who receive their laboratory experience throughout the four years of the college curriculum with that of those whose laboratory experience is confined to the last two of the four years.

# BIBLIOGRAPHY

ALEXANDER, THOMAS. "Application of Some Principles Which Underlie Practice Teaching." Address delivered before the New York Association of Teachers Colleges and Normal School Faculties, Syracuse, N. Y., October 13, 1930.

ALEXANDER, THOMAS. "Practice-Teaching in Germany for Elementary and Secondary Teachers." *Educational Administration and Supervision*, Vol. 13, pp. 289–309, May, 1927.

ALEXANDER, THOMAS. "The Training of Teachers in Europe." *National Survey of the Education of Teachers*, Vol. 5, Part VIII, pp. 385–455. Office of Education Bulletin 1933, No. 10. United States Department of the Interior, Washington, D. C., 1935.

ALEXANDER, THOMAS. "What May Teacher-Training Institutions in the United States Learn from Similar Institutions in Other Countries?" *Proceedings of the National Education Association*, Vol. 70, pp. 736–741, 1932.

ALEXANDER, THOMAS. "What Valid Principles Have We to Guide Us in the Construction of Curricula for Normal Schools and Teachers Colleges?" *Problems in Teacher-Training*, Vol. 2, pp. 77–84. Eastern-States Association of Professional Schools for Teachers, 1927.

ALEXANDER, THOMAS. "A Wider Extension of the Content of Student-Teaching." *Educational Administration and Supervision*, Vol. 16, pp. 352–358, May, 1930.

AMERICAN ASSOCIATION OF TEACHERS COLLEGES. *Minimum Standards for Accrediting Teachers Colleges and Normal Schools*. Revised, February, 1938.

AMERICAN ASSOCIATION OF TEACHERS COLLEGES. *Yearbook, 1926*, Standard VII.

AMERICAN NORMAL SCHOOLS. *Proceedings of the First Annual Convention of the American Normal School Association*, 1860.

ARMENTROUT, WINFIELD D. *The Conduct of Student Teaching in State Teachers Colleges*. Colorado Teachers College Education Series, No. 2. Colorado State Teachers College, Greeley, Colo., 1927.

BAGLEY, WILLIAM C. "Nature and Extent of Curriculum Differentiation in the Training of Rural-School Teachers." *Professional Preparation of Teachers for Rural Schools*, pp. 16–21. Office of Education Bulletin 1928, No. 6. United States Department of the Interior, Washington, D. C., 1928.

BAGLEY, WILLIAM C. "The Place of Applied Philosophy in Judging Student Teaching." *Educational Administration and Supervision*, Vol. 17, pp. 330–335, May, 1931.

BAGLEY, WILLIAM C., ALEXANDER, THOMAS, and FOOTE, J. M. *Report of the Survey Commission on The Louisiana State Normal College, The Louisiana Polytechnic Institute, The Southwestern Louisiana Institute*. The State Department of Education, Baton Rouge, La., 1924.

BAKER, FRANK E. "Selective Admission and Promotion." *Education of Teachers, Twenty-Third Yearbook* of the National Society of College Teachers of Education, pp. 16–65. University of Chicago Press, 1935.

BARNARD, HENRY. "First Annual Report of the Secretary of the Board of Commissioners of Common Schools of Connecticut." *Connecticut Common School Journal*, Vol. 1, pp. 153–176, June 1, 1839.

BARNARD, HENRY. *Normal Schools, and Other Institutions, Agencies, and Means Designed for the Professional Education of Teachers*, Part I. Hartford, Conn., 1851.

BARNARD, HENRY. "State Normal School at Salem, Mass." *American Journal of Education*, Vol. 17, pp. 697–700, 1867–1868.

BARR, A. S. and BURTON, WILLIAM H. *The Supervision of Instruction.* D. Appleton and Company, New York, 1926.

BAUGHER, JACOB I. *Organization and Administration of Practice-Teaching in Privately Endowed Colleges of Liberal Arts.* Contributions to Education, No. 487. Bureau of Publications, Teachers College, Columbia University, 1931.

BERNARD, LLOYD DUCKWORTH. "Relative Cost and Effectiveness of Campus and Off-Campus Plans of Student Teaching in California." Library manuscript, University of California, Berkeley, 1935.

*Biennial Survey of Education, 1932–34*, Vol. II, Chaps. II and IV. Office of Education Bulletin 1935, No. 2. United States Department of the Interior, Washington, D. C., 1937.

*Biennial Survey of Education, 1934–36*, Vol. II, Chaps. II and IV. Office of Education Bulletin 1937, No. 2. United States Department of the Interior, Washington, D. C., 1939.

BOYDEN, ARTHUR C. *The History of Bridgewater Normal School.* Bridgewater Normal Alumni Association, 1933.

BRESLICH, ERNEST R. and others. "The Supervision and Administration of Practice-Teaching." *Educational Administration and Supervision*, Vol. 11, pp. 1–12, January, 1925.

BRIDGEWATER NORMAL SCHOOL. *Semi-Centennial Exercises.* Address by Albert G. Boyden. Wright and Potter Printing Company, Boston, 1890.

BRIM, ORVILLE G. "Guiding Principles in Rural Education." *Thirtieth Yearbook of the National Society for the Study of Education*, Part I, pp. 257–272, 1931.

BUTTERWECK, JOSEPH S. "Apprenticeship Teaching in Secondary Schools." *School Review*, Vol. 37, pp. 377–387, May, 1929.

CARNEY, MABEL. "The Preparation of Teachers for Small Rural Schools." *National Survey of the Education of Teachers*, Vol. 5, Part VII, pp. 341–384. Office of Education Bulletin 1933, No. 10. United States Department of the Interior, Washington, D. C., 1935.

CHARTERS, W. W. and WAPLES, DOUGLAS. *The Commonwealth Teacher-Training Study.* University of Chicago Press, 1929.

CLEVENGER, A. W. "A Review of the Governor Langer Suit." *The North Central Association Quarterly*, Vol. 13, pp. 505–517, April, 1939.

COLE, MARY I. *Cooperation Between the Faculty of the Campus Elementary Training School and the Other Departments of Teachers Colleges and Normal Schools.* Contributions to Education, No. 746. Bureau of Publications, Teachers College, Columbia University, 1939.

CONNECTICUT. *Fifth Annual Report of the Superintendent of the Common Schools of Connecticut to the General Assembly*, May Session, p. 14. 1850.

COOK, JOHN W., Chairman. "The Kind and Amount of Practice-Work and Its

Place in the Normal School Course." *Journal of Proceedings and Addresses of the National Education Association*, pp. 501–509. 1895.

DEARBORN, NED H. *The Oswego Movement in American Education*. Contributions to Education, No. 183. Bureau of Publications, Teachers College, Columbia University, 1925.

DYER, W. P. "What Changes in Our Teacher-Training Programs Need to Be Made to Meet the Demands of Progressive Schools?" *Problems in Teacher-Training*, Vol. 10, pp. 246–254. Eastern States Association of Professional Schools for Teachers, 1936.

EDWARDS, NEWTON. *The Courts and the Public Schools*. University of Chicago Press, 1933.

ENGLEMAN, J. O. "A Study of Student Teaching in State Normal Schools and Teachers' Colleges." *The Elementary School Journal*, Vol. 26, pp. 256–263, December, 1925.

EUBANK, LOUIS ALLEN. *The Organization and Administration of Laboratory Schools in State Teachers Colleges*. Northeast Missouri State Teachers College Bulletin, Vol. 31, No. 4, Kirksville, Mo., April, 1931.

EVENDEN, E. S. "Cooperation of Teachers of Academic Subjects with the Training School." *Educational Administration and Supervision*, Vol. 11, pp. 307–319, May, 1925.

EVENDEN, E. S. "The Critic Teacher and the Professional Treatment of Subject-Matter—A Challenge." *Educational Administration and Supervision*, Vol. 15, pp. 373–382, May, 1929.

EVENDEN, E. S. "The Education of Teachers in the United States—Principles and Problems." *Problems in Teacher-Training*, Vol. 10, pp. 2–16. Eastern States Association of Professional Schools for Teachers, 1936.

EVENDEN, E. S. "Findings of the National Survey of the Education of Teachers: Implications for the Improvement of Current Practice." *Twelfth Yearbook of The American Association of Teachers Colleges*, pp. 99–133, 1933.

EVENDEN, E. S. "Issues in Teacher-Training Programs." *Educational Administration and Supervision*, Vol. 17, pp. 530–534, October, 1931.

EVENDEN, E. S. "Making the Preparation of Teachers More Professional." *National Survey of the Education of Teachers*, Vol. 6, Chap. III, pp. 72–190. Office of Education Bulletin 1933, No. 10. United States Department of the Interior, Washington, D. C., 1935.

EVENDEN, E. S. "Professional Elements in the Education of Teachers." *Twenty-fourth Yearbook* of the National Society of College Teachers of Education, pp. 7–9, 1936.

EVENDEN, E. S. "Proposals for Correcting Professional Myopia of Subject-Matter Teachers in Teachers Colleges." *Educational Administration and Supervision*, Vol. 16, pp. 372–382, May, 1930.

EVENDEN, E. S. *Special Report on Curriculum Practices in Normal Schools and Teachers Colleges*. American Association of Teachers Colleges (Unpublished), 1940.

EVENDEN, E. S. "What Courses in Education Are Desirable in a Four-Year Curriculum in a State Teachers College?" *Yearbook of The American Association of Teachers Colleges, 1926*, pp. 57–71.

EVENDEN, E. S., GAMBLE, GUY C., and BLUE, HAROLD G. "Teacher Personnel in the United States." *National Survey of the Education of Teachers*, Vol. 2,

Part I, pp. 1–111. Office of Education Bulletin 1933, No. 10. United States Department of the Interior, Washington, D. C., 1935.

FITCH, HARRY N. *An Analysis of the Supervisory Activities and Techniques of the Elementary School Training Supervisor.* Contributions to Education, No. 476. Bureau of Publications, Teachers College, Columbia University, 1931.

FLOWERS, JOHN G. *Content of Student-Teaching Courses Designed for the Training of Secondary Teachers in State Teachers Colleges.* Contributions to Education, No. 538. Bureau of Publications, Teachers College, Columbia University, 1932.

FOSTER, FRANK K. "The Training School in the Education of Teachers." *National Survey of the Education of Teachers*, Vol. 3, Part IV, pp. 367–401. Office of Education Bulletin 1933, No. 10. United States Department of the Interior, Washington, D. C., 1935.

GARRISON, NOBLE L. *Current Practice in Coordination of College and Training School Work.* The Author, Ypsilanti, Mich., 1930.

GARRISON, NOBLE L. *Status and Work of the Training Supervisor.* Contributions to Education, No. 280. Bureau of Publications, Teachers College, Columbia University, 1927.

GOOD, H. G. "The Legal Status of Practice Teaching." National Society of College Teachers of Education, *Educational Monographs*, No. 9, pp. 13–17, 1920.

GORDY, JOHN P. *Rise and Growth of the Normal-School Idea in the United States.* Bureau of Education, Circular of Information No. 8. Washington, D. C., 1891.

GREENOUGH, J. C., Chairman. "Training Schools in Connection with Normal Schools." *Addresses and Journal of Proceedings of the National Education Association*, pp. 229–233, 1874.

HAERTTER, LEONARD D. and SMITH, DORA V. "An Investigation into the Methods of Student Teaching in 32 Colleges and Universities." *Educational Administration and Supervision*, Vol. 12, pp. 577–595, December, 1926.

HALL-QUEST, ALFRED L. *Professional Secondary Education in Teachers Colleges.* Contributions to Education, No. 169. Bureau of Publications, Teachers College, Columbia University, 1925.

HECKERT, J. W. "Extra-Mural Practice Teaching at Miami University." *Supervisors of Student Teaching, Fourth Annual Session, 1924*, pp. 25–31.

HENDERSON, ELISHA L. *The Organization and Administration of Student Teaching in State Teachers Colleges.* Contributions to Education, No. 692. Bureau of Publications, Teachers College, Columbia University, 1937.

HENDERSON, JOSEPH L. "A Statistical Study of the Use of City School Systems by Student-Teachers in Colleges and Universities." *Educational Administration and Supervision*, Vol. 12, pp. 326–339, May, 1926.

HIGBEE, E. C. "Twenty Years of Progress in Providing Adequate Training School Facilities, 1907–1927." *Yearbook of The American Association of Teachers Colleges, 1928*, pp. 39–47.

HILL, CLYDE M. *A Decade of Progress in Teacher Training.* Contributions to Education, No. 233. Bureau of Publications, Teachers College, Columbia University, 1927.

HOLLIS, A. P. "The Present Status of Practice Teaching in State Normal Schools." *Pedagogical Seminary*, Vol. 8, pp. 495–509, 1901.

HUMPHREYS, HARRY C. *The Factors Operating in the Location of State Normal*

*Schools.* Contributions to Education, No. 142. Bureau of Publications, Teachers College, Columbia University, 1923.

HUNT, CHARLES W. "Practice, A Control for the Selection of Subject-Matter." *Educational Administration and Supervision,* Vol. 16, pp. 359–363, May, 1930.

JARMAN, ARTHUR M. *The Administration of Laboratory Schools.* George Wahr, Ann Arbor, Mich., 1932.

JARMAN, ARTHUR M. "Cooperation of Public Schools with State Universities in the Training of Teachers." *Educational Administration and Supervision,* Vol. 19, pp. 282–289, April, 1933.

JARRETT, R. P. "How May Teachers Colleges Expand Their Training School Facilities." *The Texas Outlook,* Vol. 11, pp. 12–13, October, 1927.

JUDD, CHARLES H. "Preparation of School Personnel." *The Regents Inquiry,* p. 145. The Regents Inquiry into the Character and Cost of Public Education in the State of New York. McGraw-Hill Book Company, New York, 1938.

JUDD, C. H. and PARKER, S. C. *Problems Involved in Standardizing State Normal Schools.* Bureau of Education Bulletin, No. 12. Department of the Interior, Washington, D. C., 1916.

KANDEL, I. L. *The Training of Elementary School Teachers in Germany.* Contributions to Education, No. 31. Bureau of Publications, Teachers College, Columbia University, 1910.

KELLY, F. J. and SCOTT, IRA O. "What Training School Facilities Are Provided in State Normal Schools." *Educational Administration and Supervision,* Vol. 1, pp. 591–598, November, 1915.

LEARNED, WILLIAM S. and BAGLEY, WILLIAM C. *The Professional Preparation of Teachers for American Public Schools.* Bulletin No. 14, Carnegie Foundation for the Advancement of Teaching, New York, 1920.

LIGON, M. E., Chairman. *Training of High School Teachers.* Association of Colleges and Secondary Schools of the Southern States, Birmingham, Ala., 1931.

LIVINGOOD, FRED G. "An Internship for Education." *School and Society,* Vol. 38, pp. 639–640, November 11, 1933.

LUCKEY, G. W. A. *The Professional Training of Secondary Teachers in the United States.* The Macmillan Company, New York, 1903.

MCCARREL, FRED. *The Development of the Training School.* Abstract of Contributions to Education, No. 126. George Peabody College for Teachers, Nashville, Tenn., 1934.

MCGUFFEY, VERNE. *Differences in the Activities of Teachers in Rural One-Teacher Schools and of Grade Teachers in Cities.* Contributions to Education, No. 346. Bureau of Publications, Teachers College, Columbia University, 1929.

MARSHALL, EDNA M. *Evaluation of Types of Student-Teaching.* Contributions to Education, No. 488. Bureau of Publications, Teachers College, Columbia University, 1932.

MASSACHUSETTS. *Ninth Annual Report of the Board of Education,* 1845; *Fourteenth Annual Report of the Board of Education,* 1850; *Eighteenth Annual Report of the Board of Education,* 1855. Boston, Mass.

MEAD, A. R. "Advantages and Disadvantages of Campus and 'Off-Campus' Laboratory Schools." *Educational Administration and Supervision,* Vol. 16, pp. 196–207, March, 1930.

MEAD, A. R. *Practice Teaching for Teachers in Secondary Schools.* Bulletin 1917,

No. 29. Bureau of Education, United States Department of the Interior, Washington, D. C., 1917.
MEAD, A. R. *Supervised Student-Teaching.* Johnson Publishing Company, Richmond, Va., 1930.
MERIAM, JUNIUS L. *Normal School Education and Efficiency in Teaching.* Contributions to Education, No. 1. Bureau of Publications, Teachers College, Columbia University, 1905.
MOONEY, EDWARD S. *An Analysis of the Supervision of Student Teaching.* Contributions to Education, No. 711. Bureau of Publications, Teachers College, Columbia University, 1937.
MORRISON, ROBERT H. "Fundamental Issues in the Professional Education of Teachers." *Problems in Teacher-Training*, Vol. 10, pp. 254-269. Eastern-States Association of Professional Schools for Teachers, 1936.
MYERS, ALONZO F. "The Course in Observation and Participation in Its Relationship to Courses in Principles of Teaching, Methods, School Management, etc." *Educational Administration and Supervision*, Vol. 14, pp. 404-412, September, 1928.
NELSON, ESTHER M. *An Analysis of the Content of Student-Teaching Courses for the Education of Elementary Teachers in State Teachers Colleges.* Contributions to Education, No. 723. Bureau of Publications, Teachers College, Columbia University, 1939.
NORTON, ARTHUR O. *The First State Normal School in America: The Journals of Cyrus Pierce and Mary Swift.* Harvard University Press, Cambridge, Mass., 1926.
PALMER, JAMES B. "The Responsibility of Teacher-Training Institutions During the Depression." *Proceedings of the National Education Association*, Vol. 70, pp. 435-437, 1932.
PAYNE, BRUCE R. "Twenty Years of Progress in the Service Rendered by Normal Schools and Teachers Colleges." *Addresses and Proceedings of the National Education Association*, pp. 917-920, 1928.
PEIK, W. E. "Integration of the Pre-Service Curriculum for Teaching in Separate and Intensive Professional Courses." *Seventeenth Yearbook* of the Supervisors of Student Teaching, pp. 25-35, 1917.
PEIK, W. E. "Teacher Education Curricula in Universities, Colleges, and Junior Colleges." *National Survey of the Education of Teachers*, Vol. 3, Part III, pp. 155-365. Office of Education Bulletin 1933, No. 10. United States Department of the Interior, Washington, D. C., 1935.
PHELPS, WILLIAM F. "Report on a Course of Study for Normal Schools." *Journal of Proceedings of the American Normal School, and the National Teachers' Association*, pp. 11-20, 1870.
PRYOR, HUGH CLARK. *Graded Units in Student-Teaching.* Contributions to Education, No. 202. Bureau of Publications, Teachers College, Columbia University, 1926.
PURDOM, J. LESLIE. "Teacher-Training Through Directed Observation of Teaching, Through Teaching under Faculty Supervision, and Through Teaching as an Apprentice." *Report of Seventh Annual Session of Supervisors of Student Teaching*, pp. 32-36, 1927.
PUTNAM, DANIEL. *History of the Michigan State Normal School.* 1899.
*Report of the Commissioner of Education.* Government Printing Office, Washing-

ton, D. C. For the Year 1867–68, 1868. For the Year 1873, 1874. For the Year 1883–84, 1885. For the Year 1893–94, Vol. 2, 1896. For the Year 1900–01, Vol. 2, 1902.

REYNOLDS, HELEN M. "Recruiting the Teaching Corps—The Cadet Plan." *Educational Method*, Vol. 9, pp. 290–297, February, 1930.

RHODE ISLAND. *Annual Report of the Commissioner of Public Schools of Rhode Island, January, 1856.* Providence, R. I.

RHODE ISLAND COLLEGE OF EDUCATION. *Bulletin No. 63*, January, 1934. Providence, R. I.

ROBERTS, D. H. "Observation and Practice at Michigan State Normal College, Ypsilanti, Michigan." *Educational Administration and Supervision*, Vol. 10, pp. 310–314, May, 1924.

ROBINSON, WILLIAM MCKINLEY. *Practices and Trends in the Preparation of Teachers for Rural Elementary Schools in the State Teachers Colleges and Normal Schools.* Western State Teachers College, Kalamazoo, Mich., 1936.

ROCKWELL, H. W. "Report of the Committee on Accrediting and Classification." *Yearbook of the American Association of Teachers Colleges, 1927*, pp. 118–124.

ROUNDS, C. C. "Practice Schools in Connection with Normal Schools." *Journal of Proceedings and Addresses of the National Education Association*, Vol. 24, pp. 429–436, 1885.

RUGG, EARLE U. "Curricula of Normal Schools and Teachers Colleges." *National Survey of the Education of Teachers*, Vol. 3, Part II, pp. 32–154. Office of Education Bulletin 1933, No. 10. United States Department of the Interior, Washington, D. C., 1935.

RUGG, EARLE U. and PEIK, W. E. "The Plan and Scope of Curriculum Studies." *National Survey of the Education of Teachers*, Vol. III, Part I, Office of Education Bulletin 1933, No. 10. United States Department of the Interior, Washington, D. C., 1935.

RUGGLES, CLYDE O. *Historical Sketch and Notes, Winona State Normal School, 1860–1910.* Minnesota Normal School Board, Winona, Minn., 1910.

RUTLEDGE, SAMUEL A. *The Development of Guiding Principles for the Administration of Teachers Colleges and Normal Schools.* Contributions to Education, No. 449. Bureau of Publications, Teachers College, Columbia University, 1930.

RYAN, H. H. "A Century of Laboratory Schools in the United States." Unpublished study, June 1, 1929.

RYAN, H. H. "The Practice-Teaching Load in Laboratory Schools." *Educational Administration and Supervision*, Vol. 24, pp. 143–146, February, 1938.

SANDERS, W. H. "A Study of Professional Work as Presented in the State Normal Schools of the United States" (and bibliography). *The Pedagogical Seminary*, Vol. 20, pp. 48–57, March, 1913.

SANTEE, A. M. "The Organization and Administration of Practice Teaching in State Normal Schools." *School and Home Education*, Vol. 37, pp. 8–13, September, 1917.

SCHORLING, RALEIGH. "Directed Teaching." *Education of Teachers, Twenty-third Yearbook* of the National Society of College Teachers of Education, pp. 127–178. 1935.

SCHUTTE, T. H. "The Distribution of Time of Student-Teachers in a State

Teachers College." *Educational Administration and Supervision*, Vol. 8, pp. 215–222, April, 1922.

SEERLEY, HOMER H. and STONE, CLIFF W. "Co-operation Between Normal Schools and City School Systems in Teacher Training." *Educational Administration and Supervision*, Vol. 4, pp. 116–117, February, 1918.

SHANNON, J. R. "Demonstration Teaching and Directed Observation" (and bibliography). *Educational Method*, Vol. 14, pp. 355–362, April, 1935.

SHERROD, CHARLES C. "Patterns of Student Teaching." *Fourteenth Yearbook of The American Association of Teachers Colleges*, pp. 28–35, 1935.

SOMERS, G. T. *Pedagogical Prognosis: Predicting the Success of Prospective Teachers.* Contributions to Education, No. 140. Bureau of Publications, Teachers College, Columbia University, 1923.

STEARNS, EBEN S. and others. *Historical Sketches of the Framingham State Normal School.* 1914.

STONE, MASON S. "The First Normal School in America." *Teachers College Record*, Vol. 24, pp. 263–271, May, 1923.

STOUT, KATE D. "Organization of Training Schools and Practice Teaching." *Journal of Proceedings and Addresses of the National Education Association*, pp. 700–706, 1895.

STRATEMEYER, FLORENCE B. "A Proposed Experiment in Teacher-Training." *Educational Administration and Supervision*, Vol. 18, pp. 353–358, May, 1932.

STREBEL, RALPH F. *The Nature of the Supervision of Student-Teaching in Universities Using Cooperative Public High Schools.* Contributions to Education, No. 655. Bureau of Publications, Teachers College, Columbia University, 1935.

SUHRIE, AMBROSE L. "Laboratory Facilities of Our Teacher Training Institutions." *Educational Administration and Supervision*, Vol. 12, pp. 340–344, May, 1926.

TAPE, H. A. "New Training School Buildings and Equipment of the Michigan State Normal College, Ypsilanti, Michigan." *Eighth Annual Session of Supervisors of Student Teaching*, pp. 39–46, 1928.

TARBELL, HORACE S. "Report of the Sub-Committee on the Training of Teachers." *Journal of Proceedings and Addresses of the National Education Association*, pp. 238–253, 1895.

ULLMAN, ROY ROLAND. *The Prognostic Value of Certain Factors Related to Teaching Success.* A. L. Garber Company, Ashland, Ohio, 1931.

WADE, N. A. and FRETZ, R. M. "Some Practices in the Administration and Supervision of Student-Teaching." *Educational Administration and Supervision*, Vol. 12, pp. 124–130, February, 1926.

WALK, GEORGE E. "Practice Teaching and Observation in Normal Schools." *Education*, Vol. 38, pp. 69–85, October, 1917.

WALTERS, RAYMOND. "Statistics of Registration in American Universities and Colleges." *School and Society*, Vol. 42, p. 802, December 14, 1935; Vol. 44, p. 793, December 19, 1936; Vol. 46, p. 770, December 18, 1937.

WARD, CHARLES C. "Technics and Facilities of the Training School." *Thirteenth Yearbook of The American Association of Teachers Colleges*, pp. 89–96, 1934.

WELBORN, E. L. "Co-operation with Local Schools in Student Teaching." *Educational Administration and Supervision*, Vol. 6, pp. 445–470, November, 1920.

WEST, ROSCOE L. "The Value of a Demonstration School." *Fifth Yearbook of the*

*Department of Elementary School Principals*, pp. 279–286. National Education Association, Washington, D. C., 1926.

WHITE, E. E. *Report of the Commissioner of Public Schools of Ohio to the General Assembly*. Columbus, Ohio, 1866.

WHITNEY, F. L. "The Prediction of Teaching Success." *Journal of Educational Research Monographs*, No. 6. Public School Publishing Company, Bloomington, Ill., 1924.

WICKERSHAM, JAMES P. *A History of Education in Pennsylvania*. Inquirer Publishing Company, Lancaster, Pa., 1886.

WILLIAMS, E. I. F. "Demonstration Teaching and Observation in Teacher Training Institutions of the United States." Society of College Teachers of Education, *Educational Monographs*, No. 11, pp. 103–121, 1922.

WILSON, LESTER M. *Training Departments in State Normal Schools in the United States*. The Normal School Bulletin, No. 66. Eastern Illinois State Normal School, Charleston, Ill., 1919.

# APPENDIX

# APPENDIX A

*INSTITUTIONS FROM WHICH DATA WERE RECEIVED WHICH WERE MEMBERS OF THE AMERICAN ASSOCIATION OF TEACHERS COLLEGES, 1933-34*

## NEW ENGLAND DIVISION

| | | |
|---|---|---|
| Connecticut | Danbury | State Normal School |
| | New Haven | State Normal School |
| Massachusetts | Bridgewater | State Teachers College |
| | Salem | State Teachers College |
| New Hampshire | Keene | State Normal School |
| | Plymouth | State Normal School |
| Rhode Island | Providence | Rhode Island College of Education |

## MIDDLE ATLANTIC DIVISION

| | | |
|---|---|---|
| New Jersey | Jersey City | State Normal School |
| | Newark | State Normal School |
| | Trenton | State Teachers College |
| | Upper Montclair | State Teachers College |
| New York | Albany | State College for Teachers |
| | Brockport | State Normal School |
| | Fredonia | State Normal School |
| | Geneseo | State Normal School |
| | New Paltz | State Normal School |
| | Oneonta | State Normal School |
| Pennsylvania | Bloomsburg | State Teachers College |
| | California | State Teachers College |
| | Clarion | State Teachers College |
| | East Stroudsburg | State Teachers College |
| | Edinboro | State Teachers College |
| | Indiana | State Teachers College |
| | Kutztown | State Teachers College |
| | Lock Haven | State Teachers College |
| | Mansfield | State Teachers College |
| | Millersville | State Teachers College |
| | Shippensburg | State Teachers College |
| | Slippery Rock | State Teachers College |

## EAST NORTH CENTRAL DIVISION

| | | |
|---|---|---|
| Illinois | Carbondale | Southern Illinois State Normal University |
| | Charleston | Eastern Illinois State Teachers College |

242  THE USE OF LABORATORY SCHOOLS

|  |  |  |
|---|---|---|
|  | DeKalb | Northern Illinois State Teachers College |
|  | Macomb | Western Illinois State Teachers College |
|  | Normal | Illinois State Normal University |
| Indiana | Muncie | Ball State Teachers College |
|  | Terre Haute | Indiana State Teachers College |
| Michigan | Kalamazoo | Western State Teachers College |
|  | Marquette | Northern State Teachers College |
|  | Mt. Pleasant | Central State Teachers College |
|  | Ypsilanti | Michigan State Normal College |
| Ohio | Athens | College of Education, Ohio University |
|  | Bowling Green | Bowling Green State College |
|  | Kent | Kent State College |
|  | Oxford | School of Education, Miami University |
| Wisconsin | La Crosse | State Teachers College |
|  | Menomonie | The Stout Institute |
|  | Milwaukee | State Teachers College |
|  | Oshkosh | State Teachers College |
|  | Platteville | State Teachers College |
|  | Superior | State Teachers College |

**WEST NORTH CENTRAL DIVISION**

|  |  |  |
|---|---|---|
| Iowa | Cedar Falls | Iowa State Teachers College |
| Kansas | Emporia | Kansas State Teachers College |
|  | Hays | Fort Hays Kansas State College |
|  | Pittsburg | Kansas State Teachers College |
| Minnesota | Bemidji | State Teachers College |
|  | Duluth | State Teachers College |
|  | Mankato | State Teachers College |
|  | Moorhead | State Teachers College |
|  | Winona | State Teachers College |
| Missouri | Cape Girardeau | Southeast Missouri State Teachers College |
|  | Kirksville | Northeast Missouri State Teachers College |
|  | Maryville | Northwest Missouri State Teachers College |
|  | Warrensburg | Central Missouri State Teachers College |
| Nebraska | Chadron | Nebraska State Normal College |
|  | Kearney | Nebraska State Teachers College |
|  | Peru | Nebraska State Teachers College |
| North Dakota | Dickinson | State Teachers College |
|  | Ellendale | State Normal and Industrial School |
|  | Mayville | State Teachers College |
|  | Minot | State Teachers College |
| South Dakota | Aberdeen | Northern Normal and Industrial School |
|  | Madison | Eastern State Normal School |
|  | Spearfish | State Normal School |
|  | Springfield | Southern State Normal School |

## SOUTH ATLANTIC DIVISION

| | | |
|---|---|---|
| Georgia | Statesboro | South Georgia Teachers College |
| Maryland | Frostburg | Maryland State Normal School |
| North Carolina | Cullowhee | Western Carolina Teachers College |
| | Greenville | East Carolina Teachers College |
| Virginia | East Radford | State Teachers College |
| | Farmville | State Teachers College |
| | Fredericksburg | State Teachers College |
| | Harrisonburg | State Teachers College |
| West Virginia | Athens | Concord State Teachers College |
| | Fairmont | Fairmont State Teachers College |
| | Huntington | Marshall College |
| | Shepherdstown | Shepherd State Teachers College |

## EAST SOUTH CENTRAL DIVISION

| | | |
|---|---|---|
| Alabama | Florence | State Teachers College |
| | Jacksonville | State Teachers College |
| | Troy | State Teachers College |
| Kentucky | Bowling Green | Western Kentucky State Teachers College |
| | Morehead | Morehead State Teachers College |
| | Murray | Murray State Teachers College |
| | Richmond | Eastern Kentucky State Teachers College |
| Mississippi | Hattiesburg | State Teachers College |
| Tennessee | Johnson City | State Teachers College |
| | Memphis | State Teachers College |

## WEST SOUTH CENTRAL DIVISION

| | | |
|---|---|---|
| Arkansas | Arkadelphia | Henderston State Teachers College |
| | Conway | Arkansas State Teachers College |
| Louisiana | Lafayette | College of Education, Southwestern Louisiana Institute |
| | Natchitoches | Louisiana State Normal College |
| Oklahoma | Ada | East Central State Teachers College |
| | Alva | Northwestern State Teachers College |
| | Durant | Southeastern State Teachers College |
| | Tahlequah | Northeastern State Teachers College |
| | Weatherford | Southwestern State Teachers College |
| Texas | Alpine | Sul Ross State Teachers College |
| | Canyon | West Texas State Teachers College |
| | Commerce | East Texas State Teachers College |
| | Denton | North Texas State Teachers College |
| | Huntsville | Sam Houston State Teachers College |
| | Nacogdoches | Stephen F. Austin State Teachers College |
| | San Marcos | Southwest Texas State Teachers College |

## MOUNTAIN DIVISION

| | | |
|---|---|---|
| Arizona | Flagstaff | Arizona State Teachers College |
| | Tempe | Arizona State Teachers College |

| | | |
|---|---|---|
| Colorado | Greeley | Colorado State Teachers College |
| Idaho | Lewiston | Lewiston State Normal School |
| Montana | Dillon | State Normal College |
| New Mexico | Las Vegas | New Mexico Normal University |
| | Silver City | New Mexico State Teachers College |
| Utah | Salt Lake City | School of Education, University of Utah |

### PACIFIC DIVISION

| | | |
|---|---|---|
| California | Arcata | Humboldt State Teachers College |
| | Fresno | State Teachers College |
| | San Diego | State Teachers College |
| | San Francisco | State Teachers College |
| | San Jose | State Teachers College |
| Oregon | Ashland | Southern Oregon Normal School |
| | La Grande | Eastern Oregon Normal School |
| | Monmouth | Oregon Normal School |
| Washington | Bellingham | Washington State Normal School |
| | Cheney | Washington State Normal School |
| | Ellensburg | Washington State Normal School |

## INSTITUTIONS FROM WHICH DATA WERE RECEIVED WHICH WERE MEMBERS OF THE AMERICAN ASSOCIATION OF TEACHERS COLLEGES, 1937-38

### NEW ENGLAND DIVISION

| | | |
|---|---|---|
| Connecticut | Danbury | State Teachers College |
| | New Britain | Teachers College of Connecticut |
| | New Haven | State Teachers College |
| | Willimantic | State Teachers College |
| Maine | Gorham | State Normal School |
| Massachusetts | Bridgewater | State Teachers College |
| | Fitchburg | State Teachers College |
| | Framingham | State Teachers College |
| | Salem | State Teachers College |
| | Westfield | State Teachers College |
| New Hampshire | Keene | State Normal School |
| | Plymouth | State Normal School |
| Rhode Island | Providence | Rhode Island College of Education |
| Vermont | Castleton | State Normal School |
| | Johnson | State Normal School |

### MIDDLE ATLANTIC DIVISION

| | | |
|---|---|---|
| New Jersey | Glassboro | State Teachers College |
| | Jersey City | State Teachers College |

APPENDIX

|  |  |  |
|---|---|---|
|  | Newark | State Teachers College |
|  | Paterson | State Teachers College |
|  | Trenton | State Teachers College |
|  | Upper Montclair | State Teachers College |
| New York | Albany | State College for Teachers |
|  | Cortland | State Normal School |
|  | Fredonia | State Normal School |
|  | Geneseo | State Normal School |
|  | New Paltz | State Normal School |
|  | Oneonta | State Normal School |
|  | Oswego | State Normal School |
|  | Potsdam | State Normal School |
| Pennsylvania | Bloomsburg | State Teachers College |
|  | California | State Teachers College |
|  | Clarion | State Teachers College |
|  | East Stroudsburg | State Teachers College |
|  | Edinboro | State Teachers College |
|  | Indiana | State Teachers College |
|  | Kutztown | State Teachers College |
|  | Lock Haven | State Teachers College |
|  | Mansfield | State Teachers College |
|  | Millersville | State Teachers College |
|  | Shippensburg | State Teachers College |
|  | Slippery Rock | State Teachers College |
|  | West Chester | State Teachers College |

EAST NORTH CENTRAL DIVISION

|  |  |  |
|---|---|---|
| Illinois | Carbondale | Southern Illinois State Normal University |
|  | Charleston | Eastern Illinois State Teachers College |
|  | DeKalb | Northern Illinois State Teachers College |
|  | Macomb | Western Illinois State Teachers College |
| Indiana | Muncie | Ball State Teachers College |
|  | Terre Haute | Indiana State Teachers College |
| Michigan | Kalamazoo | Western State Teachers College |
|  | Marquette | Northern State Teachers College |
|  | Mt. Pleasant | Central State Teachers College |
|  | Ypsilanti | Michigan State Normal College |
| Ohio | Bowling Green | Bowling Green State University |
|  | Kent | Kent State University |
|  | Oxford | School of Education, Miami University |
| Wisconsin | Eau Claire | State Teachers College |
|  | La Crosse | State Teachers College |
|  | Milwaukee | State Teachers College |
|  | Oshkosh | State Teachers College |
|  | River Falls | State Teachers College |
|  | Stevens Point | State Teachers College |
|  | Superior | State Teachers College |

## THE USE OF LABORATORY SCHOOLS

### WEST NORTH CENTRAL DIVISION

| | | |
|---|---|---|
| Iowa | Cedar Falls | Iowa State Teachers College |
| Kansas | Emporia | Kansas State Teachers College |
| | Hays | Fort Hays Kansas State College |
| | Pittsburg | Kansas State Teachers College |
| Minnesota | Bemidji | State Teachers College |
| | Duluth | State Teachers College |
| | Moorhead | State Teachers College |
| | Winona | State Teachers College |
| Missouri | Cape Girardeau | Southeast Missouri State Teachers College |
| | Kirksville | Northeast Missouri State Teachers College |
| | Maryville | Northwest Missouri State Teachers College |
| | Springfield | Southwest Missouri State Teachers College |
| Nebraska | Chadron | Nebraska State Teachers College |
| | Kearney | Nebraska State Teachers College |
| | Peru | Nebraska State Teachers College |
| | Wayne | Nebraska State Teachers College |
| North Dakota | Ellendale | State Normal and Industrial School |
| | Mayville | State Teachers College |
| | Minot | State Teachers College |
| | Valley City | State Teachers College |
| South Dakota | Aberdeen | Northern State Teachers College |
| | Madison | Eastern State Normal School |
| | Springfield | Southern State Normal School |

### SOUTH ATLANTIC DIVISION

| | | |
|---|---|---|
| Georgia | Milledgeville | Georgia State College for Women |
| | Statesboro | South Georgia Teachers College (Collegeboro) |
| Maryland | Frostburg | State Teachers College |
| | Salisbury | State Teachers College |
| | Towson | State Teachers College |
| North Carolina | Boone | Appalachian State Teachers College |
| | Greenville | East Carolina Teachers College |
| Virginia | Farmville | State Teachers College |
| | Fredericksburg | State Teachers College |
| | Harrisonburg | State Teachers College |
| West Virginia | Athens | Concord State Teachers College |
| | Glenville | Glenville State Teachers College |
| | Huntington | Marshall College |
| | Shepherdstown | Shepherd State Teachers College |
| | West Liberty | West Liberty State Teachers College |

## EAST SOUTH CENTRAL DIVISION

| | | |
|---|---|---|
| Alabama | Florence | State Teachers College |
| | Jacksonville | State Teachers College |
| | Troy | State Teachers College |
| Kentucky | Bowling Green | Western Kentucky State Teachers College |
| | Murray | Murray State Teachers College |
| | Richmond | Eastern Kentucky State Teachers College |
| Mississippi | Cleveland | Delta State Teachers College |
| | Hattiesburg | State Teachers College |
| Tennessee | Johnson City | State Teachers College |
| | Memphis | State Teachers College |

## WEST SOUTH CENTRAL DIVISION

| | | |
|---|---|---|
| Arkansas | Arkadelphia | Henderson State Teachers College |
| | Conway | Arkansas State Teachers College |
| Louisiana | Lafayette | College of Education, Southwestern Louisiana Institute |
| | Natchitoches | Louisiana State Normal College |
| Oklahoma | Ada | East Central State Teachers College |
| | Durant | Southeastern State Teachers College |
| | Edmond | Central State Teachers College |
| | Tahlequah | Northeastern State Teachers College |
| | Weatherford | Southwestern State Teachers College |
| Texas | Denton | North Texas State Teachers College |
| | Huntsville | Sam Houston State Teachers College |
| | San Marcos | Southwest Texas State Teachers College |

## MOUNTAIN DIVISION

| | | |
|---|---|---|
| Arizona | Flagstaff | Arizona State Teachers College |
| | Tempe | Arizona State Teachers College |
| Colorado | Greeley | Colorado State College of Education |
| | Gunnison | Western State College |
| Idaho | Lewiston | State Normal School |
| Montana | Dillon | Montana State Normal College |

## PACIFIC DIVISION

| | | |
|---|---|---|
| California | Chico | Chico State College |
| | Fresno | Fresno State College |
| | San Francisco | San Francisco State College |
| Oregon | Ashland | Southern Oregon Normal School |
| | La Grande | Eastern Oregon Normal School |
| | Monmouth | Oregon Normal School |
| Washington | Bellingham | Western Washington College of Education |
| | Cheney | Eastern Washington College of Education |
| | Ellensburg | Central Washington College of Education |

# APPENDIX B

## SELECTED LEGISLATION CONCERNING LABORATORY SCHOOLS

Capital letters, in parentheses following the name of the states whose laws are quoted below, refer to items according to the following key:

A. Legislation granting authority to contract for the use of laboratory schools
B. Mandatory laboratory schools
C. Mandatory on communities to furnish laboratory facilities
D. Laboratory schools a part of public school system
E. Financial obligations of teachers colleges and school districts
F. Joint administration and control, teachers college and board of education
G. Transportation of student teachers
H. Student teachers authorized to teach without a certificate

### STATE OF ARIZONA (D, E, F, H)

*Teacher training schools.* Every teachers' training school established in connection with such colleges (i.e., state teachers colleges) shall be a part of the public school system and a branch of the public schools of the school district within which such training school is located, and shall be governed by the laws and regulations relating to public schools, except as otherwise provided herein, and students in said college may teach in such training schools though not certificated teachers, under such rules as the board of education of the college prescribes.

*Training schools to be under teachers college boards; compensation and payment of salaries.* Every such training school shall be under the supervision and management of the board of the college in connection with which it is established; but all teachers in such school, except the principal thereof, shall be employed by the board of education of the college and the trustees of the school district in which such training school is located, acting jointly. The school district shall pay towards the expense of same an amount equal to one-half of the school money which it shall be entitled to have apportioned to it on account of the attendance at such training school during the preceding school year; provided, that pupils attending from another school district shall not be accredited with attendance in the school district in which said college is situated.

*Rules and regulations.* The board and the trustees of the district in which such training school is located, shall jointly prescribe rules and regulations governing the admission and attendance at such training school. . . .

—School Laws of Arizona, Article 11, sections 1109–1111, pp. 103–104. Phoenix, Arizona, 1931.

## STATE OF CALIFORNIA (A)

The governing board of any elementary school district within which a state teachers college is located may contract with the state teachers college for the education by the state teachers college of pupils eligible to attend school in the elementary school district. The pupils educated by the state teachers college under such contract may be housed on the campus of the state teachers college or in a building of the school district.

—School Code of the State of California, Division III, Chapter II, Article I, p. 147. Sacramento, California, 1935.

## STATE OF CONNECTICUT (C)

... the board (State Board of Education) shall not expend any money for any other normal school (except at New Britain, New Haven, Willimantic, and Danbury) until the town, city or school district, in which such school is situated, shall have agreed in writing with said board to furnish, and shall have furnished schools in suitable and sufficient buildings in connection with the training department in said school, the terms of such agreement to be satisfactory to said board; and every such town, city or city school district is authorized to make and execute such agreements.

—Section 30, Connecticut School Document No. 2, p. 18. Hartford, Connecticut, 1931.

## STATE OF MASSACHUSETTS (C, E)

North Adams, Fitchburg, Lowell and the town of Barnstable shall each make written agreements with the department to provide suitable and sufficient school buildings and model and practice schools in connection with the training departments of state teachers colleges therein. The department may, if requested by towns near such teachers colleges, make written agreements with such towns for the maintenance of practice schools therein in connection with such state teachers colleges, and may provide for the payment of part of the compensation of supervising teachers employed in such practice schools. This section shall not prevent the establishment and maintenance of model, practice, or training schools in connection with state teachers colleges, with or without the cooperation of local school authorities. All money payable to towns under such agreements shall be paid to the commonwealth.

—General Laws Relating to Education. Bulletin of the Department of Education, No. 7, Chapter 73, Section 3, p. 29. Boston, Massachusetts, 1931.

## STATE OF NEW YORK (A)

The commissioner of education is authorized to enter into a contract with the board of education of a city or district in which a state normal school is located for the education by the State for such period of time as may be agreed upon, of all or part of the children of legal school age residing in such city or school district. Before such contract becomes binding, it must be approved by the Board of Regents. Such contract must be executed in duplicate and one contract filed with the commissioner of education and the other with the state comptroller. A board of education in such a city or district is hereby authorized and empowered to enter into such contracts with the said commissioner of education and to perform all necessary acts to carry out the purposes of this act.

—Educational Laws, Section 834. Bulletin of the University of New York, No. 782, June, 1923. Albany, New York.

## STATE OF NORTH DAKOTA (E)

That all students attending any model high, graded or elementary school which is operated, maintained or in any manner connected with the state university, any normal school, publicly maintained educational institution of higher learning in this state in which model high, graded or elementary school members of the faculty or student body of such university, normal school or institution of higher learning teach, there shall be paid by the school district in which said pupils reside to said institution as tuition for such attendance as follows: Not less than two and one half dollars per month of actual membership per pupil in such model high school, and not less than two dollars per month of actual membership per pupil in any such graded or elementary school provided, however, that such tuition is payable at the close of each term or semester.

—General School Laws, State of North Dakota, Section 1221a, p. 59. Bismarck, North Dakota, 1931.

## STATE OF OREGON (A, H)

Any district school board may at its discretion authorize the use of all or any part of the public schools under its jurisdiction for training school purposes, and for this purpose may enter into a contract with the board of regents for normal schools upon such terms as may be mutually agreed upon.

\* \* \* \* \*

Any student of a state normal school who is assigned to teach in a training school is hereby vested with full authority to teach, during the time such student is so assigned, and such assignment shall have the same effect in all respects as if such student were the holder of a valid teacher's certificate. Any contract entered into by such school district board and such board of regents shall in all other respects have the same effect and be subject to the same requirements as a contract between a teacher and a school district board.

—School Laws of Oregon, Section 35—1135-37, p. 56. Salem, Oregon, 1931.

## STATE OF PENNSYLVANIA (A, B, F, G)

Each college shall provide practice teaching facilities so organized and administered that the students of the college shall acquire therein a practical knowledge of the art of teaching under the instruction and supervision of their proper teachers. It shall be lawful for the board of trustees of any college and the board of school directors of any district in this Commonwealth to enter into an agreement between such board of trustees and board of school directors by which all or part of the pupils of such school district may be instructed in the training school in such college upon terms mutually agreeable to the board of trustees and the board of school directors concerned. It also shall be lawful for the board of trustees of any college and the board of school directors of any district or districts to enter into an agreement, upon terms mutually satisfactory, in accordance with which all or part of the classes of such district or districts may be available for practice teaching facilities for the students of such college. Such actions of the said school district or school districts and the boards of trustees of such colleges shall be entered respectively upon the minutes of the said respective boards and must be approved by the Superintendent of Public Instruction. The board of trustees of any college may provide for the transportation of students of the college to and from the place or places where such practice teaching facilities are available.

—The School Laws of Pennsylvania, Section 2004, p. 152. Department of Public Instruction, Harrisburg, Pennsylvania, 1935.

## STATE OF WASHINGTON (C)

It shall be the duty of the board of the school district (i.e., in which normal school is located) to apportion for attendance to the said training school, a sufficient number of pupils from the public schools under the supervision of said board as will furnish to such normal school the number of pupils required in order to maintain such training school; provided that the principal of said normal school may refuse to accept such pupils as in his judgment by reason of incorrigibility, or mental defects would tend to reduce the efficiency of said training department.

—Code of Public Instruction, Sections 154–157, Olympia, Washington, 1923.

# APPENDIX C

*SELECTED CONTRACTS\* AND AGREEMENTS BETWEEN LOCAL BOARDS OF EDUCATION AND THE AUTHORITIES GOVERNING STATE TEACHERS COLLEGES FOR THE USE OF LABORATORY SCHOOLS IN EFFECT IN THE ACADEMIC YEAR, 1937-38, OR LATER*

CONTRACT A. WESTERN STATE COLLEGE OF COLORADO, GUNNISON, COLORADO

(Contract deals almost exclusively with financial matters)

GUNNISON, COLORADO
AGREEMENT
Between
SCHOOL DISTRICT NO. 1, GUNNISON COUNTY, COLORADO
and
WESTERN STATE COLLEGE OF COLORADO
for
TRAINING SCHOOL PURPOSES

The following agreement is hereby entered into by and between School District Number One of Gunnison County, Colorado, and Western State College of Colorado for Training School purposes:

School District Number One agrees to furnish the following services for the regular school year:

1. As much of the time of their seventeen (17) teachers as the needs of the teacher training program of Western State College demands for all practice teachers in the grades from the kindergarten through Junior High School. All of the salary of said teachers to be paid by said District Number One.

The training program to provide for all training students of the college facilities for: (a) practice teaching, (b) observation, (c) participation, (d) demonstration teaching, (e) experimental school work.

2. Teacher qualifications: All teachers employed by said school district must be approved by the college administration as fully meeting their requirements for critic teachers.

3. School District Number One further agrees to provide all necessary buildings, equipment, supplies, maintenance, and operation necessary for these training schools. For the summer quarter, School District Number One agrees to furnish

---

\* Copies of these contracts were furnished by the authorities of the institutions concerned and are published with their consent.

all the above services except the salary of the critic teachers. For all these above enumerated services for the regular school year of 1937-38, and for the summer quarter of 1938, Western State College of Colorado agrees to pay to School District Number One of Gunnison County, Colorado, forty-one hundred dollars ($4100). This is to be paid as follows:

>     November 1, 1937................... $1,000
>     February 1, 1938...................  1,500
>     May 1, 1938.......................  1,000
>     June 15, 1938......................    600

SIGNED .............................. SIGNED ..............................
Western State College of Colorado    School District No. One
by C. C. Casey, President    Gunnison County, Colorado
   by H. T. Hatch, Supt.

## CONTRACT B. MADISON COLLEGE, HARRISONBURG, VIRGINIA

(Contract includes primarily financial and administrative details)

The City School Board of Harrisonburg agrees that the State Teachers College of Harrisonburg shall have the privilege of doing student teaching in the elementary and junior high school grades of the public schools of the City provided:

1. The student teaching in each grade be under the supervision and direction of a supervising teacher who shall (a) be selected, advanced or dismissed jointly by the contracting parties; (b) be paid 60% by the College and 40% by the City School Board, either party being allowed to pay more at their own volition if it appears desirable to get a better teacher.

2. That the curriculum to be used in the training grades shall be the State adopted curriculum, any variation from this to be approved by the City School Board, the same regulation to apply to the selection and use of textbooks.

3. That the number of student teachers assigned at any time to any one class group shall not exceed five.

4. That all materials and supplies necessitated by student-teaching and not furnished by the School Board to other grades shall be furnished by the Teachers College and may remain the property of the Teachers College.

5. That the dates of opening and closing the training grades shall be left to the determination of the City School Board.

6. That the Teachers College shall supply a director of training with such assistants as may be necessary, the same to be paid entirely by the Teachers College.

7. That the Teachers College shall provide entirely for the salaries of the supervising teachers in the vacation or summer school.

8. That such matters as school fees, dismissal of students, enforcing compulsory attendance laws, keeping records, enforcing quarantine and vaccination

regulations, etc. shall be dealt with in the manner usual with public school teachers of the city.

9. That all observation, teaching, suggestions, or other contacts of the college students or faculty with the training school grades shall be handled through the Director of Training and that all criticism, suggestions, and instructions of the Supt. of Schools or of the City School Board collectively or individually concerning student-teaching be conveyed through the Director of Training.

10. That this contract may be modified or terminated by the mutual consent of the contracting parties at any time.

11. That either party to this contract may terminate this contract without the consent of the second party provided a notice of at least three years is given to the other party by the party desiring to terminate this agreement.

AMENDMENT:
Under the provision of Article 10 above, it is mutually agreed upon by the contracting parties that the State Teachers College shall pay, in addition to the sums provided for in paragraph one of this contract, three hundred and fifty dollars annually to the City School Board as a supplement to the salary of the Supt. of Schools for his services in connection with the training of teachers for the college.

AMENDMENT—SECTION B OF PARAGRAPH ONE:
The above forty per cent to be paid by the City School Board to apply to salaries not in excess of $1500.00.

Madison College<br>was formerly<br>The State Teachers College<br>Harrisonburg, Virginia

## CONTRACT C. STATE TEACHERS COLLEGE, MINOT, SOUTH DAKOTA

(Contract emphasizes instruction and supervision in the laboratory school)

### AGREEMENT

This agreement, made in duplicate by and between the State Teachers College, Minot, North Dakota (hereinafter designated as "First Party") and ............................................................ Witnesseth: (hereinafter designated as "Second Party")

That the First Party, seeking the privilege of using ..................... within the ................. School District of Ward County for purposes of observation, participation, and practice teaching for teacher-training activities agrees to pay the teacher of ............................. the sum of $............. per month for the school year.

First Party further agrees to provide adequate supervision to safeguard the interests and welfare of the pupils of said school ................. and that the methods of training shall be carefully controlled by First Party's Rural Supervisor.

Second Party agrees to employ a teacher for School .................. who shall have had at least two years' preparation for teaching beyond high school graduation and one who meets the approval of the First Party.

Second Party further agrees to maintain a clean, well kept building and grounds and to exercise such authority with the teacher of said school as to insure a wholesome school situation in which students and enrolled pupils may receive the fullest benefit.

First party further agrees to purchase any additional supplies made necessary by the presence of student-teachers in the school or required by the supervisor of such work and not regularly furnished by the school.

The parties to the above mutually agree that the local teacher shall always be in complete charge of the school; that such teacher shall teach under the supervision of the Rural Supervisor and the administration of the School Board; that all teaching done by cadets in training shall be with the local teacher's full approval and sanction; that lesson plans shall be submitted by cadets and scrutinized by the teacher in charge preliminary to teaching by the cadets; and that at no time shall the amount of teaching done by cadets amount to more than 40% of the total amount of all teaching done during school time in said School ....................................

The school year, during which this agreement is to be in full effect and operative, is mutually determined to be as follows:

Witness our signatures on this, the ...... day of ........................., 19....

................................................
President

................................................
Director of Training for the State Teachers College

................................................
For the ..................... School District

................................................
Clerk

## CONTRACT D. IOWA STATE TEACHERS COLLEGE, CEDAR FALLS, IOWA

(Limited to finances, the school district compensating the college)

### Agreement for Cooperating in the Training of Teachers

This contract made and entered into by and between the Iowa State Board of Education, governing body of the Iowa State Teachers College, and the Independent School District of Hudson, Iowa, in accordance with Chapter 187 of the Laws of the Thirty-Eighth General Assembly.

WITNESSETH: That the said State Board of Education hereby agrees to supply the schools of Hudson, Iowa, with *six* supervisors, each assisted by not more than four to eight student teachers each term, during the school year of nine months beginning September, 1938.

That the Independent School District of Hudson, Iowa, agrees to cooperate in the training of student teachers according to the law referred to above, and agrees to pay to the Iowa State Board of Education for the use of the Iowa State Teachers College the sum of Three Thousand Dollars ($3000) for these services, one-half to be paid on November 1, 1938, and the balance on or before May 1, 1939.

........................, 1938      ........................................ President
Date signed                Iowa State Teachers College on the part
                           of the Iowa State Board of Education

........................, 1938      ........................................
Date signed                On the part of the Independent School
                           District of Hudson, Iowa

## CONTRACT E. STATE TEACHERS COLLEGE, FRAMINGHAM, MASSACHUSETTS

(Comprehensive contract for use of a city public school as a laboratory school)

AGREEMENT BETWEEN THE COMMONWEALTH AND THE TOWN OF FRAMINGHAM RELATIVE TO THE USE OF THE JONATHAN MAYNARD SCHOOL AS A SCHOOL OF OBSERVATION AND PRACTICE FOR THE STATE TEACHERS COLLEGE AT FRAMINGHAM.

This agreement made this ........ day of ............ in the year nineteen hundred and thirty-four between the Commonwealth of Massachusetts, by its Department of Education, constituted under General Laws, Chapter 15, and by authority of the General Laws Chapter 73 and acts in addition to an amendment thereof for the said Commonwealth, and the Town of Framingham, a municipal corporation in the County of Middlesex and said Commonwealth by its School Committee, thereof duly authorized, witnesseth that the parties to this agreement, each in consideration of the agreements on the part of the other herein contained, do hereby agree, the Commonwealth of Massachusetts for itself and the Town of Framingham for itself as follows:

(1) The Town of Framingham agrees to the use of the Jonathan Maynard School as a school of observation and practice by the State Teachers College at Framingham.

(2) The Town of Framingham agrees that the Commonwealth by its Department of Education, shall have joint authority with the School Committee of said Town in the general management of the Training School, including courses of study, text books and supplies, methods of instruction, grading, promotion, attendance, discipline, and other matters of administrative detail mutually agreed upon by the parties to this agreement.

It is agreed that the rules and regulations governing other schools and teachers in Framingham shall apply similarly to the Training School and its teachers.

It is also agreed that the courses of study and regular text books used at the Jonathan Maynard School shall be the same as those used in other Framingham schools of similar grade, and that the text books and supplies furnished by the

# APPENDIX

Framingham School Department shall be of like quantity and quality to those provided the other Framingham schools of the same grade.

The Department of Education will furnish such additional books and special supplies as it may deem necessary, without further expense to the Town of Framingham, that methods and materials may be enriched and thus the Training School made more valuable for teacher training purposes.

(3) It is also agreed that the instruction in the special subjects of Music, Drawing, Penmanship, Household and Manual Arts and Physical Education, similar in time and extent to that furnished in the other schools in Framingham of corresponding grade, shall be under the supervision of instructors from the State Teachers College, whose services shall be rendered without expense to the Town of Framingham. All materials used in the course of Manual Arts shall be supplied by the Framingham School Department.

(4) It is agreed that the principal and teachers of the said Training School, shall with the approval of the Department of Education, be nominated by the President of the State Teachers College at Framingham, with the approval of the Superintendent of Schools, and appointed by the School Committee of the Town of Framingham.

(5) Commencing September 1, 1934, and continuing until August 31, 1936, the Town of Framingham agrees to pay one half and the Commonwealth one half, of the salary of the Principal and each of the regular teachers of the Jonathan Maynard School.

(6) Commencing September 1, 1936, and thereafter, the Town of Framingham agrees to pay the principal and teachers in the Training School the same salaries paid teachers in the same grades in the public schools of the Town of Framingham. Any sums in excess of these salaries shall be provided by the Commonwealth in accordance with General Laws, Chapter 73, Section 3.

This agreement shall become operative September 1, 1934, with the exception of section six, and shall remain in force until amended or superseded on twelve months' notice, which may be given in writing either by the Commonwealth or the Town of Framingham. Section six shall become operative on September 1, 1936.

In witnesseth whereof the parties hereunto set their hands and seals, the Department of Education executing these presents through the Commissioner of Education, who incurs no personal liability by reason of the execution thereof, or anything herein contained or done hereunder, and the Town of Framingham by its School Committee duly authorized by Town meeting held a certified copy of which is attached.

Commonwealth of Massachusetts
Department of Education
By .........................................
Commissioner of Education

Approved as to matters of form:  Town of Framingham
.................................  .........................................
Assistant Attorney General  (Lines for signature by six members of)
School Committee

## CONTRACT F. EAST STROUDSBURG STATE TEACHERS COLLEGE, EAST STROUDSBURG, PENNSYLVANIA

(Comprehensive contract providing for the use of a college-owned school building as one of the city schools)

CONTRACT BETWEEN EAST STROUDSBURG STATE TEACHERS COLLEGE, EAST STROUDSBURG, AND SCHOOL DISTRICT OF EAST STROUDSBURG, PENNSYLVANIA.

Contract entered into this ........ day of ...................., 1937, between the East Stroudsburg State Teachers College, East Stroudsburg, Pennsylvania, party of the first part, and the School District of East Stroudsburg, party of the second part.

I. Party of the first part agrees to admit to its Training School, located on the college campus, all children of the District of East Stroudsburg enrolled below the seventh grade, residing in that part of East Stroudsburg east and south of the following line, beginning at the Brodhead Creek bridge extending up Washington Street to the corner of Washington and Crystal streets, thence north to the corner of Crystal and Analomink streets, thence east on Analomink street to the East Stroudsburg borough line. It is understood and agreed that all children of school age *below the seventh grade* residing in the aforesaid district shall be required to attend the Training School of the East Stroudsburg State Teachers College provided they can be accommodated.

II. Party of the first part agrees to teach all children admitted from the aforesaid district, and being below the seventh grade, without any charge whatever to the party of the second part, furnishing adequate room accommodations, with heat, light and janitor service, text books and all other supplies and sufficient number of training school teachers and supervisors to guarantee instruction up to the standard of the same grades in the best city schools.

III. It is further understood and agreed that the Supervising Principal employed by the District of East Stroudsburg shall have authority to inspect the work done in the Training School and make any suggestions in regard to the teaching, course of study, and general conduct of the work as he may see fit, which suggestions and recommendations shall receive due consideration from the authorities of the East Stroudsburg State Teachers College.

IV. Party of the second part agrees to permit student teaching in as many rooms in the elementary schools as may be desired by the College. The teachers of all rooms thus used shall be paid additional compensation in accordance with the State Salary Schedule for cooperative training teachers in school districts of the third class. This compensation shall be over and above the amount paid by the East Stroudsburg School District. The teachers used for training purposes are to be selected by the President of the East Stroudsburg State Teachers College after consultation with the Supervising Principal of the East Stroudsburg Public Schools. Party of the second part agrees that no new teachers shall be employed in the elementary school unless they are normal graduates with two years of teaching experience and are approved by the President of the State Teachers College. However, this requirement and approval will not be necessary unless the East Stroudsburg State Teachers College selects such new teachers as cooperative training teachers. Party of the first part agrees to provide adequate supervision in order to safeguard the interests of both parties.

V. The party of the second part agrees to permit the use of the Junior High School, comprising grades seven, eight and nine, for training purposes. The party of the first part agrees to pay the party of the second part the sum of eight hundred ($800) dollars per annum as compensation for additional expense made necessary by this use of the Junior High School; the same to be paid in equal quarterly installments, beginning on July 1, 1937.

The teachers of all rooms in the Junior High School, used for training purposes, shall be paid additional compensation in accordance with the State Salary Schedule for cooperative training teachers. This compensation shall be over and above the amount paid by the school district of East Stroudsburg as required by law for third class school districts. Party of the second part agrees that no new teachers shall be employed in the Junior High School unless they meet the educational requirements of the schedule for State Teachers Colleges and are approved by the President of the State Teachers College. This applies only to the fields in which the college is preparing teachers. The teachers used in the Junior High School for training purposes are to be selected by the President of the East Stroudsburg State Teachers College after consultation with the Supervising Principal of the East Stroudsburg Public Schools. Party of the first part agrees to provide adequate supervision in order to safeguard the interests of both parties.

VI. The party of the first part agrees to provide instruction in Health Education and proper supervision in the elementary schools and the junior and senior high schools. It is understood and agreed that the Supervising Principal employed by the District of East Stroudsburg shall have authority to inspect the work done in Health Education and make any suggestions with regard to the teaching, course of study, and general conduct of the work as he may see fit, which suggestions and recommendations shall receive due consideration from the authorities of the East Stroudsburg State Teachers College.

VII. It is further understood and agreed that both parties to this contract shall do all in their power to further the interests of the East Stroudsburg State Teachers College and the School District of East Stroudsburg.

VIII. This contract shall take effect on June 1, 1937 and continue to May 31, 1939, with the distinct understanding that both parties to this contract express full intent and purpose to renew the contract at the time of expiration for a period of two years with such alterations and additions as experience may indicate as advisable.

This Agreement is executed by the first party pursuant to a resolution duly adopted ..............., 1937, and entered upon the minutes of the Board of Trustees of the East Stroudsburg State Teachers College

SIGNED: PARTY OF THE FIRST PART
EAST STROUDSBURG STATE TEACHERS COLLEGE

............................... President

............................... Secretary

This Agreement is executed by the second party pursuant to a resolution duly adopted ..............., 1937, and entered upon the minutes of the Board of School Directors of the East Stroudsburg School District

SIGNED: PARTY OF THE SECOND PART
EAST STROUDSBURG SCHOOL DISTRICT

............................... President

............................... Secretary

Approved: Superintendent of Public Instruction ...............................